BETTER Bed & Breakfast Inns

Covering Northern California, Oregon,
Washington, Idaho, Montana, and Wyoming

By

Jimmy Don Franklin

Illustrations by Sally Clarke

HOMESTEAD PUBLISHING
Moose, Wyoming

DEDICATION

This book is dedicated to my wife, Jan, who did the proofreading and has supported and encouraged me to follow my dream; to Lloyd Woods, editor of *The Gresham Outlook*, who hired Jimmy Don as its first outdoor columnist and made a dream come true; and to my physician, Dr. Mary Bodie, who has always made sure I had the best medical care possible. I will always be indebted to all three.

ISBN 0-943972-31-0
Library of Congress Catalog Card Number 93-81011
Printed in the United States of America
on recycled, acid free paper.

Published by
Homestead Publishing
Box 193
Moose, Wyoming 83012

CONTENTS

INTRODUCTION

This complete guidebook offers everything you wanted to know about the Better Bed & Breakfast Inns, including maps, information about where to go, activities, things to see, and history of the area. All to help you plan that perfect vacation!

"Anytime of the year is a good time to plan a vacation to a Better Bed & Breakfast Inn."

———————————— ૨ঌ ————————————

RATES

The folowing table is a guide to the rates of Better Bed & Breakfast Inns.

0 to $50.00	$51.00 to $100.00	$101.00 to $150.00	Over $151.00
$	$$	$$$	$$$$

MAP LOCATIONS

The following guide locates towns and bed & breakfast inns to regions of their respective states.

NW=Northwest	NE=Northeast
SE=Southeast	SW=Southwest
E=East	W=West

BETTER
Bed
&Breakfast
Inns

NORTHERN CALIFORNIA

ALTURAS, CALIFORNIA

Dorris House Bed & Breakfast Inn
P.O. Box 1655
Alturas, California 96101
(916) 233-3786

Dorris House is a two-story ranch dwelling built in 1912 by descendants of Presley and Carlos Dorris, founders of Alturas (originally called Dorris Bridge). The Inn is on the shores of Dorris Lake, with the majestic Warner mountains in the background.

It is quiet and private here, unless migratory friends from Canada fly over to say hello. The drive on country roads along the federal bird refuge and past grazing cattle put you in touch with nature.

The decor in the four guest rooms reflects the historic setting. It is accented by great grandma's quilts and a collection of Indian beadwork. The bedrooms are large, airy and are furnished with antiques—with a family story behind every one. Each bedroom is furnished with a double bed.Three bedrooms have an extra twin bed, and there are shared baths.

If you are coming to relax, try the quiet screened front porch. It's great for reading, visiting or a little dozing. Or spend some time in the parlor playing the piano, antique pump organ or Victrola.

If you're interested in something more energetic, take your alpine or cross-country skis, ice skates, ski boat, sailboat, fishing pole, bicycle, horses, golf clubs or backpack. Dorris Lake is 15 miles around. Fish for channel catfish, bass and trout, or get directions to mountain streams for pan-sized trout. Pasture is available if you are traveling on horseback; just give forewarning. Backpacking or day hikes in the primitive area offer great adventures that put you in touch with nature. Cedar Pass Ski Area is only a 20-minute drive away.

Continental plus breakfast and complimentary wine in the evening.

Rates - $ Map Location - E

ANDERSON, CALIFORNIA

The Plantation House
1690 Ferry Street
Anderson, California 96007
1-800-950-2827 or (916) 365-2827 or (916) 365-8229

This beautiful historic landmark is a two-story Victorian house, offering a romantic step into the past. You will be greeted with true Southern hospitality by hosts attired in authentic costumes of the Civil War era. In your room, you'll find breathtaking splendor. The period furniture will invite you to relax in tranquility. The furnishings include a radio, cassette player and TV. Awaiting your culinary pleasure will be a complimentary bottle of the finest Napa Valley wine, chilled to perfection, plus fresh fruit, cheeses and nuts. In the evening, go to the downstairs parlour for complimentary hors d'oeuvres—cold cuts, cheeses, tea, coffee, hot chocolate and sherry.

After a soothing and refreshing slumber, you will—at your leisure—be served a sumptuous repast in the dining room. A full continental breakfast (European style) of fresh fruits, juices, homebaked muffins and rolls, croissants, yogurt, boiled eggs, prunes, cold cuts, cheeses, granola, coffee, tea, hot chocolate and milk.

Rates - $$ Map Location - E

ARCATA, CALIFORNIA

The Lady Anne
902 14th Street
Arcata, California 95521
(707) 822-2797

The Lady Anne is a stately Victorian mansion built in 1888, and occupies a place of prestige on the hill overlooking the Humboldt Bay. A glass veranda bids you welcome.

Just a few blocks from the university and the downtown plaza, The Lady Anne is a welcome respite from a hurried world. The round-corner tower, upper-story patterned shingles and projecting third story typify a pure example of Queen Anne architecture. Inside, you are transported into the romantic elegance of a Victorian home. Unlike many Victorians, however, the rooms are large, light and airy. Antiques, burnished woods, English stained glass, Oriental rugs and delicate lace curtains await you.

The Lady Anne is in a quiet residential area and within walking distance of the downtown plaza, with many fine shops and restaurants, and Humboldt State University. The lovely campus is alive with concerts, plays, art openings and sporting events. The city's swimming pool (complete with hot tub and workout room), several parks, playgrounds, picnic areas and a fine museum are just a few blocks away. You may choose to hike through the majestic redwood forest or explore the many trails and backroads. Pack a picnic lunch and use one of The Lady Anne's bicycles to tour the award-winning Arcata Marsh and Wildlife Sanctuary on Humboldt Bay. A short drive south will take you to Eureka's Old Town or to the fairyland Victorian Village of Ferndale. Drive north just 12 miles to the quaint fishing village of Trinidad. Charter a boat for deep-sea fishing, explore the beaches, hunt agates, dig for clams and swim or sail in the many lagoons. Continue north to explore the redwood forests, Roosevelt elk and Fern Canyon, which offers spectacular ferns, waterfalls and native plants.

A full breakfast is served in the grand dining room, warmed with a fireplace, inlaid floors and delicious aromas. Linger over fresh-ground coffee, homebaked muffins, quiche or the inn's famous Belgian waffles topped with fresh fruit.

Rates - $$ to $$$ Map Location - W

BURNT RANCH, CALIFORNIA

Madrone Lane Bed & Breakfast
H.C.R. #34
Burnt Ranch, California 95527
(916) 629-3642

The Madrone Lane Bed & Breakfast is ideally located in a secluded fir and hardwood forest near the gateways of the Trinity Wilderness, just one mile from the scenic and wild adventures of the Trinity River.

Your hosts invite you to enter a world resplendent with the quiet, restorative sounds of nature. You may wish to relax around the pool or use the sauna. You might enjoy casual walking and nature exploration, or you might choose to spend a day swimming and sunning on the river. River-adventure companies offer guided excursions and rentals. A challenging year-round golf course also is available.

Other guests have enjoyed the spectacular views of a drive on Ironside Mountain, or the drive that leads to the Hoopa Indian Reservation. If it's a wilderness experience you're seeking, try the Ammon Family backpacking service, complete with 14 well-disciplined horses.

For the fisherman, there are the seasonal runs of salmon and steelhead, and you may smoke your catch in the alder fed smokehouse. Your hosts invite you to join them in their studio for an experience with watercolor or airbrush, or perhaps take a sketching trip along the river.

The Madrone Lane facilities are situated on a year-round creek amidst abundant wildlife. Deer, birds, and a pair of foxes make their home nearby. The beautiful grey squirrels delight in being handfed. Your hosts offer an expanded Continental breakfast of fresh fruits, gourmet bakery goods, coffees, teas, and a wide variety of juices. The refrigerator is stocked with soft drinks, beer, hard-boiled eggs and, when available, smoked salmon, as well as complimentary California wines, cheese and crackers. The accommodations include a 750-square-foot studio located in a separate building and tastefully decorated to include a large lounge area. Or there's the suite of rooms in the main house, which includes a private bath, jacuzzi and immediate access to the pool and sauna. Both accommodations have access to laundry facilities, refrigerators, toaster ovens, VCRs and a large film library. Get away from business and the harried schedules and crowds of demanding vacations for a chance to relax, reflect and restore.

Rates - $$ Map Location - W

CHESTER, CALIFORNIA

The Bidwell House
Number One Main Street
P.O. Box 1790
Chester, California 96020
(916) 258-3338

The Bidwell House is named in honor of General John Bidwell. Venturing to California in 1841, he first worked for John Sutter in his sawmill. A love for agriculture coaxed him north to the foothills of the Sacramento Valley, where he later founded the town of Chico.

While on a trip to Washington D.C., the long-affirmed bachelor fell in love with Annie Kennedy of Massachusetts. John and his new wife escaped the intense summer heat of the valley by spending their summers in the mountains east of Chico. They loved the area of the Feather River and, in 1901, built a summer home in the meadow near the river.

When John died, Earl McKenzie bought the house and moved it to its current location in the town of Chester. The home served for many years as ranch headquarters for the Stover-McKenzie Cattle Company, one of the largest cattle operations in Northern California. As such, the home became the hub of lavish summer parties and community rodeos.

The Bidwell House is located in a "yet-to-be-discovered" area on the southeastern slope of Mount Lassen. Chester and its surrounding area are rich in the history of gold mining, ranching and logging. The inn provides a great resting spot between the valley of California and points east. It's perfect for hideaway seekers and honeymooners.

Each distinctly different guest room, the swing on the porch, the unusual collection of antiques and attention to details all improve your comfort. At your leisure, you may choose to enjoy the privacy of your room, catch up on the latest news, spend time in a cozy reading nook or just sit on the porch with company to enjoy a beautiful view and witness the distant foraging of Canada geese.

To help you greet the day, gourmet coffee or special tea will be served in the privacy of your room. Then, join your hosts for a full breakfast featuring the inn's specialties—freshly baked breads and muffins.

This area also offers diverse recreational activities. Near the inn are opportunities for hiking, boating, water-skiing and bike riding. Premier views of wildlife and possibly the best fly-fishing in California also are at your fingertips. During the winter, the inn offers immediate access to cross-country skiing, with downhill skiing and snowmobiling nearby as well. Take a tour of Mount Lassen Volcanic National Park, Lake Almanor, Pacific Crest Trail and the Feather River.

Rates - $$ to $$$ Map Location - E

DORRIS, CALIFORNIA

The Hospitality Inn
200 South California Street
Dorris, California 96023
(916) 397-2097

The Inn was built by the Evans family and later became a boarding house, with the front-end extension and bathrooms added. When the lumber mills were flourishing and the town needed a local doctor, the doctor bought the largest building in town and turned it into office space and hospital. The last doctor (Dr. Drader) had his ashes buried in the back yard. Your hosts periodically dig up artifacts, since the place also was an old dumping ground.

Four rooms are available for your comfort and pleasure in this historically renowned turn-of-the-century home. You'll also enjoy a wholesome breakfast.

The Hospitality Inn is situated at the corner of California and Second streets, one block off Highway 97. It is 50 miles north of Weed, California and 22 miles south of Klamath Falls, Oregon.

For the wildlife enthusiasts, the Inn is just minutes away from Lower Klamath Refuge, Tule Lake Refuge, Meiss Lake Refuge and Lava Beds National Monument. The Hospitality Inn is centrally located within the finest fishing and hunting area of Northern California.

Rates - $$ Map Location - E

DUNSMUIR, CALIFORNIA

Dunsmuir Bed & Breakfast Inn
5423 Dunsmuir Avenue
Dunsmuir, California 96025
(916) 235-4543

Take a step back to a time when neighbors were friends and everyone in town was a neighbor. Stroll down Main Street past buildings that date back 100 years. Enjoy the historic atmosphere of the railroad town, and when you return "home," stop in at Rosie's Ice Cream Parlor for an old-fashioned soda or delicious ice-cream cone. Relax in the pleasant atmosphere of the restored Dunsmuir Inn. Your hosts will serve you a delicious continental breakfast in your room—or outdoors on warm days. Reward yourself with a soothing soak in the claw-foot tubs. Feel free to use the bright kitchen anytime; enjoy the garden barbecue, or try any of the area's fine restaurants.

If you're interested in skiing, fishing, or some of the most beautiful scenery in the country, you've found it. Excellent downhill and cross-country skiing and ice skating are just 20 minutes away. Fishing in the crystal waters of the Upper Sacramento River is within walking distance of the inn. Your hosts can suggest any number of hikes and driving tours to mountain lakes, waterfalls, Castle Crags State Park, and magnificent Mount Shasta. Discover the excitement of gold-panning. They'll supply the pan!

Dunsmuir is home to the best water on earth. A spring above Mossbrae Falls is fed by melting glaciers on Mount Shasta. The water flows through hundreds of miles of lava tubes, never seeing daylight until the tap is turned on.

Twin Room: Two twin beds, private bath with claw-foot tub and shower across the hall.

Double Room: Double bed, private bath with claw-foot tub and shower across the hall.

King Room: King-size bed, private bath with claw-foot tub and shower.

The Suite: Spacious two-room suite with king-size bed and private bath with claw-foot tub and shower.

Expanded continental breakfast and use of kitchen and barbecue facilities.

Rates - $ to $$ Map Location - E

Riverwalk Inn Bed & Breakfast
4300 Stage Coach Road
Dunsmuir, California 96025
(916) 235-4300

The Riverwalk Inn is a Victorian farm house built in 1929 on Hudson Bay Trappers

Old Town Bed & Breakfast Inn, Eureka, CA

Mineral Springs. This is one of three architecturally unique homes in Dunsmuir, which was established as a stagecoach stop to the gold fields in Yreka and as a railroad head to Oregon and Washington. This is one of the historical towns on the Oregon Trail.

The upstairs features three charming bedrooms with quaint dormer windows and one traditional cozy bath. Downstairs is one semi-modern bath and shower combo, a nice country dining room for a complete and satisfying breakfast, and a comfortable sitting room with piano, TV and VCR, plus interesting nooks and crannies throughout the house. Antiques and family heirlooms abound and surround a warm fireplace

The Inn is within walking distance of the historic railroad town, falls, park, tennis courts, antique art and craft boutiques and eateries. You'll also be offered self-guided tours of Siskiyou County fishing, rock hounding, lakes, volcanic points of interest and general sight-seeing. You may wish to ski nearby Mount Shasta, whitewater raft on the Sacramento River just 200 yards from your room or take a train ride on the Blue Goose Express. Enjoy beautiful lake Siskiyou with beaches, swimming and boat rentals.

Rose Room: Take time to smell the roses in the specially decorated Rose Room.

Violet Room & Sunshine Room: Let violets satisfy your sense and fill your soul with their essence or feel old-fashioned warmth as you stir in the morning to the sounds and smells of breakfast from the kitchen.

Children's Room: Recapturing the time of yesterday filled with games and toys for girls and boys.

All have shared bath or can be used as a personal suite for $ extra.

Rates - $ to $$ Map Location - E

EUREKA, CALIFORNIA

The Daly Inn
1125 'H' Street
Eureka, California 95501
(707) 445-3638 or 1-800-321-9656

This lovely Colonial revival home was built in 1905 by Cornelius Daly for his wife, Annie, and their five children. Mr. Daly owned and operated the Daly Department Stores with locations throughout the Pacific Northwest. The home has been beautifully restored to its original elegance, with modern conveniences added tastefully. The five guest rooms are furnished with queen beds and antiques with the charm of the early 1900s.

If you're traveling California's north coast looking for a relaxing getaway or celebrating a special occasion, consider Eureka's beautiful Daly Inn. It is located in the historic section of Eureka, a few blocks from the Pacific and close to the majestic Redwoods. Eureka's Old Town offers unique shops and restaurants within walking distance.

Miss Martha's Room: This delightful room was the nursery of the Daly home. The room has opaque glass windows through which light from the hall would illuminate the room. No gas for light or heat was supplied to the nursery, and electricity was only recently added. Bleached pine antiques from Holland furnish this cheery room.

Annie Murphy's Room: Originally the master bedroom of the Daly home, this sunny room has a fireplace and overlooks the lovely garden and fish pond. The room has an ornate bedroom suite, hand-carved in Belgium.

The Guest Room: This bedroom was reserved for visiting friends, family and business associates of the Dalys It is adjoined by a private bath with the original clawfoot. It is decorated with turn-of-the-century American Oak antiques and accented with framed quilt patterns and templates. This is a charming room with large windows overlooking the surrounding Victorian architecture.

The Victorian Rose Suite: This beautiful three room suite is decorated with white wicker furniture and various black floral wall coverings and fabrics. These rooms often are used as a bridal suite and consist of a bedroom, sitting room, and a large bath.

The Garden View Suite: A tasteful return to the Victorian Era. This three-room suite (bedroom, sitting room, and bath) is decorated with English walnut antiques and Victorian reproduction wall coverings and accessories.

Recapture the charm of the Victorian family breakfast at the Daly Inn. Enjoy a leisurely morning meal in the sunlit breakfast parlor or on the beautiful garden patio. On cooler days, you may be served in the elegant dining room, seated before a crackling fire.

Rates - $$ to $$$ Map Location - W

Hollander House Bed & Breakfast Inn
2436 'E' Street
Eureka, California 95501
(707) 443-2419

The coastal city of Eureka bears California's state slogan—meaning "I found it"— ·the cry of the forty-niners who poured into California during the Gold Rush. It lies in the heart of the breathtaking forests of California's state tree, the Giant Coastal Redwood. The area enjoys year-round moderate temperatures with a gentle ocean breeze.

The gracious Queen Anne Victorian that is the Hollander House Bed & Breakfast Inn was constructed in 1906 by the Hollander family, owners of Eureka's first jewelry store, which remained in business for nearly a hundred years.

Hollander House features the experience of traditional Victorian elegance with modern conveniences. Antiques and artifacts from world travels grace virtually every room; sunny south-facing sitting rooms offer a delightful escape into a full variety of books and magazines. The secluded deck provides a quiet space to take in the fresh air, read, dine, or enjoy a sunset. Other available amenities include a guest refrigerator, cable TV in the parlor, and a variety of toys and games for children.

The Serenity Suite: This suite consists of the Serenity Room, the tower room and the master bath. The Serenity Room features a comfortable queen-size bed and walk-in closet, as well as a sink in the room. Two large south-facing windows add plenty of cheer to the room's natural softness. Adjoining is a large sitting room called the Tower Room, where five lovely bay-type windows set off a unique rounded alcove, part of the home's architectural "tower." Here you'll find a couch, settee and king-size or two twin beds. The Serenity Suite boasts a particularly beautiful master bath, replete with a luxurious soaking tub and a separate, tiled shower. Comfy robes are available upon request.

The Rose Room: Here you'll find a full size bed, walk-in closet and private bath. Three large windows face south and west, allowing plenty of afternoon sun to filter in through delicate lace curtains. This room has a table and chairs in the corner that is perfect for reading from the in-room library.

The Ivy Room: On the north side of the house, the Ivy Room is a very special place, with a charming window overlooking the back yard. Ideal for families, it has two twin beds and a walk-in closet. This room is available with a shared bath only.

Enjoy a full breakfast including a hot entree, fresh fruit and homebaked goodies, juice, freshly ground coffee or tea. Your hosts can accommodate dietary needs as well.

Rates - $$ to $$$ Map Location - W

Iris Inn Bed & Breakfast
1134 'H' Street
Eureka, California 95501
(707) 445-0307

Just a few blocks from Old Town, the Iris Inn is a welcome respite from a hurried world. This elegantly restored Queen Anne Victorian was built in 1900 for William Haw, Humboldt's first county clerk.

Victorian antiques and contemporary art help create a setting of quiet and peaceful splendor. Each guest room is uniquely decorated with beauty and comfort as priorities. Your innkeepers are knowledgeable and willing to help with dinner and entertainment plans. Relax on the shaded veranda or snuggle up with a good book in the library. Whatever you choose, rest assured your utmost privacy and comfort are important.

Nothing is too fine for the Iris Inn guest, from the expertly arranged flowers in your room to the beautiful china and silver used during breakfast and afternoon tea.

In the morning, you are greeted with a gourmet breakfast in the dining room, the parlor, or in the privacy of your room.

Rates - $ to $$ Map Location - E

Old Town Bed & Breakfast Inn
1521 Third Street
Eureka, California 95501
(707) 445-3951 or 1-800-331-5098

Old Town Bed & Breakfast Inn is one of the few remaining Greek Revival Italianate Victorian structures in the area, and was the original home of the pioneer Lumber Baron extraordinaire, William Carson. Carson's mill supplied much of the wood used to build San Francisco and then rebuild it after the 1906 earthquake. Carson also was responsible for the county seat moving from Arcata to Eureka, an event Arcata still remembers.

This home was built in 1871 on an unknown location, by one of Carson's accountants. The accountant's wife, however, died within six months of its construction, and he sold it to William Carson. The house was moved to the site of the previous Carson Bank, directly across the street from the Ingomar Club. The Carsons lived in this home until 1886, when they moved into the mansion. The house remained adjacent to the mansion and was used as part of the Bay Mill until 1915.

When he died in 1912, William Carson left the house to an injured mill foreman, John Gillis. The Gillis family moved it to its current location in 1915 and lived here the early 1950s. During the following 30 years, the house changed hands several times, and was used as a family home, a boarding house, and possibly a brothel (unconfirmed report by previous owners and local residents). In 1982, Bob and Agnes Sobrito renovated the building and converted it to a bed & breakfast inn. Agnes—who now does color consulting for major hotel chains—chose the color scheme. Bob is a general contractor, restoring Victorians in San Diego. The inn's birthday is July 4; the city is kind enough to provide the fireworks!

The inn's exterior walls are four inches of solid virgin redwood, and the hardwood floors are Douglas fir. The construction is balloon-type post and beam, and the fireplaces are original. The fireplace in the front parlor (previously the ladies parlor) is a coal fireplace; the men had the wood fireplace in their parlor.

The William Carson Room: Named after the original owner, this room includes a queen-size bed and private bath with Victorian claw-foot tub and shower.

Gerri's Room: A ginger-peachy room featuring a whimsical collection of stuffed animals, king or twin poster beds, and private detached bath with shower.

Sarah's Rose Parfait Room: A warm elegant room with morning sun, queen-size bed, and shared bath with Victorian claw-foot tub. Named for William's wife.

The Maxfield Parrish Room: A charming room featuring Maxfield Parrish artwork and oak antiques, queen-size bed, and shared bath with tub.

Sumner's Room: An intimate, cozy room with antique brass double bed and private bath with shower. Named after Carson's middle son.

Carlotta's Room: The Inn's largest room, named after Carson's only daughter. Perfect for first or second honeymoons. This lavender and lace room features king-size brass feather bed, antiques, private bath, tub and shower, plus woodstove and sunsets.

Chetola Hold: Downstairs with a private entrance, this room includes a queen-size Victorian Mansion bed, private bath with his and her shower, and cable TV. The name is a Native American word meaning "a place of peace and rest."

Full country gourmet breakfast served family style in the country kitchen.

Rates - $$ to $$$ Map Location - W

Shannon House Bed & Breakfast
2154 Spring Street
Eureka, California 95501
(707) 443-8130

A Norwegian carpenter built this inn in 1891 for himself and his family. It is a Queen Anne style Victorian, constructed almost entirely of redwood. In 1989, the inn was restored—using period wallpaper and antiques—to the way it might have looked in 1891.

The Shannon House offers three rooms outfitted with queen-size beds and one room, the Melinda Room, with a twin bed. The Melinda and Marilyn rooms share the same bath, and the Esther Room has its own private bath.

The Inn is located on a quiet residential street in Eureka, just two blocks off Broadway (Highway 101 through Eureka).

Within an hour's drive north or south of Eureka are areas of virgin redwoods, where the public is free to hike for miles. Boating, swimming, whitewater rafting, and fishing are available as well. A full breakfast and an afternoon tea are offered.

Rates - $ to $$ Map Location - W

A Weaver's Inn
1440 'B' Street
Eureka, California 95501
(707) 443-8119

A Weaver's Inn—a stately Queen Ann/Colonial Revival house built in 1883 and remodeled in 1907—is the home and studio of a fiber artist and her husband. Amid a spacious garden, it is airy and light, yet cozy and warm when veiled by wisps of fog. Visit the studio, try the spinning wheel before the fire, or weave on the antique loom.

The Victorian Parlor offers a piano and elegant relaxing, and the city of Eureka offers many fine restaurants. Or dine at the Inn if dinner is offered that evening.

The Pamela Suite: Two romantic rooms with sliding door, fireplace, bath with tiled shower, queen-size bed and sofa bed in the sitting room.

The Amy Room: Delightful cozy country comfort for the single traveler, with two full-size beds, cable TV and shared bath.

The Cynthia Room: Sunny bay window and wicker furnishings, fireplace, king-size bed or long twins and shared bath with Victorian claw-foot tub.

The Marcia Room: Welcoming window seat, restored family furniture, queen-size bed, and bath with soaking tub.

A delectable full breakfast may include treats from the garden and is served in the gracious dining room or on the sunlit porch.

After breakfast, play croquet, contemplate the Japanese garden, and explore the the Victorian Era in Old Town, where you can play golf, fish from a boat, or comb a beach.

Rates - $ to $$ Map Location - W

FERNDALE, CALIFORNIA

The Gingerbread Mansion
400 Berding Street , P.O. Box 40
Ferndale, California 95536
(707) 786-4000 or 1-800-952-4136

The Gingerbread Mansion, built in 1899, is everything the discriminating inngoer has come to expect—elegance, quiet, charm, warm hospitality, comfort, attention to detail, antiques, romance, beautiful gardens, and a location that invites an extended stay.

Fountain Suite: This large, luxurious front-corner room features a bay-window view of the Victorian Village and a side-garden view of the fountain. Also included is a bathroom with antique Franklin fireplace, a fainting couch, side-by-side twin claw-foot tubs for "his and her" bubble baths, and a canopied queen bed.

Rose Suite: This elegant front-corner room includes a fireplace and offers views over the veranda and the hills. A deluxe garden-like bathroom with claw-foot tub is in the center of the room, which includes mirrored ceiling and walls, and a queen bed.

Gingerbread Suite: The twin "his and her" claw-foot tubs are positioned toe-to-toe in the bedroom of this large, romantic suite on the main floor. Queen bed.

Heron Suite: In a more authentic style, two rooms have been opened up into one very large, sunny suite with sitting area and writing desk. Queen bed.

Hideaway Room: This architecturally unique room features many angled details, beveled and stained glass windows, and its own stairway. Queen bed and bathroom downstairs. Single bed and sitting area on upper level.

Lilac Room: You'll find shades of lilac and a claw-foot tub beneath a beautiful stained glass window in this spacious bedroom overlooking the garden. Queen bed.

Strawberry Hill Room: Lots of windows and light in this large green and peach room with dressing area and tub-and-shower combination.

Garden Room: This conveniently located main-floor room includes a Franklin stove and French windows overlooking the formal garden, plus a large bathroom with step-in shower. Queen bed.

Zipporah's Room: An intimate room in blue looking out toward the hills. Named for a Ferndale settler. Queen bed.

Afternoon tea with cake served at 4 p.m. in the Victorian parlor, plus a generous continental breakfast of homemade delights, an early morning tray of coffee in your room, and various little extras to make your stay ever-so-memorable!

Enjoy fishing, hiking, biking and visit the many shops and galleries.

Rates - $$ to $$$$ Map Location - W

Grandmother's House Bed & Breakfast
861 Howard Street
P.O. Box 1004
Ferndale, California 95536
(707) 786-9704

Ferndale was settled by dairy farmers and lumbermen in the 1800s, and the area remains dairy country today. In the 1960s, many artists and craftspeople moved to

The Gingerbread Mansion Inn, Ferndale, CA

Ferndale and opened shops.

Grandmother's House was built in 1901 and is made entirely of redwood. The original three bedrooms, parlor and dining room are yours to enjoy during your visit. Individuals or friends and families with children traveling together are welcome to share this lovely turn-of-the-century Queen Anne home.

One bedroom has detached private bath. Two bedrooms share a bath.

Come afternoons and evenings; serve yourself crackers, cookies, cheese and your choice of beverage. Breakfast includes waffles, fresh fruit, juice, coffee, tea, hot chocolate, muffins , cereal or yogurt.

Enjoy hiking, fishing, biking and car tours of the beautiful countryside surrounding Ferndale.

Rates - $$ Map Location - W

The Shaw House Inn
703 Main Street, P.O. Box 1125
Ferndale, California 95536
(707) 786-9958

Located in the historical village of Ferndale, five miles from Highway 101, this inn is near the site of annual festivals representing the various cultures that settled and still occupy this verdant valley. The three-block-long Main Street business section is a delight to explore. Craft studios, shops, galleries, service facilities, restaurants, and the Village Playhouse all are housed in historical buildings.

The Shaw House was built in 1854 by the founder of Ferndale, and continues the tradition of hospitality. This historic and architecturally significant home now is listed on the National Register of Historic Places. The gabled Gothic carpenter house is situated on a beautiful garden acre of trees along Frances Creek. As you drive along Main Street, you will be drawn by its dignified and inviting appearance.

You'll want to open the gate under the seemingly ancient Buckeye tree and go up the walk to a V-shaped cutting garden between the two old-fashioned porches. The jutting gables, bays, and numerous balconies excite the imagination, suggesting the graciousness of this charming and romantic home.

Inside, you'll enjoy the tastefully decorated rooms overflowing with the owners' lifelong collection of art, antiques, books and other memorabilia. The secluded deck overlooking the creek offers a perfect place for daydreaming. In the garden, there is room to spread a blanket, read quietly by the shade of a tree, or just relax and enjoy the sunshine.

The sleeping rooms are wallpapered havens nestled under the gables. The honeymoon room has its own bath with a claw-foot tub and shower, and the Shaw Room has the famous honeymoon bed that has always been in the house.

A homemade breakfast is served in the dining room warmed by collections of baskets, old prints, and Chinese and Japanese antiques.

Rates - $$ to $$$ Map Location - W

GARBERVILLE, CALIFORNIA

The Ranch House 'a' Country Inn
2906 Alderpoint Road
Garberville, California 95542
707) 923-3441

Established in the 1870s by the Robertson family, a once 7,000-acre sheep ranch played an important part in the early settlement of Humboldt County, passing through three family generations. The current two-story ranch house, on 43 acres, was built in 1902, with barns and outbuildings representing the heart of the homestead. The ranch has been restored and provides an elegant and private atmosphere. Guest rooms are airy and comfortable, and furnished with queen beds and private baths with claw-foot tubs.

Enjoy the ranch and its historical charm as you stroll through the orchard, around the pond, through the pepperwoods, and survey the vast view of the valleys below. The ranch is located 2.5 miles up the Alderpoint Road leaving Garberville. As you quickly ascend to 1,702 feet, the view is spectacular.

Accommodations include a morning breakfast and beverage at your convenience.

The surrounding area provides numerous activities including Avenue of the Giants, Benbow Valley and Shelter Cove.

Rates - $$ Map Location - W

LEGGETT, CALIFORNIA

Bell Glen Bed & Breakfast In The Redwoods
70400 Highway 101
Leggett, California 95455
(707) 925-6425

The Bell Glen is situated on 10 acres and enjoys a quarter mile of beach and riverfront. The grounds are complemented with beautiful gardens, a duck pond and a trail leading across the Japanese bridge to a love seat in the gazebo. As you stroll along the rose-lined pathways, enjoy the beautiful beds of botanical delights.

The shallow upstream section of the river is heated to about 80 degrees and then flows into a deep swimming hole; it's perfect for a morning dip or midnight swim. The beach offers lounge chairs, free inner tubes, a gazebo, face masks and snorkels and—best of all—a European style sauna that's open 24 hours.

Cottages are nestled under the giant trees, with magnificent views of the Eel River and the mountains it flows through. Each cottage is secluded from the next, and is unique in decor and ambience, all with antiques, flowers, Vienna roasted coffee, tea, California wine, hot chocolate, marshmallows and even bubble bath!

Most of the cottages sit on the river bluffs. Guests say they've never slept so well. "It's the sound of the river."

Rise and shine at your convenience; your breakfast basket was thoughtfully delivered to you the night before. The basket includes in-season fresh fruit, muffins and cheese, to go with fresh coffee or chocolate in your room. Enjoy your breakfast on your private deck and watch the river go by.

Enjoy birdwatching, photography, fishing, and hiking, and visit micro-breweries.

Rates - $$ to $$$ Map Location - W

LEWISTON, CALIFORNIA

Old Lewiston Inn 'a' Bed & Breakfast
P.O. Box 688
Lewiston, California 96052
(916) 778-3385

The Old Lewiston Inn is located in Trinity County, beside the Trinity River in the heart of the National Historic Mining town of Lewiston. Trinity is unique to all of California with more than 3,220 square miles of parks, forest reserves and wilderness areas. There are no stop lights or parking meters here. Travel back in time. This area, rich in frontier history and protected wilderness is the perfect setting for your family's retreat.

The Baker House, built in 1875, is located in the heart of this once ruckus and rowdy mining town. The inn features large rooms with private entrances, private baths, and individual decks with sweeping views of the surrounding mountains and Trinity River. The river, just 100 feet from the inn, will lull you to sleep at night. A continental breakfast of fresh fruit will await you in the morning.

Historic Lewiston offers something for the whole family. Nearby is Lewiston Lake, where the trout fishing is the finest in all of California. This lake is an environmentalist's dream, where development has been restricted and day camps abound.

The Trinity River offers excellent rafting and swimming. The finest salmon and steelhead fishing hole in the country also is located behind the inn. Just down the way is a fishing-supply store whose owners will show you the tricks of the fish. Fishing guides and drift-boat services are available, and the inn's barbecue will await your evening catch.

Water-ski, cross-country ski, go whitewater rafting, camping, or backpacking.

Historical Visits: Old Bridge, Park & Honeymoon Cabin, Old Cemetery, Lewiston Congregational Church, Old School House, The Siligo Chamberlin House, The Goetze Butcher Shop, Paulson Store, The Phillips House, Baker House and Lewiston Hotel.

Rates - $ to $$ Map Location - W

McCLOUD, CALIFORNIA

Joanie's Bed & Breakfast
417 Lawndale Court
McCloud, California 96057
(916) 964-3106

Joanie's log home is situated among tall pines on a hill overlooking town, an enclave of old-fashioned Southern hospitality.

The great room is large and inviting, with a fireplace and piano, an extensive library of books and games, and plenty of space to enjoy lone or group activities. Retire to one of the spacious chambers, each unique with its own decor. After a peaceful night's sleep enjoy a country-style breakfast and a view of Mount Shasta in the dining area, or outside on the deck. Visitors take in pure mountain air, scenic beauty and plenty of relaxation.

Two bedrooms with private bath, one with half bath and two with shared baths.

Enjoy skiing Mount Shasta, fishing, hunting, golf, whitewater rafting, swimming, boating and hiking.

Rates - $ to $$ Map Location - E

The McCloud Guest House
606 West Colombero Drive, P.O. Box 1510
McCloud, California 96057
(916) 974-3160

Nestled among stately oaks and lofty pines on the lower slopes of majestic Mount Shasta, this beautiful old country home overlooks the once-thriving mill of McCloud. Built in 1907, it originally served as personal residence of Mr. J.H. Queal, president of the McCloud River Lumber Company.

After Mr. Queal's death in 1921, it became known as the "Guest House" when the company staffed the house with a cook and housekeeper and used it to accommodate visiting VIPs and lumber executives.

VIPs who stayed at the Guest House during the 60-plus years it was owned by the company include President Herbert Hoover, actress Jean Harlow, California Gov. James Rolph and various members of the Hearst Family.

Acquired in 1984 by its present owners, the McCloud Guest House is open to the public, following extensive renovations to recapture thet warmth and country-inn charm of its past.

On the first floor is one of Siskiyou County's finer dining establishments. The second floor is for the enjoyment of overnight guests and features a large parlor with a pool table from the Hearst Collection. Surrounding the parlor are five individually decorated bedrooms, each with its own bath. Three of the rooms have claw-foot tubs and two have showers. Continental breakfast-plus included witt your room.

Enjoy downhill and Nordic skiing, trout fishing, bicycling, golfing, spelunking, hiking, swimming, or just kick back and enjoy the beautiful scenery.

Rates - $$ Map Location - E

Stoney Brook Inn
309 West Colombero, P.O. Box 1860
McCloud, California 96057-1860
(916) 964-2300 or 1-800-369-6118

On the south slope of majestic Mount Shasta, in the heart of the Shasta-Cascade Wonderland is the Stoney Brook Inn. It is located in historical McCloud, California, a mill town dating back to the late 1800s. The town now is being rediscovered as a home base for the area's vast natural beauty and recreational activities.

The Stoney Brook Inn is truly unique. The building, which has received historical designation, has been fully restored, yet retains its cozy, homey character. Its soothing atmosphere invites you to unwind and relax in the outdoor hot tub under the pines, in the sauna, on the spacious front porch, or inside by the fire in the winter. Serve yourself breakfast as you listen to the sounds of nature in this alpine setting.

The atmosphere is that of a bed & breakfast, yet there are 16 rooms total, 14 with private baths, and five with kitchenettes.

Go hiking, boating ,swimming, fishing, hunting, golfing and skiing.

Rates - $ to $$ Map Location - E

MOUNT SHASTA, CALIFORNIA

Mount Shasta Ranch Bed & Breakfast
1008 W.A. Barr Road
Mount Shasta, California 96067
(916) 926-3870

The ranch was built in 1923 by H.D. "Curley" Brown as a thoroughbred horse ranch. Its a two-story ranch home in a historical setting, just a stone's thrown from Lake Siskiyou.

The Mount Shasta Ranch Bed & Breakfast is located minutes from downtown Mount Shasta City. The mountain offers a spectacular backdrop for the Mount Shasta Ranch. Logging and mill work has been the main industry, though it now is being replaced with tourism, skiing and recreation.

This bed and breakfast includes nine bedrooms, plus a two-bedroom cottage. In the main lodge are four rooms with private baths; in the Carriage House are five rooms with two shared baths; plus there's a two-bedroom cottage.

Enjoy cross-country and downhill skiing, fishing, hunting, sailing, swimming, hiking, biking, golf, museums, railroad nostalgia and visiting the fish hatchery.

Rates - $ to $$ Map Location - E

RED BLUFF, CALIFORNIA

The Faulkner House
1029 Jefferson Street
Red Bluff, California 96080
(916) 529-0520

Built by jeweler Herman H. Wiendieck in the 1890s, Dr. and Mrs. James L. Faulkner bought this Queen Anne Victorian in 1933. They raised their family and he ran a medical practice for years, occasionally examining patients in the downstairs sitting room.

Inspired by the lovely little Victorian town of Red Bluff, your hosts have created an inviting setting for your holiday escape to this Sacramento River town. After a delicious breakfast, enjoy antique shops, a Victorian museum, the Victorian House Tour or a visit to the Ide Adobe, the home of California's first and only president. A short trip to nearby Redding or Chico completes your day before returning to the tree-shaded setting of this beautiful Queen Anne house.

Enjoy relaxing in the parlor or on the screened porch before choosing one of the fine restaurants in the area for dinner. You may be lucky enough to hear the nearby church bells chime the hour.

Make new friends in the comfortable parlor or a take a magazine or book to your lovely antique-filled bedroom.

Arbor Room: Queen-size bed, private bath and shower.

Rose Room: Queen-size bed, private bath with tub and shower.

Wicker Room: Queen-size bed, private bath with shower.

Tower Room: Double bed, private bath with shower.

Enjoy fishing , hunting hiking, canoeing, golfing and whitewater rafting. Visit museums, antique shops, the National Fish Hatchery, Lassen Volcanic National Park, Woodson Bridge Park, Black Butte Lake/Dam, Shasta Caverns and Cascade Wonderland, Burney Falls, Lake Almanor, Trinity Alps/River and Mendocino National Forest.

Rates - $$ Map Location - E

Jarvis Mansion Bed & Breakfast
1313 Jackson Street
Red Bluff, California 96080
(916) 527-6901

The Jarvis Mansion is a Victorian home built in 1870. It boasts a classic Italianate architectural design, and is completely refurbished and tastefully decorated in Victorian era antique furnishings to give you a taste of 1800s' charm.

This spacious Inn is easily accessible from Interstate 5, located in the Victorian Home Tour area of Red Bluff. The main house has three rooms, each with a private, adjoining bath, and equipped with air conditioning, heating, electric blankets, clock/ radio, TV and telephone upon request. Your hosts also have a cottage for total privacy, with its own sitting room and kitchen.

The beautiful grounds and historic gazebo are designed for your relaxation and are available for garden parties, weddings and receptions.

Guests arriving by 5 p.m. will be served hors d'oeuvres and a complimentary glass of wine or another favorite beverage. An expanded continental breakfast plus choice breakfast served in elegant surroundings will start your day.

The Inn is just a leisurely stroll from historic downtown Red Bluff, where the old mercantile stores and livery stables fronting Main, Oak and Walnut streets—built in the 1800s—now house modern shops behind their Victorian facades. Antiques stores, novelty shops, restaurants and much more are located in the downtown area. Five miles from town is the state historic monument and the reconstructed adobe of William B. Ide, the only president of the California Bear Flag Republic. The Sacramento River is a quarter mile from the Inn and offers fishing, boating and water-skiing. Mount Lassen Volcanic National Park and ski resort are less than an hour's drive.

A convenient drive north will take you to Shasta Lake, Mount Shasta, Whiskeytown Lake and Burney Falls, with other quaint and historic towns along the way.

Rates - $$ Map Location - E

REDDING, CALIFORNIA

The Cabral House
1752 Chestnut Street
Redding, California 96001
(916) 244-3766

At the Cabral House, you'll enter a world of the nostalgic past—the 1920s-1940s— an era of the golden years, elegance and spirit. The setting is in a quiet, historic residential area of Redding.

Settle in to the warmth and hospitality created by your hosts. Greeting you are photographs of beautiful, intriguing women, which are displayed throughout the house. Big Band music sets the tone for the evening.

Relax in your uniquely decorated bedroom, each with a private bath and an unforgettable woman's name. Enjoy the company of other guests in the comfortable living room filled with vintage furnishings and memories of a vanished time. Refreshments and conversation await you prior to your evening on the town. Sample interesting hors d'oeuvres and wines. Review the selection of area restaurant menus, and ask about places you may want to visit. Your hosts will assist you in arranging activities.

During your stay, enjoy the beauty of the flowering gardens. Although no smoking is allowed inside the home, areas are provided on the front porch and the patio. And because the hosts have a household dog and cats, they cannot accommodate traveling pets.

Breakfast is served at 8:30 a.m., either in the dining room or the patio gazebo. Each guest will have a distinct place setting of china and flatware. A sumptuous breakfast is presented with flavorful entrees, homemade breads, muffins, fruits, and blended coffee or tea.

Rates - **$$**   Map Location - E

Palisades Paradise
1200 Palisades Avenue
Redding, California 96003
(916) 223-5305 or 1-800-382-4649

Enjoy a breathtaking view of the Sacramento River, city and surrounding mountains from this beautiful, newly decorated contemporary home with its garden spa, fireplace, wide-screen TV and VCR and homelike atmosphere. Palisades Paradise is a serene settling for a quiet hideaway, yet conveniently located one mile from shopping and Interstate 5.

Come and enjoy fishing, whitewater rafting, swimming and boating on Whiskeytown Lake, Shasta Lake and the Sacramento River. For those who love hiking, Lassen National Park, Mount Shasta, Castle Crags, Lake Shasta Caverns, Trinity Alps and Burney Falls State Park are all within driving distance.

Sunset Suite: From this room, you have a panoramic view of the city lights from two sliding doors that open onto a 50-foot patio and spa. The setting is a romantic and spacious bedroom with a queen-size bed and a mixture of contemporary and antique furnishings. It also includes a comfortable sitting area.

Cozy Retreat: This exquisite room features soft, muted colors and a comfortable queen-size bed. Before retiring, enjoy the moonlight from the garden spa or the restful porch swing suspended from a native oak tree overlooking the Bluffs of the Sacramento.

Rates - **$$**   Map Location - E

Redding's Bed & Breakfast Inn
1094 Palisades Avenue
Redding, California 96003
(916) 222-2494

A unique and memorable experience for someone special! Welcome to a 'Private Home Bed & Breakfast,' with a chamber maid to service your stay in the most comfortable manner. Its location on the Bluffs overlooking Redding's city lights and the Sacramento River sets a romantic and sparkling view for guests in the evening! Bedrooms are decorated in country-living style with a very comfortable queen bed. Breakfast served in your room

Rate $ to $$ Map Location - E

Tiffany House
1510 Barbara Road
Redding, California 96003
(916) 244-3225

Nestled among large spreading oaks, high on a hilltop with a panoramic view of Mount Lassen range, sits this late Victorian two-story home, architecturally designed for comfort and gracious living. A large shaded deck with an old-fashioned porch swing, comfortable chairs and a quaint gazebo create a sense of nostalgia and tranquility. For the more active, there is a refreshing swimming pool, half basketball court, table tennis, badminton and volleyball.

Relax in the Victorian parlor or the drawing room, decorated with 19th century antiques and Tiffany lamps. There you'll find an organ with old sheet music, plus parlor games, a variety of classic and current books and a cable TV and VCR with a collection of old movie classics. Two Victorian fireplaces add warmth to chilly evenings.

Within the city are art and science museums, small theater groups, a summer Shakespeare Festival and world-class entertainment at the beautiful convention center. Ideal for the outdoors person, Redding is in the prime recreational area of Northern California. Within the city are several golf courses, tennis courts, hiking and biking opportunities along the Sacramento River Trail, plus river rafting and canoeing on the serene river.

Hiking, fishing, swimming, boating, downhill and cross-country skiing all are available at nearby lakes, rivers, streams, mountains, parks and wilderness areas. Mount Shasta, Mount Lassen and the Trinity Alps all are within an hour and a half drive. Lake Shasta and Whiskeytown Lakes are nearby, as are Castle Crags , and McArthur-Burney Falls state parks.

The upstairs bedrooms are fully carpeted, have private baths, queen-size beds, guest robes and sitting areas.

The English Wicker Room: Calm and restful in peach, rose and soft greens, this room overlooks branching oaks and, as the sun rises, waves of color from the pool below reflect on the ceiling through an etched stained glass window. The private bath features a stall shower, pedestal sink, antique oak washstand and solid brass fixtures.

The Victorian Rose Room: Decor has mauves, pinks and blacks that flow together to create an ambience of Victorian elegance, eliciting nostalgia and romance. The feeling of bygone days is further enhanced with an antique oak and marble dry sink and a claw-foot tub replete with brass fixtures, resting in the window cupola. This affords a panoramic view of a star-filled sky or beautiful sunrise, from bath and bed.

Wisteria Cottage: This cottage is decorated in lavender, white and soft greens, inspired by the Claude Monet water lily prints on the walls and the wisteria fabrics and plants throughout. Tranquility and romance pervade the Suite, which includes a seven-foot spa tub and separate bath with stall shower.

The queen bed has a hand-painted, scrolled, pine headboard and is smothered in goose down in winter. The spacious sitting area overlooking the pool has a comfortable sofa-bed, two chairs and a table. You enter through a small, private garden with a flowing fountain. This is what dreams and memories are made.

An elegant gourmet breakfast is served in the dining room or in the outdoor gazebo.

Rates - $$ to $$$ Map Location - E

SHINGLETOWN, CALIFORNIA

Weston House
P.O. Box 276
Shingletown, California 96088
(916) 474-3738

Conveniently located at the 3,000-foot elevation on one of Mount Lassen's volcanic ridges, Weston House offers an intimate retreat on five and a half mountaintop acres. This secluded luxury is set in the quiet mood of green lawns, radiant gardens, fruit trees and vineyard.

Whether you are relaxing by the pool, sunning on the deck, or reading in your room, breathtaking panoramic views await you. Designed for the discriminate traveler, Weston House blends the warmth and romance of a spectacular mountain setting with the luxury and comfort of elegant accommodations.

The Victorian suite is an engaging hideaway complete with private entrance, bath and balcony, antique woodburning stove, plus sitting area and wet bar. You'll discover the wonderful attention to detail in this lovely suite with its delicate floral wallpaper, sumptuous eyelet fabrics, linen and embroidered pillows, all in soft pastels. Upon your arrival, complimentary refreshments are yours as you relax and settle in. After a peaceful slumber, a bountiful breakfast is served in the sunny dining room, at the poolside or in the privacy of your room.

Shingletown was a small community set up many years ago to make cedar shingles. While visiting Northern California, enjoy an adventure to Mount Lassen National Park or McArthur-Burney Falls State Park, considered by some to be the eighth wonder of the world. Mount Shasta, the Trinity Alps and Whiskeytown Lake all are within an hour and a half drive.

Enjoy hiking, fishing, swimming, boating, biking, horseback riding, golf, nature walks, picnics and tennis. Experience a visit to California's only wild-horse sanctuary or enjoy the tranquility of a guided boat tour along the beautiful Sacramento River.

During the winter months, spend a day cross-country skiing or discover the excitement of downhill slopes at Mount Lassen or Mount Shasta ski parks.

Rates -$$ Map Location - E

TRINIDAD, CALIFORNIA

The Lost Whale Bed & Breakfast Inn
3452 Patrick's Point Drive
Trinidad, California 95570
(707) 677-3425

This cozy Cape Cod style inn features wood-planked flooring and a charming country decor enhanced by the work of local artisans. Choose one of four spacious suites with full bath or shower, then step out on the balcony or sitting alcove for breathtaking ocean views. Wake up to the barking of sea lions on Turtle Rock, and have your hearty breakfast in the sunny Great Room or out on the deck, while watching for migrating whales. Enjoy homebaked bread and muffins, bagels and locally smoked salmon and quiches made from fresh eggs and vegetables.

After you stroll along the bluff through native rhododendrons, azaleas and fuchsias, take a private path to the beach. This is one of the few inns that can boast of a scenic, wooded trail to a secluded and primitive cove of jutting rocks, tide pools and sea lions. Or you may choose to walk out the front door, turn left and, in minutes, arrive at the beautiful Patrick's Point State Park. Take the long winding staircase down to Agate Beach. Collect driftwood or compete with the locals, who are masters at hunting the illusive agate and jade. And while the tide is out, explore the bountiful marine life in the tide pools.

Shaw House Inn, Ferndale, CA

While you are here, visit the quaint fishing village of Trinidad. At the marina, you can charter a boat for deep-sea fishing. If you prefer, try surf fishing; or bring your own boat and cast off from one of the many lagoons in the area, where you can also swim, sail or windsurf.

Don't miss hiking the trails through the majestic redwood forests, a 20-minute drive north. In the same area is Fern Canyon, with literally thousands of ferns and spectacular waterfalls that provide photo opportunities galore. Or use one of your hosts' bicycles to cruise the quiet coastal roads overlooking miles of unspoiled beach.

Visit the lively college town of Arcata, or Eureka's Old Town; a wonderful array of restored Victorian with a variety of delightful shops, restaurants and art galleries.

Watch the glorious sunset on the deck with cappuccino or sherry and homebaked pastries. Then, before your evening out on the town, relax in the jacuzzi while you watch the crashing waves. Indulge in the culinary expertise of award-winning restaurants and head out for a night of dancing, entertainment and music. Or just lounge in the spacious Great Room with a glass of wine and listen to music or engage in conversation with other guests. You also may choose to curl up with a good book from an eclectic library or pull out a chessboard or a deck of cards.

If you're bringing the kids, rest assured there are endless ways to channel their boundless energies. While you're sunbathing on the deck, they'll have the run of the enclosed grounds as they pick berries or have fun in the playhouse and playground or feed bunnies and lambs. They'll also hear about the "Legend of the Lost Whale" and delight in sleeping in their very own loft. The Great Room is filled with books, puzzles and games that will entertain and satisfy their curious minds. For your romantic evening out, childcare can be arranged. For those of you who come in the winter, the excitement of ocean storms is an added attraction.

Rates - $$ to $$$ Map Location - W

Trinidad Bed & Breakfast
P.O. Box 849
Trinidad, California 95570-0849
(707) 667-0840

Anchored on an ancient bluff overlooking the rugged California coast with Trinidad's picturesque fishing harbor below, the Trinidad Bed & Breakfast offers two suites, one with fireplace, and two upstairs bedrooms, all with private baths.

Surrounded by beaches, trails and the Redwood National Park, this inn is within steps of the restaurants and shops. A pleasant trail around Trinidad Head offers superb spots for picnicking or whale and sea-lion watching as well. Summer and late spring are filled with hearty outdoor activity. Fall and winter are especially appealing times in Trinidad for those who savor cozy, rainy nights and moody, fog-laden days.

Mauve Fireplace Suite: This large front-corner room with wraparound windows overlooks Trinidad Bay, which provides spectacular coastline views and sunsets. A king-size bed and a private bath with shower are featured. Two comfy rockers in front of your large brick fireplace add a cozy touch. Your private entrance affords you the luxury of breakfast delivered to your door and enjoyed at an ocean-view table for two.

Peach Master Bedroom: This special upstairs corner room built for the original owners boasts warm knotty-pine paneled walls and captures a view of the memorial lighthouse that clings to the bluff. It includes a queen-size bed and a large private bath with shower, as well as a bay-view dormer window with a cozy table for two to enjoy the beautiful sunsets behind the Trinidad Headland. Each morning, you will enjoy a hearty breakfast at a family-style table downstairs.

Blue Bay View Suite: This large upstairs all-windowed room overlooks beautiful Trinidad Bay and offers a spectacular view of historic Indian Beach and its rocky shoreline. It includes a queen-size bed and private bath with shower-tub combination, plus two comfy rockers alongside a telescope for whale watching in the bay. Your outside private entrance allows the hosts to bring breakfast up each morning for you to enjoy at your bay-view breakfast table.

Green Window Seat Room: This cozy second-floor bedroom has a large pillow-filled window seat built into the Cape Cod style dormer window. The view looks down the coast for miles, enabling you to enjoy the often tranquil or sometimes angry ocean. A queen-size bed wrapped with knotty pine walls and a private bath with a shower are featured. Come downstairs to a hearty breakfast of fresh-baked bread, muffins, baked fruits and a bottomless coffee pot.

Rates - $$$ Map Location - W

WEAVERVILLE, CALIFORNIA

Granny's House
313 Taylor Street, P.O. Box 31
Weaverville, California 96093
(916) 623-2756

Enjoy this two-story Victorian style home with your hosts. Built Queen Anne style in 1897, it still retains much of the flavor of its historical past.

Featuring three elegantly decorated turn-of-the-century rooms for a restful return to the past. The softly lighted parlors and dining room invite you to curl up by the fireplace with a good book or enjoy your sumptuous breakfast, including smoked meats, cheeses, croissants, muffins, fresh fruit, beverages and other delicacies.

Rates - $$ Map Location - W

YREKA, CALIFORNIA

McFadden's Bed & Breakfast Inn
418 Third Street
Yreka, California 996097
(916) 842-7712

McFadden's Bed & Breakfast Inn is an old Victorian house in a quiet neighborhood in the historic district near the center of Yreka—a town established during the California Gold Rush of the 1850s.

The Inn has one bedroom furnished in Victorian style, featuring a double bed with goose-down Duvet and a private bath.

Continental breakfast and complimentary wine & cheese are served.

Enjoy fishing, hunting, photography, boating, bird watching, or try your hand at climbing Mount Shasta, Mount Eddy and Black Butte.

Rates - $$ Map Location - W

BETTER

Bed

Breakfast

& Inns

OREGON

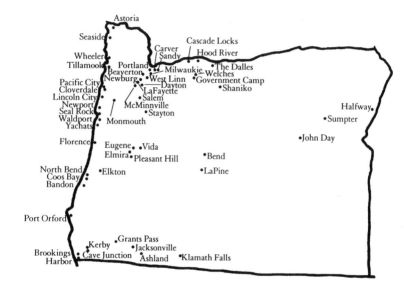

ASHLAND, OREGON

Edinburgh Lodge
586 East Main Street
Ashland, Oregon 97520
(503) 488-1050 or 1-800-643-4434

The spirit of early Ashland has left its warm glow of hospitality on Edinburgh Lodge, which originally was the J.T. Currie Boarding House, built in 1908. Here, your hosts welcome you to a bed and breakfast experience in the British tradition, with a touch of Scotland and their own special brand of Southern hospitality. The six cozy bedrooms are named for Scottish castles and offer air conditioning with queen-sized or twin beds. Each room has a private bath, one of which includes the original Victorian tub and an added shower.

Culinary delights may include scones and cakes with tea, peaches-and-cream french toast, fresh berry crepes or baked herb eggs with pumpkin heavenly surprise muffins for breakfast.

Enjoy the finest of Shakespeare and off Bard's way theatre, varied shopping, whitewater rafting on the famous Rogue River and the challenge of mountain biking, hiking, or skiing. Located one block from downtown, enjoy an easy walk to shopping and theatres. Airport and ski shuttle service available without charge.

Rates - $$ - Senior/Group Discount   Map Location - SW

McCall House Bed & Breakfast
153 Oak Street
Ashland, Oregon 97520
(503) 482-9296

This McCall House Bed & Breakfast is a beautifully restored historic Inn built by

General John McCall. A splendid example of Italianate architecture, the McCall House once has hosted many a prominent visitor, including General Sherman, Rutherford B. Hayes and William Jennings Bryan.

Here you'll find spacious, smoke-free rooms in a grand Victorian home. Private or shared bath and full homemade breakfast.

One block to Shakespearean theatres, restaurants, shops, and Lithia Park.

Rates - $$ Map Location - SW

Romeo Inn
295 Idaho Street
Ashland, Oregon 97520
(503) 488-0884

The Romeo Inn is romantically set in one of Ashland's quiet residential neighborhoods, just eight blocks from the nationally acclaimed Oregon Shakespearean Festival. This classic Cape Cod house sits elegantly amid towering Ponderosa pines on half an acre overlooking the Rogue Valley.

Guests are encouraged to relax in the living room, curl up with a good book from the library, or play a favorite song on the baby grand piano. The mild Southern Oregon weather allows guests to sit or stroll in the Inn's beautiful gardens and enjoy the lovely patio, pool and spa year-round.

Built in the early 1930s, the Inn is completely equipped with modern conveniences, yet still retains its gracious Cape Cod style. Its four large guest rooms and two luxurious suites have central air conditioning, king-sized beds and private baths. Each is decorated with a blend of antique and traditional furnishings, including a collection of hand-stitched Amish quilts.

Two of the rooms are upstairs in the main house. The Bristol is a cheerful English country guest room, decorated in blue and white, with views of the pines and valley. The Coventry is done in antiques and earth tones. Guests look out from this spacious room onto the flower garden and mountains.

Located on the first floor, the Canterbury and Windsor rooms each have a private outside entrance and a daybed, in addition to the king. The Windsor room is designed around several distinctive Oriental rugs, emphasizing blue and taupe. In the airy Canterbury room, done in white and forest green, a hand-crafted oak poster bed faces a floor-to-ceiling brick fireplace.

The Cambridge Suite features a blue and mauve decor and vaulted ceiling. Its comfortable sitting area includes overstuffed chairs in front of a tiled fireplace. The view of the pool and the Cascades, and French doors opening onto a private garden patio, create a quiet and relaxing setting.

The Stratford Suite is detached from the Inn for complete privacy. It is high above street level to take full advantage of the views of the Cascades, the Rogue Valley, and the Inn's lovely gardens. A graceful vaulted ceiling, marbled fireplace, two-person whirlpool bath with a skylight view, comfortable living room and complete kitchen are some of the elegant features of the suite. The bedroom showcases a handmade Amish quilt that reflects the suite's contemporary teal and peach color theme.

Breakfast is quite an event at Romeo Inn. Freshly squeezed orange juice, a plate of melon with blueberry sauce, eggs Florentine, tasty farm sausage, freshly baked breads, and fresh-ground coffee or tea is a typical breakfast served in the Inn's cheerful dining room. It's guaranteed to give you second thoughts about having lunch.

Comfortable.... Quiet.... Elegant.

Rates - $$$ to $$$ Map Location - SW

The Woods House Bed & Breakfast Inn
333 North Main Street
Ashland, Oregon 97520
(503) 488-1598

This 1908 Craftsman style home with a carriage house across the courtyard was occupied for almost 40 years by the Woods family. Dr. and Mrs. Woods had four sons, most of whom lived and raised families in Ashland. Third- and fourth-generation members still live in the area.

The Woods House is nestled on a landscaped half acre. The extensive grounds are patterned after a traditional English garden, comprising a grape arbor, pergola, rose garden, summer house, and other secluded nooks.

You are welcome to relax in the quiet elegance of the living room, where a cheery fire awaits you on chilly days. A selection of books is at hand, as well as the daily newspapers for your quiet perusal. Hot coffee, tea and treats are available in the dining room throughout the day.

A delectable breakfast is served promptly at 9 a.m. in the gracious dining room or, on warm summer mornings, in the garden under a spreading walnut tree. Your hosts provide convenient off-street parking behind the Carriage House. In addition, there is central air conditioning and heating in the main house and individual units in the Carriage House.

The Victorian Room is the original master bedroom, with a windowed, walk-in closet. The bath has a large soaking tub and pedestal sink. Lace-curtained windows give views of the garden, and a lace-canopied, queen-sized bed, reading chair, and side table provide ease and comfort.

The charming Courtyard Room—with a private entrance and plenty of lace—is perfect for honeymooners. The generous front window provides delightful views of the cloud-dappled hills of Ashland. A queen-sized bed, piled with pillows, completes this lovely chamber.

In the Bouquet Room, a skylight brings the romance of the moon and stars to the queen-sized bed. A secluded daybed and comfortable chair are perfect for reading and relaxing. From here, you also have access to the covered porch overlooking the garden, where you might sip afternoon sherry.

In the Monet Room, a soothing and serene ambiance is created with soft tones of blue and mauve. A lace canopy and skylight enhance the queen- and twin-sized beds. This room also has access to the private, upstairs porch.

The Cottage Room is cozy, with a private entrance, and is located in the Carriage House. The antique, queen-sized bed, with lace canopy, will transport you to dreams of yesteryear.

The Cupid's Chamber also is located in the Carriage House, with a private entrance. Here, you will find a romantic, canopy-topped, king-sized bed. A twin bed and comfy reading chair complete this spacious and restful room.

The Shakespearean Festival theatres all are an easy four-block walk from the Inn, and Lithia Park is seasonless. Spend a day discovering the shaded paths and hidden ponds with ducks and turtles. Return time and time again as you explore the beauties of this 100-acre sylvan idyll.

Winter events include: (Nov.) Fall Performing Arts Festival; (Dec.) Come Home for the Holidays Festival; (Jan.) A Taste of Ashland, Winter Wine, Food & Arts Festival; (May) Spring Festival.

Moreover, downtown Ashland offers a wide variety of excellent restaurants for your dining pleasure, in addition to eight intriguing bookstores and numerous antique, gift, and clothing shops.

Weisingers and Ashland Wineries are open year-round and are just a short drive from the Inn. Tour maps are available.

Jacksonville, a National Historic Landmark is home to a museum, galleries, antique shops, and unusual restaurants, all housed in original brick buildings and delightful, restored Victorian houses.

Exploring the town and surroundings is a pleasant day excursion from Ashland. The Britt Music Festival takes place during the summer months at the Peter Britt Estate in Jacksonville, and local restaurants offer picnic lunches.

Rates - $$$ to $$$$ Map Location - SW

ASTORIA, OREGON

Grandview Bed & Breakfast
1574 Grand Avenue
Astoria, Oregon 97103
1-800-488-3250
(503) 325-0000 or (503) 325-5555

When Tall Ships still plied the Columbia River and salmon runs were plentiful, Eben Tallant and his brother, Nathan Tallant, came to Astoria to build a salmon-packing cannery much larger than the cannery Eagle Cliff, Washington had before it burned down. Andrew Ferguson designed the Eben Tallant family residence at 682 Arch Street in the Richardson Shingle style. The home features a bullet turret, inset balconies, open staircase and bay windows. During the past 40 years, the home has been divided into eight apartments.

The Northwest tower, now capped with an open balcony, makes one feel like a captain on the prow of a ship as the house steers toward the mouth of the Columbia River.

The Garden: This sunny south-side room, with bay windows and a lilac and Iris motif, provides views of the Astoria Column, treetops and nearby Victorian homes. Queen bed, daybed and private bath.

The Refuge: Bird-call records, bird books and wallpaper.

The Gazebo: A spacious room with a view of the Columbia River from tower windows or balcony. Queen bed and private bath.

The Treetops: Spacious room with spectacular view from the balcony overlooking the river and grove. Queen bed and private bath.

Cloud 9: This room offers a wonderful view of Washington's mountains and river. Queen bed, daybed and shared bath.

The Cove: A large, but cozy and peaceful room with shells and art. Queen bed and private or shared bath.

Anastasia's Room: This is the smallest, coziest room, with pink petal paper, pictures and comforter. View of Victorian homes, treetops and the Astor Column. Queen bed and shared bath.

TWO-BEDROOM SUITES

Little Hummers: Sleeps six. Old fashioned claw-foot tub in private bath. Two queen beds and two twin beds. View of historic buildings and mini view of river.

Cloud 9 Suite: Sleeps five. Two individual bedrooms with a shared bath between them. Wonderful view of the mountains and river. Queen bed and daybed.

"Treetops Suite:" Sleeps four. Two single bedrooms with shared bath between them. Spacious room with spectacular view from balcony overlooking the river and grove.

Continental breakfast "plus" is complimentary and consists of five coffee choices, five teas, hot cocoa or cider, milk, fruit juices, fruit, and a variety of fresh muffins.

The Grandview is located on the Historic Homes Walking Tour. A superb Maritime Museum, Heritage Museum, Columbia Lightship, and 100-year-old churches are close by. Ships from many nations dock here. Some allow Sunday tours.

Golf, clam-digging, beachcombing and surfing opportunities, plus fishing boats, are a short drive away. You can hike to the Astor Column, stroll on the college campus, read books, and watch boats or birds.

Rates - $ to $$ Map Location - NW

BANDON, OREGON

Lighthouse Bed & Breakfast
650 Jetty Road S.W.
Bandon, Oregon 97411
(503) 347-9316

The Lighthouse Bed & Breakfast is located on the beach across from Bandon's historic lighthouse, at the mouth of the Coquille River. The panoramic view encompasses the Pacific Ocean and Coquille estuary, complete with shorebirds, marine wildlife, fishing boats crossing the jetty, sport fishermen, and occasional sailboarders.

A short walk to the ocean will give you a glimpse of the ancient sea-stacks jutting from the water just offshore, a wondrous environment for those who like to beachcomb or jog along the water's edge.

Your hosts believe in getting guests off to a good start with a heart-healthy breakfast and ideas about what to do and see in Bandon. The local chamber of commerce also has a wealth of information about the area.

Greenhouse Room: Romantic and spacious king room. Adjoining private bath with shower and whirlpool tub for two. Fireplace, river view, and T.V.

Sunset View Room: Sunny queen room with lighthouse and ocean views. Adjoining private bath with shower.

Deck Room: The sliding-glass door leads to a private east-facing deck. Queen bed, adjoining private bath with shower and a river view.

Karen's Room: Cheerful queen room with ocean and lighthouse views. The private bath across the hall includes tub and shower.

The unique location and romantic rooms provide guests with a quiet setting to relax amid plants, original artwork and unsurpassed views. And remember, "A good rest is half the work".

Things to do: Shore bird watching, West Coast Game Park Petting Zoo, Festival of Lights in December, concerts and other events at Harbor Hall, clamming, fishing, crabbing, golfing, antique and gallery shopping, cheese factory tours, sternwheeler cruises, Old Town specialty shops, mountain and beach horseback riding, gourmet dining in fine restaurants, whale watching, beach-rock and driftwood collecting, and local aerobics and Jazzercise classes.

Rates - $$ Map Location - SW

Sea Star Guest House
375 Second Street
Bandon, Oregon 97411
(503) 347-9632

The Sea Star is a uniquely designed coastal getaway in historic Old town Bandon, with an incredible view of the harbor and beach from each unit and deck. Bandon-by-the-Sea is a coastal artist colony on Oregon's most scenic beach, with miles of pure sandy beaches, dunes, cliffs, an ocean of legendary rock formations and incredible sunsets.

Sleeping rooms or full suites are offered here, all with private baths, cable TV and queen-sized beds.

Room 1 - Upper level suite, queen bed in loft, hide-a-bed in living room, plus kitchen, skylight, open beam . A fantastic setting.

Room 2 - Upper level , queen-sized bed, open beam. A romantic getaway.

Room 3A - Ground-level suite, queen bed, hide-a-bed in living room, kitchen. A homey retreat.

Room 3B - Ground level, queen bed, and a cozy, hide-a-bed.

Things to do: Cheese factory, museum, art galleries, wild animal game park, historic lighthouse, performing-arts center, cranberry sweets factory, swimming, surfing, fishing, crabbing, clamming, beachcombing, whale watching, and shopping in unique shops.

Rates - $$ Map Location - SW

BEAVERTON, OREGON

The Yankee Tinker Bed & Breakfast
5480 S.W. 183rd Avenue
Beaverton, Oregon 97007
(503) 649-0932

The Yankee Tinker is located just 10 miles west of Portland, yet is in the heart of wine country. You'll enjoy a quiet street and fresh country air, with easy access to farmers' markets, colorful festivals, and numerous historical sites. From here, visit the famed Washington Park Rose Gardens, the dramatic Columbia River Gorge, Mount Hood, local wineries and the fine array of Oregon beaches!

The spacious deck, surrounded by an ever-changing array of colorful flowers, is a fun place to relax, chat, catch up on reading, or even have a meeting.

The Massachusetts Room: The master suite with queen-sized bed, private adjoining bath, a handmade dusty rose and blue quilt and a view of the flower garden.

The Maine Room: Deep teal and burgundy handmade comforter and oversize pillows grace the queen-sized bed in this spacious room with rocker and antique dresser.

The New Hampshire Room: An antique four-poster single bed, a soft pink and blue quilt and other collectibles give this room a charm all its own.

All rooms feature a warm antique New England decor and air conditioning.

Your gourmet breakfast may be mouth-watering blueberry pancakes or muffins, peaches and cream french toast, herb omelets, or some other equally delightful choice. Following an old Yankee tradition, pie often is included for the hearty eater. And the pleasing aromas, superb service, and pure taste enjoyment will stay with you long after your trip is over.

Rates - $ to $$ Map Location - NW

BEND, OREGON

Farewell Bend Bed & Breakfast
29 N.W. Greeley
Bend, Oregon 97701
(503) 382-4374

Farewell Bend Bed & Breakfast is a Dutch Colonial style house built in the 1920s and recently remodeled. It is located just four blocks from the unique shops and abundant restaurants of downtown Bend and the picturesque banks of the Deschutes River, where it meanders through Drake and Mirror Pond parks. Wild geese, ducks and a pair of mute swans glide serenely on the water, and a variety of activities are offered nearby during summer months. Bend also offers whitewater rafting, hiking, fishing, and windsurfing. And in the winter months, downhill skiing is available at magnificent Mount Bachelor, just 22 miles away. In addition, you'll find endless miles of cross-country skiing and snowmobile trails in close proximity.

Rooms have private baths with terry bath robes for each guest. Each room is unique, though all are warm and include colorful handmade quilts on the beds. Relax in the living room with one of many books, watch T.V., or plus a movie into the VCR.

Enjoy breakfast in the family dining room, or on the deck in the summer. Your hosts will serve a full breakfast with homemade jams, muffins and bread. You may request a picnic basket 24 hours in advance. Special attention will be given to dietary needs if you notify your hosts in advance.

Rates - $$ Map Location - SE

BROOKINGS, OREGON

Chetco River Inn Bed & Breakfast
21202 High Prairie Road
Brookings, Oregon 97415
(503) 469-8128

Relax in the peaceful seclusion of this private 35-acre forest, bordered on three sides by the Chetco River. The Inn is small, so guest numbers are limited. The river—where you can fish for salmon, trout or steelhead from a private bank—is just a stone's throw from the front door. You may choose to practice at horseshoes, darts or archery, or enjoy birdwatching, hiking on one of the many nearby trails, or watching the grey squirrels play in the myrtlewood grove.

These accommodations offer a delightful combination of "old-world" hospitality and "new-world" comfort. Spacious rooms feature comfortable queen- and twin-sized beds, private baths and spectacular views of the mountains and river.

A complete country-style, home-cooked breakfast, served family style, gets your day off to a good start. Upon request, your hosts offer picnic lunches and delicious five-course dinners. The large common room welcomes you with games, books, comfortable furniture, television, videos, a scenic view, and a crackling fire.

Fishing and hunting packages can be individually tailored to your needs—including early breakfasts, hearty box lunches and generous dinners. Your hosts also will help you arrange for fishing and hunting guides, deep sea charters, or general transportation. Sportsmen may be interested in the special catch-and-release discount program.

Brookings is the southern-most community on the beautiful Oregon Coast. Enjoy ocean fishing, crabbing, clamming, whale watching, and windsurfing. A bit further inland, you can try trekking, tennis, golf, bowling, fine restaurants, and antique shops.

The area is famous for Easter lilies, wildflowers, and myrtlewood trees. Brookings also has its own airport.

Rates - $$ Map Location - SW

Lowden's Beachfront Bed & Breakfast
14626 Wollam Road
Brookings, Oregon 97415
(503) 469-7045 or 1-800 453-4768

Lowden's Beachfront is located on the ocean, where the Winchuck River enters the Pacific. Every season offers new entertainment, as pelicans, seals, whales, salmon and the like perform for you.

Walk the beach, clam, fish, swim or hunt for seashells. Visit numerous state parks or browse in the many galleries and craft shops. You'll certainly enjoy the "Banana Belt" of the Northwest.

Rooms include river and ocean views, private baths, queen-sized beds with comforters, remote-control TV, on the beach refrigerator, microwave and coffee pot.

A continental breakfast is breakfast placed in your room each night, so you can have it whenever you like.

Rates - $$ Map Location - SW

The Ward House Bed & Breakfast Inn
Box 86, 516 Redwood Street
Brookings, Oregon 97415
(503) 469-5557

The Ward House was built in 1917 by William Ward, then president of the Brookings Lumber Mill. It is one of the few old, distinguished homes in the town of about 4,700 people.

This inn overlooks downtown Brookings, offering a view of the Pacific Ocean a few blocks away. Walk to one of the many restaurants, shops, the town movie house, beautiful Azalea Park or the harbor at the mouth of the Chetco River.

The beautifully decorated, spacious bedrooms located upstairs have ocean views, queen beds, televisions or radios. Bathrooms feature old-fashioned tubs or convenient showers.

Breakfast is elegantly served in the dining room from 8-9:30 a.m., and the menu includes such delicacies as Norwegian waffles with special sauce and fresh jams or eggs Benedict.

The Ward House is sure to provide you with a delightfully happy experience. Also available here are hot tub and sauna, picnic baskets, prearranged, guided hikes along the coastline or inland, and airport pickup.

Rates - $$ Map Location - SW

CARVER, OREGON

Kipling Rock Farm Bed & Breakfast
17000 S.E. Hwy. 224
Carver, Oregon 97015
(503) 658-5056

"And I have lived! The rest of the American Continent may now sink under the sea, for I have taken the best that it yields and the best was neither love, nor money, nor real estate." Rudyard Kipling upon catching a salmon at Carver, Oregon in the late 1800s.

For a real immersion in country life along the Clackamas River, visit this 1938 cottage home. Kipling Rock Farm stands on seven acres of hillside above the river, and includes vegetable/herb gardens, ponds, an orchard, and a cheerful barnyard at the bottom of the hill. A short walk through the woods reveals a private beach at the river's edge.

One special guest room ensures a renewal of the senses. You'll find a large view room with a fireplace, down quilt, antiques, flowers, private bath, entrance and sitting porch, complete with a small refrigerator.

Even if it's only for a day and a night, this idyllic escape—less than a 10-minute drive from I-205 (Clackamas Exit 12A)—will make you feel as if you've had a refreshing vacation.

Rates - $$ Map Location - NW

CASCADE LOCKS, OREGON

Foster House Bed & Breakfast
369 Forest Lane
P.O. Box 391
Cascade Locks, Oregon 97014
(503) 374-8834

Foster House is located in the heart of the Columbia Gorge Scenic Area. Here, you'll stay in an old-fashioned country home, and have your choice at breakfast.

Cascade Locks is more then just a place; it's an experience! It's the home of the Sternwheeler "Columbia Gorge," and is a friendly community with many tourist facilities.

Dining: Excellent restaurants, drive-ins, deli, cocktail lounges, tavern, and catering services are located throughout the community.

Windsurfing is great both for the beginner and the expert. The Gorge Cities Blow Out starts in Cascade Locks.

A boat marina located next to the Port Visitors' Center offers a public launch and pump station. And an airport for small aircraft is located on Forest Lane, just down the road from this Bed & Breakfast. Portland International Airport is 35 minutes away.

Cascade Locks has a grocery store, convenience stores, a fish market, liquor store, gift shops, beauty shop, and bait and tackle shops. Additional services include garages, services stations, hardware, towing, video mart, locksmith, and laundromat.

Rates - $ Map Location - NE

CAVE JUNCTION, OREGON

Out 'n' About Bed & Breakfast Resort
300 Page Creek Road
Cave Junction, Oregon 97523
(503) 592-2208

At Out 'n' About, it's all or nothing! You can relax to your heart's content in the cozy cabin, which features either electric or wood heat, a full bath, and a panoramic view of a peaceful meadow and surrounding mountains. Or, if you prefer, take advantage of the many activities the Illinois Valley has to offer. But at Out 'n' About, the word is horses!

Depending upon your experience, you can take a short lesson in the meadow, a longer ride down a wooded path, or a trek to the top of a mountain on any of the hundreds of miles of national forest trails!

Anytime of the year is the perfect time to visit this rustic bed & breakfast. Come for a day, or make it your destination resort!

In the spring, wildflowers abound: The unique ecology and geography of Southwestern Oregon nurtures a variety of rare, prehistoric flowers, grasses and succulents found nowhere else in the world. You can walk, take a mountain bike, ride a horse, or drive to some of the most beautiful country in the world. And in the spring, you can raft the Illinois River, one of the most scenic and exciting rivers in the Pacific Northwest!

In the summertime, the livin' is easy, but hardly dull. Come for a week and learn to ride, or cool off in one of the numerous secluded swimming holes.

With the autumn comes the beautiful colors and the outset of the greening rain. During this season, you also can experience the annual salmon and steelhead runs, the first game hunts, and the hunt for edible mushrooms, which grow in abundance throughout fire-scarred areas. The early nights in front of a cozy fire make for romance as well.

Winter in this special corner of Oregon can be as quiet or as fun-filled as you'd like. Relax and enjoy the pristine beauty of the snow-covered Siskiyou Mountains looming ancient above the rivers. Enter headlong into the heart of the wilderness winter on a cross-country skiing trek or horse ride, or catch the wilder side of winter sports on a snowmobile, sled, snowboard, toboggan or tube!

Out 'n' About features: A deluxe cabin that sleeps five, a delightful "Swiss Family Robinson" adult treehouse, complete RV hook-ups, buggy rides, mountain bikes, cross-country skis, river raft trips, cottage industry craft tour, and horseback riding for two to seven people.

Rates - $$ Map Location - SW

CLOVERDALE, OREGON

The Hudson House Bed & Breakfast Inn
3700 Highway 101, South
Cloverdale, Oregon 97112
(503) 392-3533

The Hudson House was completed in 1906 by the Hudson family and, through the years, has become a landmark in south Tillamook County. Your stay in this Victorian home will be a delightful one.

All rates include a full gourmet breakfast for two, with the famous Hudson House Oats, British bangers sausage, fresh-baked fruit muffins, fresh fruits and cheese, and egg specialties. If you have a particular menu preference, just let your hosts know in advance and they'll do their best to accommodate you. Breakfast is served in the Victorian dining room from 8 to 10 a.m. An earlier breakfast may be served if prior arrangements are made. Complimentary teas and homemade cookies are offered in the afternoon.

The Hudson House specializes in good food. If you would like to take the flavor of the inn home with you, Hudson House Oats and other recipes are available for purchase.

The Inn has rooms with both private and shared baths. Each room with a shared bath is furnished with comfortable robes for your convenience, as well as baskets of fresh, fluffy towels.

Both Hudson House and the rugged surrounding of coast and country require at least two nights to explore. Although they are really a "grown-up" fantasy, children are fondly welcomed with prior arrangement as well. The Hudson House will need to know in advance if there will be more than two of you. When possible, the hosts will furnish an extra bed and another place at breakfast for an additional charge.

Other amenities available include wake-up service, a lending library and table games in the parlor, lawn croquet and badminton, full use of common areas, such as the garden, orchard, forest, and veranda porches, and local maps and fishing guides upon request.

The immediate area offers numerous hiking trails, Three Capes Scenic Loop, the dory fleet, golf, wine touring, boating, beachcombing, kite festivals, clam digging, and some of the best salmon and steelhead fishing on the Oregon Coast. Many choice restaurants and antique shops are nearby as well.

Rates - $$ Map Location - NW

COOS BAY, OREGON

Coos Bay Manor Bed & Breakfast
955 South Fifth Street
Coos Bay, Oregon 97420
(503) 269-1224

This historic Colonial-style house was built in 1911 by two Finish brothers, the Nerdrums, who worked for the C.A. Smith Lumber Company, where they pioneered the use of saltwater from the bay in making pulp.

The Victorian Room: Lace, ruffles, and romance. The largest room, featuring late 19th century charm and elegance. A sitting area overlooks rolling hills in the distance. Queen canopy bed and shared bath.

Cattle Baron's Room: Bed yourself down in the tradition of the Old West. Authentic bear and coyote rugs grace the walls of this room. Queen bed and private bath includes tub with shower.

The Country Room: Warm and inviting, the old-fashioned country softness enhances this cozy room just like Grandma's house, complete with spinning wheel. Brass queen-sized bed adorned with authentic handmade quilts. Shared bath with shower.

The Garden Room: Capture the freshness of a spring garden in the blue room, accented with beautifully woven white rattan furniture. This room overlooks a beautiful rhododendron garden in the spring. Draped queen bed and shared bath with shower.

The Colonial Room: Handsomely decorated in the timeless style of yesteryear. Two twin poster beds and shared bath. Gaze out the window at historic giant redwood trees.

Take time to enjoy the South Coast Lake, ocean, and river fishing, just minutes from the Manor. Other features include botanical gardens, art and historical museums, fine dining, sand dunes, excellent deer, elk and duck hunting, unique shops, and antique stores.

Rates - $$ Map Location - SW

CORVALLIS, OREGON

Abed and Breakfast at Sparks' Hearth
2515 S.W. 45th
Corvallis, Oregon 97333
(503) 757-7321

Located just three miles from downtown Corvallis and the beautiful Oregon State University campus, Abed and Breakfast offers you a cordial, casual stay in a peaceful country setting.

You'll share a spacious antique-furnished living room and formal dining room on the main floor. And your large second-floor bedroom will provide you peace and privacy. You can relax in the comfort of a heated spa on the south deck, where luxuriously soft body towels and terry robes are provided for your use.

From the wrap-round porch, you can enjoy the view of the Coast Range to the west or the Corvallis Golf and Country Club on the east.

Breakfast is served with a flair of elegance in the dining room, or in casual leisure on the east deck.

Rates - $$ Map Location - SW

DAYTON, OREGON

Wine Country Farm
6855 Breyman Orchards Road
Dayton, Oregon 97114
(503) 864-3446

Wine Country Farm, a 13-acre estate surrounded by miles of vineyards and orchards, is located in the heart of Oregon's wine-growing region in beautiful Yamhill County. The Inn is a restored 1910 estate and sits on a hill that commands an impressive view of the surrounding vineyards, wineries, orchards and Cascade Mountain Range.

The farm produces five varieties of grapes, in addition to raising Arabian horses. If you travel with your horse, boarding is available. And, for your enjoyment, you are invited to take a horse-drawn buggy ride for an afternoon picnic, walk the nature trails, tour the surrounding area on mountain bikes, or lounge on the inn's large deck.

The four bedrooms at Wine Country Farm vary in price. For your comfort, all rooms are spacious, tastefully furnished, and offer a view of the beautiful countryside.

In the master bedroom, you'll find a queen-sized bed, fireplace and private bath, while the second-floor bedroom includes a roomy king-sized bed and a private bath.

One of the two other rooms has two twin beds, the other a double; they share a bath. The living room, family room and reading rooms are available for your enjoyment. Read a book from the library, watch a little television, or just sit by the fire and relax. All overnight accommodations include the Country Farm Breakfast.

Things to do: Visit the many wineries, Historic Champoeg State Park, antiques shops, Oregon coast, or Portland, dine in one of many fine restaurants in neighboring towns of McMinnville, Dundee and Newberg, try your hand a golf, or rent a horse.

Rates - $$ Map Location - NW

ELKTON, OREGON

Elkqua Lodge Bed & Breakfast
P.O. Box 546
Elkton, Oregon 97436
(503) 584-2161

The Elkqua Lodge is located in Elkton on the banks of the beautiful Umpqua River on Highway 38. It has three guest rooms, all with private bath and full- and twin-sized beds. An in-ground swimming pool and a recreation room, complete with pool table, cards, games, and English darts, are available, as is satellite TV, a small library and more than 10 acres on which to walk, explore, and fish. The Lodge has a large trophy room and living room with a big-beam Cathedral ceiling.

Your hosts serve a large country-style breakfast, and lunches and dinner can be arranged for fishing guests.

Fishing or hunting guide services also are available on the Umpqua. Elkqua's guide service (Hannah Fish Camp) was named No. 1 in the state in the January, 1992 issue of *Oregon Magazine*. Your hosts have been in the fishing business for 20 years and the Bed & Breakfast business for three years.

Rates - $$ Map Location - SW

ELMIRA, OREGON

The Dome Bed & Breakfast
24456 Warthen Road
Elmira, Oregon 97437
(503) 935-3138

This Geodesic Dome is located 14 miles from Eugene, in a beautiful country setting, and 44 scenic miles from the Oregon Coast. The spacious interior of the Dome includes two suites, each with private bath and queen-sized beds. The upstairs suite has a large skylight for star gazing and a loft. The lower suite opens onto a large patio deck. Television and telephones are available in each suite. Guests can enjoy the large vaulted living room with all the comfort of home as well.

Lodging costs include a full breakfast, featuring homemade sausage and German egg cakes prepared by the Dome's chef, who promises that you'll never go away hungry. Fishing, boating and water recreation is available at nearby Fern Ridge Lake. Professionally guided fishing trips can be arranged by the owners. Airport transportation is provided as well.

Rates - $$ Map Location - SW

McGillivray's Log Home Bed & Breakfast
88680 Evers Road
Elmira, Oregon 97437
(503) 935-3564

This unique, built-from-scratch log home is located on five acres, mostly covered with fir and pine trees, in a secluded country setting. It is just 14 miles west of Eugene, on the way to the Oregon Coast.

McGillivray's offers the best of yesterday, combined with the comforts of today—king-sized beds, private bath, air-conditioning, and quiet. An old-fashioned breakfast is usually prepared on the antique wood-burning stove.

Rates - $$ Map Location - SW

EUGENE, OREGON

B & G's Bed & Breakfast
711 West 11th Avenue
Eugene, Oregon 97402
(503) 343-5739

B & G's offers convenience and a pleasant ambience, in walking distance of downtown shops and restaurants. Yet, the densely tree-shaded neighborhood makes this inn sem miles away from the city.

The house is Dutch Colonial style, recently remodeled with a distinctly Scandinavian feeling in mind.

The coffee pot is always on, and your host is available to go on walks along the river, through the rose garden or along the Ridgeline Trail. For those who enjoy biking and jogging, a trail is just two blocks away.

To help make your vacation or business trip even more enjoyable, your hosts will make restaurant and cafe suggestions or help plan a day trip west to seaside forests or east to lush, ancient mountain forests. B & G's also is just a 10-minute bus ride from the University of Oregon.

Also available are laundry facilities, three-speed bicycles, board games, novels, Scandinavian literature, maps and brochures covering events and places statewide.

Apartment: The entire second floor is an apartment available for the exclusive use of guests. It has a private entrance and bath, open-beam ceiling and kitchen facilities. This home-away-from-home has been tastefully remodeled with natural woods and greenery; the decor is blue, yellow and green with touches of red. The many nooks and crannies feature the work of local artists.

The apartment accommodates from one to six people, and is perfect for those relocating to the Eugene area or involved in short-term teaching or research projects at the university.

Cottage: The skylight and vaulted windows allow light to flood in at interesting angles. The wildflower garden in back fosters a sense of beauty, solitude and comfort. The cottage is perfect for those seeking complete privacy.

Shoji Room: The Shoji Room has a European and Japanese feel with simple but elegant decor. Shared bath.

Rates - $ to $$ Map Location - SW

Campus Cottage Bed & Breakfast Inn
1136 E. 19th Avenue
Eugene, Oregon 97403
(503) 342-5346

Campus Cottage is a homey alternative to a hotel or motel, and is just south of the University of Oregon campus.

The three guest rooms are furnished with antiques, comforters, fresh flowers, and have private baths. Guests are invited to curl up in the living room in front of a warm fire to read, visit, or work on the house jigsaw puzzle.

On warmer days and evenings, the southwest deck overlooking the cottage garden is a great place to relax. Bicycles are provided for those who want to pedal their way around town or campus.

A breakfast of fresh fruits and juices, pastries with jams and butter, special egg dishes, and plenty of fresh-ground coffee or tea will be served in the dining room or, upon request, in the guest rooms.

The cottage on 19th Avenue, built in 1922, was purchased in 1981 for the purpose of establishing Eugene's first bed and breakfast inn. All of the renovations retain the home's original character, while enhancing a country atmosphere.

The Cottage: A large, romantic retreat with queen-sized oak bed, day and trundle bed, as well as a private entrance, deck, vaulted ceiling, bay window, TV, and small refrigerator. The large bath has a claw-foot tub and shower combination.

The Suite: The original master bedroom with a queen-sized brass bed, plus a sitting room with a twin Jenny Lind bed. The large bath has a tub and hand-held shower.

The Guest Room: A cozy, south-facing room with a queen-size pine bed and a comfy reading chair by the window. The private bath has a cedar-lined shower.

Rates - $$ Map Location - SW

Duckworth Bed & Breakfast Inn
987 East 19th Avenue
Eugene, Oregon 97403
(503) 686-2451

Duckworth is a refreshing alternative to brand-name hotels and rooms that all look alike. An easy stroll from the University of Oregon campus, it's a charming English Tudor Inn, where your hosts specialize in old-fashioned hospitality. The rooms are furnished with genuine, old-world antiques, designed to make you feel as comfortable as you would at an old friend's country home.

You are free to choose a movie from a 500-plus library to watch in your room. Or you may wish to compare notes with other guests in front of the fireplace. The player piano makes everyone a musician, and folks have been known to sing along to songs of days gone by.

You may choose to curl up with a good book in the garden room, or ride a bicycle across the beautiful college campus. Join your hosts for afternoon tea in the parlor, or have them serve you in your room, if you'd prefer.

The rooms include all the amenities you would expect from the finest Inns— including full, private bath as well as semi-private bath accommodations.

Mornings begin with a sumptuously traditional American breakfast. If you're visiting friends or relatives at the university, they're welcome to join you for breakfast. The family-style kitchen is available for homemade treats throughout your stay, and your hosts are happy to cater your special event, business lunch, or family gathering.

Ask about discounts for parents of college students, or discounts for extended stays.

Rates - $$ Map Location - SW

Lorane Valley Bed & Breakfast
86621 Lorane Highway
Eugene, Oregon 97405
(503) 686-0241

This is a unique home on 22 acres of quiet, wooded hillside and meadow, featuring nine Angus cows and a Scottie dog in residence.

Single party in private suite. Full breakfast of varied menu.

King and two twin beds in spacious rooms, plus fresh cut flowers, complete kitchen with microwave, and Jacuzzi in private bath. Air conditioned.

The Inn is located just four and a half miles from the Hult Center for Performing Arts in downtown Eugene.

Rates - $$ Map Location - SW

The Lyon & The Lambe, A Bed & Breakfast Inn
988 Lawrence Street at Tenth
Eugene, Oregon 97401
(503) 683-3160

The Lyon & The Lambe is an elegant charm-filled home decorated for your pleasure and comfort. Your bed chamber is large, light, and has a private bath. In your room, you'll find Perrier, a toothsome Betthupferl on your pillow and other tasteful amenities.

Discover the luxurious tub room, and pamper yourself in the whirlpool bath with lotions and potions, heated towel bar and music of your selection.

The Lyon and Lambe's famous gourmet breakfast always includes fresh-baked croissants, bread or muffins, choice of fresh-squeezed juices, cereals, fresh-fruit compotes and, on weekends, "David Eyre Pancakes," "Kaiserschmarrn," "Eggs Florentine," and "French Toast Aphrodisia," all to the strains of Bach, Beethoven, and company.

Enjoy absolute privacy or choose conversation in the living room. You are invited to look at the menus of fine restaurants in Eugene.

Browse through the books in the library or use the TV, VCR, and compact discs as you please.

The Zephyr Room: Queen-sized bed, queen sofa bed, and private bath.

The Santana Room: Queen-sized bed, studio couch, and private bath.

The Mariah Room: Queen-sized bed and private bath.

The Scirocco Room: Twin beds and private bath.

Rates - $$ Map Location - SW

Pookie's Bed 'n' Breakfast On College Hill
2013 Charnelton Street
Eugene, Oregon 97405
(503) 686-9312

Pookie's Bed & Breakfast Inn was built in 1918 but has been remodeled. Nonetheless, inside still has that old-home charm, with period antiques in every room. Pookie's is close to downtown shopping and one short mile from the University of Oregon campus. Two local parks are within a two-block radius, and jogging and bike paths are nearby.

Rates - $$ Map Location - SW

FLORENCE, OREGON

The Edwin "K" Bed & Breakfast Inn
1155 Bay Street, P.O. Box 2687
Florence, Oregon 97439
(503) 997-8360

Built in 1914 and nestled on the rugged coastline of Oregon, the Edwin K defines the tradition of fine accommodations. It was built by the eldest son of William Kyle, one of the founders of Florence. The artistry of the wood crafters who restored The Edwin K—located across the street from the Siuslaw River and Dunes—is a pleasure to see.

You may choose from four large rooms offering custom private baths. The Edwin K has a pleasing blend of antiques and fine furnishings, and breakfast is served in the formal dining room on exquisite china, fine linens, and crystal.

Winter Room: This room will take you back in time with white and soft apricot colors on the queen-sized, four-poster bed. Soak in the claw-foot tub or shower.

Spring Room: Decorated in soft rose tones with a queen oak bed and down comforter. Wash away your cares in the double shower and whirlpool tub.

Summer Room: This room is a delight, with the soft greens, yellows and blues that dance across the room from the antique stained-glass door that leads to a large shower. The hand-carved lions on the queen-sized bed frame will guard you from nightmares.

Fall Room: Snuggle in the antique queen bed under the burgundy down comforter and enjoy the double shower.

In the Summer and Fall rooms, you can hear the waterfall in the private courtyard, which is accessible from the deck.

The Edwin K is a part of the history of old-town Florence, a small art community.

Here, visitors are reminded of the past, when beauty and workmanship were a proud tradition. You will enjoy browsing the unusual shops on Bay Street; or go 10 miles to Sea Lion Caves or 12 miles to Heceta House Lighthouse.

Visit the West End Gallery & Collectibles in the Edwin K. Located in the West Wing, the gallery exhibits a wide selection of watercolors, oils and handpainted china from local and West Coast artists.

Rates - $$ Map Location - SW

GARIBALDI, OREGON

Hill Top House Bed & Breakfast
617 Holly Avenue
P.O. Box 538
Garibaldi, Oregon 97118
(503) 322-3221

Hill Top House offers luxurious accommodations, an unforgettable breakfast, and an unequaled view of the town of Garibaldi, the docks, the bay and the ocean. Spacious bedrooms with private baths, furnished with antiques and original paintings, offer elegant comfort.

Room One: Lower level, queen bed, private bath with shower, and view overlooking bay and ocean.

Room Two: Mid-level, king bed, large and airy, furnished with antiques, no stairs to climb, private bath.

Room Three: Master suite, private balcony, king bed, private bath with Jacuzzi, antiques, and spectacular view.

Fishing, clamming, crabbing, boating, and windsurfing are just a few of the many things to do in the beautiful bay city of Garibaldi.

Rates - $$ Map Location - NW

GOLD BEACH, OREGON

Heather House Bed & Breakfast
190 11th Street
Gold Beach, Oregon 97444
(503) 247-2074

Heather House is located on the beautiful Southern Oregon Coast in the city of

Gold Beach. Here, you can comb breathtaking beaches, dine in the many fine restaurants and shop in the nearby novelty stores. If you are adventurous, bring your fishing gear and try your luck on the world-famous Rogue River.

The leisurely pace and relaxing atmosphere of the Heather House make it a perfect vacation spot for those who want to get away from it all. You'll have four uniquely decorated rooms—in a Scottish Theme—from which to choose.

Victorian Room: Romantically adorned in Old World charm, with private bath and lovely ocean view.

Tartan Room: Includes a private bath, mountain view and a peek at the ocean.

Paisley Room: Offers seaside decor and a beautiful ocean view.

Oriental Room: Offers distinctive elegance and a fantastic mountain view.

Entertainment: Fine dining, hiking, whale watching, winter storm watching, movie theater, golfing, horseback trail riding, jet-boat trips, clam digging, beachcombing, ocean sport fishing, bay crabbing, plus the Curry County Museum and Prehistoric Gardens.

Annual events include the Chowder Festival in May, the Jet Boat Marathon in June, Summer Theater in June through August, the Curry County Fair in July and August, the Quilt Show in October, and the Christmas Bazaar in December.

Rates - $$ Map Location - SW

GOVERNMENT CAMP, OREGON

Falcon's Crest Inn
87287 Government Camp Loop Highway
P.O. Box 185
Government Camp, Oregon 97028
1-800-624-7384 or (503) 272-3403

Falcon's Crest Inn is a beautiful mountain lodge/chalet-style house, architecturally designed to fit into the quiet natural-forest setting of the Cascades. Conveniently located at the intersection of Highway 26 and the Government Camp Loop Highway, it is within walking distance of Ski Bowl, a year round playground, featuring downhill skiing in the winter—including the largest night-skiing area in the country—and the Alpine Slide in the Summer! Timberline Lodge is six miles from the Inn, and Mount Hood Meadows is just 12 miles away.

A 27-hole championship golf course is just 12 miles from the Inn's front door as well. Other activities offered include fishing, hiking, tennis, swimming, whitewater rafting, mineral hot springs, wineries, antique shops, windsurfing, or just sitting back on one of two decks and taking in the fragrant Mount Hood air and scenery.

The Inn has five suites, all with private baths. Each guest room is individually decorated with unique collectibles, and each provides mountain and forest views. Telephones are available in each suite. The decors are Southwestern, Safari, French Country, Late 1800s and the 1920s, with choices of king, queen or twin beds.

Guests are invited to enjoy all the common areas of the Inn, from the airy, warm lofts to the wonderful Great Room, with its cozy wood-burning stove and an expanse of glass framing a view of Mount Hood Skibowl.

After a hard day of play, relax in the Great Room with your favorite soft drink, beer or wine and complimentary snacks. When it's time to turn in, you'll be greeted by a turned-down bed and a tray of ice water and mints. In the morning, a basket of fresh muffins and a choice of beverage is delivered to your door. Complimentary breakfasts feature items such as the host's original buttermilk pancakes, Belgian waffles, quiches, sweet rolls, along with breakfast meats, fruit juices and plenty of fresh-brewed coffee. All meals are served in the dining room, on one of the host's 12 sets of china, with crystal stemware and serving pieces and the Inn's own set of flatware. Reservations are requested for dinner.

Rates - **$$** to **$$$**   Map Location - NE

GRANTS PASS, OREGON

The Clemens House Bed & Breakfast Inn
612 N.W. Third Street
Grants Pass, Oregon 97526
(503) 476-5564

The Clemens House was built in 1905 for the town's pharmacist, Michael Clemens and his wife, who continued the tradition of fine gardens begun in the early years. In spring, the azaleas, camellias and rhododendrons comprise such a dazzling array that visitors are attracted from miles around to view the magnificent show.

Rooms are adorned with delightful antiques and family heirlooms, and are complete with all the modern amenities. Bedrooms are graced with lace curtains and handmade quilts, and feature comfortable queen-sized beds and private bathrooms. Twin beds are available if desired. The penthouse offers a spacious accommodation with more contemporary decor.

Featured on the walking tour of historic homes in Grants Pass, and listed on the National Register of Historic Places, The Clemens House is located in a quiet residential neighborhood, only five minutes from the heart of town and the Rogue River.

Guests are treated like members of the family and are encouraged to rest from the hurried pace of modern life. Curl up in the parlor with a good book, or share a nice chat.

Breakfast is a gourmet delight, always homemade, and always fresh. A variety of daily specials, with homemade bread and jam, or sliced peaches in their own honey-vanilla creme sauce are offered. On brisk mornings, you're apt to find breakfast cooking on the old, wood-burning stove.

Business travelers get a special bonus—a desk and a place to set up your computer. Enjoy the comforts of home in an ideal setting for optimum productivity away from your office.

Activities: Rogue River rafting, fishing, scenic river trips, boating to a secluded ranch for dinner, antique shopping, Crater Lake, Redwood Forest, Historic Jacksonville & Nunan Mansion, Shakespearean Festival in Ashland, winery tours, skiing, Oregon Caves, and the Britt Music Festival.

Rates - $$ Map Location - SW

Riverbanks Inn "A" Bed & Breakfast
8401 Riverbanks Road
Grants Pass, Oregon 97527
(503) 479-1118

Bird watchers, river runners and vagabonds have visited this river retreat—some for relaxation and pleasure, some for adventure, and some to renew their spirit through the scenic solitude of the mighty Rogue River.

An oriental garden is the first surprise awaiting you behind the gated, wood-slat entry at Riverbanks Inn. The Inn's decor is a rich and varied crossroads of exotic cultures, art and music. In the large living area, among a generous amount of stone, wood and glass, sits a Steinway "B" piano. The Navajo Sweat Lodge, a cedar and mud sauna shaped like a tepee, the Zen House, an Oriental tea house for meditation and rest, and a children's playhouse are available for guests.

Casablanca Room: Peruvian carved furniture, tribal carpets, and a used brick fireplace set an atmosphere of mystery and romance in the appropriately dubbed Casablanca Room. A canopied queen bed, private bath, wet bar, TV, VCR, and separate entry all add to your comfort and seclusion.

Jean Harlow Room: This flamingo colored, art-deco room has a king European bed (can be two twins) with inlaid woods, a velvet love seat and grand dressing table. Around the room, you'll find a smattering of framed Hollywood greats. French doors lead to a patio with a river view. A private bath with tub and separate shower adjoin the room.

Caribbean Dream Suite: As you enter the glass brick foyer, the stone garden room with sunken Jacuzzi draws you into the tropics. Bathe in a rainforest shower and gaze at the stars through several sky lights. A Mombasa net covers the Plantation

Canopy Queen Bed. There are videos with island themes and a collection of photos and memorabilia from the Caribbean. Private bath, patio, entrance, TV, VCR, and wet bar.

The Log Cabin: This cabin is just a few feet from the main house. On the cabin's large covered front porch, guests can curl up on the hammock for a short nap, read, talk, or prepare tackle for another day of fishing. The cabin has a pine-floored living room with wood stove. A small bath and shower with skylight connects the bedroom and den. TV and VCR included.

Grandma's Room: This cozy antique-filled room has a four-poster, extra-long double bed. The night sounds of crickets chirping and the river flowing make this a soothing place to drift into sleep.

Your host is a licensed massage therapist, and massages are available by appointment to all guests, at a minimal charge.

Rates - $$ to $$$ Map Location - SW

HALFWAY, OREGON

The Birch Leaf Lodge Bed & Breakfast
Route 1, Box 91
Halfway, Oregon 97834
(503) 742-2990

The Birch Leaf Lodge is located on a 42-acre farm at the foot of the Wallowa Mountains in Eastern Oregon. Nearby are the Hells Canyon National Recreation Area and the Eagle Cap Wilderness, two of the most rugged and beautiful places in the Western United States.

This home is a turn-of-the-century farmhouse, updated for your comfort. The character of the original house has been carefully preserved, to showcase the original woodwork, floors, and stone foundation. These have been enhanced with new decks and a sunny dining alcove looking out on the old birch trees.

You will find alpine lake and stream fishing, whitewater rafting, jet-boat trips, canoeing, hiking, backpacking, biking, hunting, birding, and cross-country skiing. Snake River reservoirs offer some of the best bass fishing in the country. Pack trips through the Wallowa Mountains are conducted by Cornucopia Pack Station and Wallowa Llamas. Hells Canyon is breathtaking from the air, and chartered plane rides can be arranged.

Lovely guest rooms have an airy country feeling. Each room offers comfortable surroundings, polished pine floors, a variety of books, and wonderful views of the surrounding valley.

Country-style breakfasts feature pancakes, local jams, honey, and fresh fruit, in season. The seating is family-style in the dining alcove or, in the summer, you may enjoy your breakfast outside on the wrap-around deck.

Guests are welcomed as family and are offered the privacy of a country retreat. Feel free to explore the old orchards, walk the farm, and study a gravity irrigation system during your stay.

Rates - $ to $$ Map Location - NE

HARBOR, OREGON

Oceancrest House
15510 Pedrioli Drive
Harbor, Oregon 97415
(503) 469-9200 or 1-800- 769-9200

Oceancrest House is located just three and a half miles from the California border, on a quiet street overlooking the Pacific Ocean.

Enjoy the sweeping view of Pelican Bay, with white waves crashing on the rocks, plus beautiful sandy beaches, pelicans, whales, birds, tidepool creatures and fishing boats.

Relax and enjoy a queen-sized brass bed in an extra-large room with a private entrance, private bath, luxurious furnishings, a refrigerator, microwave, coffee maker, cable TV and VCR. A delicious continental breakfast will make your stay complete.

Rates - $$ Map Location - SW

HOOD RIVER, OREGON

State Street Inn Bed & Breakfast
1005 State Street
Hood River, Oregon 97031
(503) 386-1899

The State Street Inn is located in the heart of Hood River, 60 miles east of Portland. The town provides the perfect launching spot for all Columbia River Gorge and Mount Hood activities—including hiking, downhill and cross-country skiing ,windsurfing, whitewater rafting, fishing, cycling, and sightseeing. Several museums and wineries also are nearby, as well as many fine restaurants and shops.

Built in 1932, the home is a traditionally styled English house with gabled roof and pitched ceilings. The oak floors and the leaded glass windows overlooking the Columbia River reflect the craftsmanship of the past. The spacious living room with sunroom provides plenty of space for guests to enjoy a warming fire in the winter or a refreshing drink in the summer. With its plate glass window capturing snowcapped Mount Adams, the guest dining room is the perfect place to enjoy a delicious breakfast. Four guest rooms have been named for states in which the innkeepers have lived. The bedrooms share two full baths.

Colorado Room: This cozy room with a full bed is decorated with the Old West and Southwest in mind.

Massachusetts Room: This quiet room with queen bed is decorated Colonial style. Maple trees surround the windows.

California Room: Sunshine and bright airy colors bring the beach to Central Oregon in this room with queen bed. You'll also get a spectacular view of the river and Mount Adams from here.

Maryland Room: This large room has an aura of Southern grace and luxury, as well as a beautiful view of the Columbia River and Mount Adams. The room has both a queen bed and a daybed.

Annual Events: April-Blossom Festival, May-May Fest, June-High Wind Classic, July- Columbia Gorge Pro-Am-Gorge Cities Blowout-Hood River County Fair, August-Naish Dash-Apple Jam, September-Columbia River Cross Channel Swim, November-Light up the Gorge.

Rates - $ to $$ Map Location - NE

JACKSONVILLE, OREGON

McCully House Inn
240 E. California Street, P.O. Box 13
Jacksonville, Oregon 97530
(503) 899-1942

When newly constructed in 1861, Dr. J.W. McCully's mansion was one of the most expensive and palatial residences in the booming Gold-Rush town of Jacksonville, Oregon. Today, visitors to Jacksonville continue to enjoy the elegance and grace of one of the town's most important historic homes. After more than 10 years of painstaking restoration, this stately mansion is once again welcoming guests.

Standing on East California Street, at the edge of Jacksonville's shopping and restaurant district, the McCully House Inn is on the National Registry of Historic Places and is one of he town's six original dwellings.

European and American antiques, polished hardwood floors, Oriental rugs, delicate lace curtains and a magnificent square grand piano help create an atmosphere of quiet elegance. Each room and its private bath has been professionally decorated to capture the historic heritage of the home.

Steiger Haus, McMinnville, OR

You'll get home-cooked breads and pastries from the Inn's kitchen. And fresh seafood from the Pacific Northwest and crisp, innovative salads are presented daily. The meat and produce are from the area's plentiful farms, and the fine wines also are of this bountiful growing region. Weddings, parties, and other special events also can be arranged to meet your individual needs.

McCully Room: A special place to spend an historic night. The original master bedroom is furnished with massive Renaissance Revival pieces of solid black walnut; these were brought around the Horn especially for this room. The soft gray walls embrace a cozy fireplace and antique claw-foot tub with a private old-fashioned water closet.

Girl's Room: Sunlight filters into the room through lace curtains, picking up the soft colors of the rose floral wallpaper. A massive wood inlaid wardrobe belonging to the McCully daughters complements the two full-sized beds. Enclosed within the room is a private bathroom and shower.

Doll Suite: This large attic space, which once housed the famous Jacksonville Doll Museum, has been transformed into a charming three-room suite, perfect for families. The main bedroom features a king-sized bed or two singles, and adjoining is a small antique iron child's bed. Enclosed within the suite is a full private bath.

In the morning, you'll be greeted with fresh-ground coffee, as you delight in a country breakfast of homemade breads, fresh fruits, eggs and other specialty items.

Rates - $$ to $$$ Map Location - SW

JOHN DAY, OREGON

Sonshine Bed & Breakfast Inn
210 Northwest Canton
John Day, Oregon 97845
(503) 575-1827 or 575-0140

Experience a Bed & Breakfast Inn in the heart of Grant County, home of the John Day Fossil Beds and National Monument and the Strawberry Wilderness Area.

Join your host for a meal you simply won't find in any restaurant. It may include anything from stuffed french toast to homemade breads and your choice of meats native to the area.

The Inn is located in the heart of John Day near the City Park, pool and Kam Wah Chung Museum.

You'll find the two rooms clean, comfortable and air-conditioned. One room has a queen bed and access directly to the spacious bath with walk-in shower. The other room has a double bed and a private grooming area and has access to the bath just out the door.

Enjoy your host's wildlife collection that graces the walls of the Inn, which once served as the offices to the Chinese Dr. Wah in the early 1900s. Your host, born and raised in Grant County, can fill you in on most any local subject.

Things to do: Visit museums, fish, raft, soak in hot springs, hike, hunt, or get out and do some photography.

Rates - $ Map Location - NE

KERBY, OREGON

Kerbyville Inn Bed & Breakfast
24304 Redwood Highway
Kerby, Oregon 97531
(503) 592-4698 or 592-4689

Guests at the newly renovated Kerbyville Inn will find true Southern Oregon hospitality. The Inn, as well as the Oregon Wine Barrel Tasting Room next door, and the Bridgeview Vineyards, are owned and operated by your hosts.

The Inn features three suites, two with spas, and a guest room. All have private baths and private entrances.

The central living area includes a wood stove and and outdoor deck. A full hearty breakfast is served daily, as is a complimentary afternoon wine tasting of Bridgeview's finest.

Tucked amid the mountains of Southwest Oregon, the Illinois Valley lies between Grants Pass (I-5) and the Oregon Coast. Visitors to the valley are quickly discovering the charms of this serene and scenic area that residents have so long enjoyed.

Tall evergreens, mountain streams, rivers and lakes, majestic vistas and the Kalmlopsis Wilderness Area create an idyllic destination for the nature lover and sportsman alike.

The valley is an ideal home base for visiting other Southern Oregon attractions. Drive through the majestic Smith Canyon to the redwoods and the rugged Oregon Coast to the west. Raft the whitewater of the Rogue River, or opt for the calmer jet-boat excursion tours. Visit Crater Lake National Park, Ashland's Shakespearean Festival, and historic Jacksonville to the east.

Burgundy Suite: King and double beds, kitchenette, and spa.

Riesling Suite: Queen bed and two twins.

Chardonnay Suite: Two queen-sized beds, kitchenette, and spa.

Inspiration Room: One king waterbed.

Local Activities: Tour area wineries, fish the Illinois River for steelhead and salmon or the Selmac for record bass and trout, hike, visit the Oregon Caves and Kerbyville museum and Noah's Ark Wildlife Park and Petting Zoo, tour Woodland Echoes Theme Park, or golf at Illinois Valley Golf Course.

Rates - $ to $$ Map Location - SW

KLAMATH FALLS, OREGON

Thompson's Bed & Breakfast
1420 Wild Plum Court
Klamath Falls, Oregon 97601
(503) 882-7938

Thompson's Bed & Breakfast overlooks beautiful Klamath Lake, and is next door to Moore Park, with its marina, tennis courts, picnic facilities, and magnificent hiking trail.

Almost within casting range are some of the world's great fishing areas and the

Mountain Lakes and Sky Lakes wilderness areas, which are alive with bald eagles, deer, and other woodland creatures.

The lake's many coves and inlets are home to pelicans, grebes, Canadian honkers, snow geese, blue herons, and countless varieties of wild ducks. Within an hour's drive is world-renowned Crater Lake and, in the wintertime, a number of the world's most pristine white ski areas.

Sunsets over the Cascade Range provide a backdrop to the spectacular view of Upper Klamath Lake. Bring your camera, as deer and bald eagle are frequent visitors to the back yard of Thompson's Bed & Breakfast.

Rates - $$ Map Location - SW

LAFAYETTE, OREGON

Kelty Estate Bed & Breakfast
675 Highway 99W
Lafayette, Oregon 97127
(503) 864-3740

James Monroe Kelty was born in Davies County, Indiana in about 1842. In the early spring of 1852, his family moved to Oregon and settled on a farm west of Carlton. James Kelty grew up on the farm following a tour of military duty during the Civil War, then moved to Lafayette in 1866 and established himself as the local druggist.

He married Sarah Maria Scott on June 23, 1869, in Lafayette. His bride was the youngest daughter of John Tucker, also a pioneer. Sarah Maria's brother, Harvey W. Scott, distinguished himself as the pioneer editor of Portland's *Oregonian*, now Oregon's largest newspaper.

James and Sarah Maria Kelty built the house that now is the Kelty Estate Bed & Breakfast sometime between their marriage in 1869 and the birth of their son, Paul, on March 27, 1872. James Kelty continued his business, and twice was elected as Yamhill County Sheriff. Mrs. Kelty was elected to the Lafayette School Board, the first woman in the town's history to have held such a position. The Keltys sold the house in 1893 and moved to Portland.

On August 17, 1934, Paul R. Kelty, son of James M. Kelty, purchased his boyhood home and converted the old farmhouse into an elegant manor, maintaining the original plan and many of the original features. Paul Kelty died on March 11, 1944, and his wife, Clara, died in Portland in 1967.

Basically unchanged since 1934, the Kelty Estate house now is a Bed & Breakfast Inn. It fronts Highway 99W, just across the street from the Lafayette Antique Mall. It is within walking distance to the Yamhill County Museum, and near the area's many fine wineries. Lafayette is 32 miles from Portland, less than an hour from the Oregon

Coast, Salem (Oregon's State Capitol) and within two hours of the world's famous and scenic Mount Hood and the Columbia Gorge.

The Inn offers two rooms, both with queen-size beds and private baths. Full or continental breakfast is available.

Rates - $$ Map Location - NE

LaPINE, OREGON

The Big Blue House Bed & Breakfast
53223 Riverview Drive
LaPine, Oregon 97739
(503) 536-3879

The quaint little town of LaPine is the home of The Big Blue House. Here, you will be greeted at the door by Buffy, the in-resident boxer, and then escorted to one of two rooms.

In one room, matching twin beds are adorned with beautiful Amish quilts from Pennsylvania. Handmade pictures add to the room's atmosphere. A king-sized bed is available in a more modern room that also sports a TV. The two share a bath.

The Big Blue House breakfast speciality is made-from-scratch blueberry pancakes. Your host is glad to cater to special diets or tastes as well.

There is plenty of yard for relaxing and enjoying the flowers, or you might choose to take a soak in the Jaccuzi.

Things to do: Fishing, hunting, whitewater rafting, skiing, snowmobiling, and hiking. And don't forget to visit Newberry Crater National Volcanic Monument.

Rates - $$ Map Location - SE

LINCOLN CITY, OREGON

The Rustic Inn Bed & Breakfast
2313 N.E. Holmes Road
Lincoln City, Oregon 97367
(503) 994-5111

The Rustic Inn is located right off Coastal Highway 101 and is just a half mile from the Pacific Ocean. It has a large front porch and is surrounded by pine trees and shrubbery to insure privacy. Each room also has a private bath.

Awake to the aroma of coffee brewing and fresh bread baking. Your host will fix a hearty breakfast at your convenience. Eat in the dining room, or enjoy a leisurely breakfast outside on the deck.

The Inn is located within walking distance of gift and antique shops and the factory-outlet stores of Lincoln City. You may spend your day on the beach, whale watching or beachcombing, or you might try your hand at kite flying or fishing for salmon, steelhead, or trout in the nearby Salmon River.

A Touch of Lace Room: Antique, queen-sized bed, lace curtains, rocking chair, private bath and color TV.

The Country Room: Antique, three-quarter bed with country quilt and hand-painted bedside lamp. This room is right next to the sitting room and features a color TV, private bath with shower, and private entrance from the outside.

Romance of Roses Room: Queen-sized bed, antique furnishings, private bath with Jacuzzi for two, color TV, and a private entrance from the outside.

Rates - $ to $$ Map Location - NW

McMINNVILLE, OREGON

Steiger Haus
360 Wilson Street
McMinnville, Oregon 97128
(503) 472-0821

Steiger Haus is nestled in a park-like town setting and has all the character and style of its European country ancestors. The theme, "A Wool and Wine Country Inn," combines the owner's interest in spinning, weaving, and knitting with a location in the heart of Oregon's wine country. From here, guests may easily visit the many wineries scattered throughout the countryside, or may walk to Linfield College, Gallery Theater, and the fine shops and restaurants of downtown McMinnville.

Peaceful, quiet, and comfortable, all rooms have access to decks and terraces surrounded by ivy, Oregon Grape and an English garden variety of flowers, shrubs, and trees. Relax on the decks or enjoy a walk through the rodies, wildflowers, and other Northwest flora.

The Garden Level Rooms share a common sitting/TV room and open onto expansive decks. All have private baths.

Finnsheep "Fireside": Fireplace, queen and hide-a-bed.

Merino "Morningsun": Cheerful room and queen bed.

Dorset "Deckside": Full-size antique brass bed.

The upper-level rooms share a common sitting/TV room and spacious bath with separate shower and tub. You may choose to enjoy the entire two-bedroom suite.

Targhee "Treetop": A comfortable, bay-window room reserved as a private suite with its own bath and sitting room.

Romney "Rooftop": Twin feather beds.

Steiger Haus is ideally located for regional day trips to Portland, North and Central Coast, Willamette Valley points of interest, Mount Hood and the beautiful Columbia River Gorge Scenic Area.

Rates - $ Map Location - NW

Youngberg Hill Farm Inn
10660 Youngberg Hill Road
McMinnville, Oregon 97128
(503) 472-2727

Youngberg Hill Farm, just minutes from McMinnville, is a working farm and vineyard on 700 rolling acres in the heart of Oregon's wine country. From high on a hill, the farmhouse overlooks vineyards, the Willamette Valley, the Cascades, and the Coast Range. Salem, Portland and the beautiful Oregon coast are each less than an hour away.

Blending the charm of turn-of-the-century architecture and decor with modern amenities, each spacious, tastefully decorated guest room offers a private bath, as well as central heating and air conditioning. Two of the five guest rooms have fireplaces. A sitting room with wood-stove warmth provides the opportunity to visit with hosts and other guests, while the spacious grounds, comfortable guest rooms and covered porches offer the opportunity for pleasant seclusion.

Guests of Youngberg Hill Farm will find miles of old logging roads for walking and, in the fall, for hunting pheasants and deer. Arrangements can be made for seasonal duck hunting, goose hunting and elk hunting in the nearby Coast Range. Or try your hand at trout, salmon and steelhead fishing in world-class waters nearby. Deer hunting and salmon fishing can be combined when reservations are made well in advance.

The private "Winelovers Winecellar" at Yongberg Hill is stocked with a collection of local and European wines of exceptional quality and value; all of the wines are available for purchase by guests.

A hearty, healthy farm breakfast is served each morning at a time agreed upon with each guest. On Monday evenings, a sumptuous dinner is offered for four or more guests, featuring the delicious fresh ingredients bountifully provided by the Willamette Valley's farms, rivers and the Pacific Ocean, with Oregon wines matched to taste.

Rates - $$ Map Location - NW

MILWAUKIE, OREGON

Historic Broetje House
3101 S.E. Courtney Road
Milwaukie, Oregon 97222
(503) 659-8860

Enjoy the romantic ambience that this magnificent turn-of-the-century Queen Anne style residence has to offer. The home was built in 1890 by noted horticulturist and floriculturist John F. Broetje.

The house's unique four-story 50-foot-high water tower added in 1909 was Clackamas County's first bonded winery and one of the first five wineries in the state of Oregon after the Great Depression.

Stroll through more than an acre of scenic grounds supporting more than 100 flowering shrubs and trees planted nearly a century ago. Relax in the gazebo nestled below the towering 100-year-old Sequoia redwood trees, the first ever planted in the Portland area.

Relive a time past in the restful furnished rooms. Step into the "Queen Anne" sitting room and enjoy the flickering fire. Feast in the airy dining room, and relax in the plant-filled sun room or in the nostalgic comfort of a real country kitchen.

Whether you are part of a group planning a special occasion, a business person requiring rejuvenating solitude, a couple planning a romantic wedding or anniversary party, someone seeking the privacy of a hideaway, or a tourist wanting the friendly environment and hospitality of a truly unique home, you'll find the elegance of the Historic Broetje House a truly classic experience.

Queen Anne Room: This charming spacious Victorian room has a queen brass bed, large private antique bath, including all brass fixtures, pedestal toilet and a six-foot double-end claw-foot bathtub, large enough to indulge even the weariest traveler.

Country Charm Room: You will feel right at home in this sunny, cheerful room filled with white wicker furniture, a white and brass queen-sized bed, and antique dressers. Share/Private bath boasts a four-foot claw-foot bathtub and a water closet.

Gazebo Garden Room: Overlooking the vast garden and gazebo, this cozy room has a white and gold daybed, antique furniture and enough warmth to make you recall grandma's home. Share/Private bath with country charm.

Located in a quiet residential area, just 15 minutes from downtown Portland.

Rates - $ to $$ Map Location - NW

MONMOUTH, OREGON

Howell's Bed & Breakfast
212 N. Knox
Monmouth, Oregon 97361
(503) 838-2085

Howell House is listed on the National Register of Historic Places as the oldest student rooming house in Oregon. Beginning in 1891 and continuing until 1984, hundreds of students lived there while attending the college.

The house now has been restored as a bed & breakfast, where guests can step back in time and enjoy a touch of the past in a warm and relaxing atmosphere.

The guest rooms, which include a private bath, are filled with traditional Victorian furnishings. The walls are covered with magnificent reproductions of authentic 1890s wallpaper. Original wood trim and moldings match throughout, depicting an era of top-notch artistic achievement.

The Inn is located 15 minutes from Salem, one hour from the Cascade Range, 45 minutes from the Pacific Ocean, and one hour from Portland and Portland International Airport.

You can fish in a number of local streams, and the Willamette River, five minutes away, offers swimming, boating, fishing, canoeing and waterskiing.

Breakfast is a real treat at Howell's. Your hostess' specialty is her raspberry and blueberry pancakes and homemade jams. Special diet requirements can be met.

Rates - $$ Map Location - SW

NEWBERG, OREGON

Hess Canyon Estate Bed & Breakfast Extraordinaire
712 Wynooski
Newberg, Oregon 97132
(503) 538-1139

In the magnificent Willamette Valley city of Newberg, the Hess Canyon Estate is a homey alternative to a hotel or motel. Tour any of the 20 wineries just minutes from your door. Visit George Fox College or see Herbert Hoover's childhood home. If water sports are your pleasure, the Willamette River offers terrific fishing, skiing, and sightseeing. Downtown, you'll find wonderful antique shops awaiting you. And, in the winter, you can ski down magnificent Mount Hood. The Oregon Coast is a lovely hour drive, and Portland and Salem are just 35 minutes down the road.

Although it is located in the city, this bed & breakfast manages to offer a true country atmosphere. Set above Hess Canyon, the 1903 Estate sits on four acres with a scenic view of rolling hills, tall pines, Hess Creek, and wildlife—including deer, wild geese, and mallard ducks. In addition, the hosts board their own horses.

The home is furnished in lovely turn-of-the-century furniture that accents the mahogany beams and moldings throughout the house. Your guest room is furnished with period antiques, fluffy comforters, pillows, and lace.

Guests are invited to curl up in the parlor in front of a warm fire to read, visit, or enjoy games. Rent a movie or watch cable TV in the den. Visit the fruit orchard or pick a rose for that special someone. On warmer days, the west porch provides spectacular sunsets, while the east deck overlooks the canyon, pool, and hot tub.

A full breakfast is offered daily, with dishes to please every palette. The meal is served family-style, beside a wood-burning stove and overlooking the canyon. Or, upon request, breakfast may be served in the privacy of your room.

The Master Suite: This spacious and inviting king-sized room is on the second floor. Its extras include cable TV with remote control, beveled glass mirrors, and plenty of closet space. The adjoining private bath will take your breath away, as you look over the best view in the inn while you enjoy a bubbling Jacuzzi bath or shower.

The Queen Anne Room: This first-floor room has a queen bed and spacious eight-foot ceiling. Heirloom quilt squares hang above the bed, and a cozy comforter and pillows invite a good night's rest. Your private hall bath has a large shower, plenty of cupboard space, and a terrific view of the canyon.

The Blueberry King Room: A large, romantic room with a king-sized bed located on the second floor. Comforters, lace, beveled-glass doors, and period antiques grace this room as it looks out toward the sunset. The large hall bath has a tub and shower and is shared with the Peppermint Room.

The Peppermint Twin: This delightful, cheery second-floor room offers two twin beds. The large hall bath has a tub and shower and is shared with the Blueberry King Room. Plenty of shelves, counter space, and modern fixtures will enhance your privacy and comfort.

Rates - $$ Map location - NW

The Partridge Farm Bed & Breakfast Inn
4300 E. Portland Road
Newberg, Oregon 97132
(503) 538-2050

The Partridge Farm—a restored turn-of-the-century farmhouse, well-appointed with period antiques—is situated on five beautifully landscaped acres. It has four guest rooms, including one suite with sitting room and private bath.

Yamhill County offers a variety of options for the traveler—wine tasting, hot-air ballooning, antique shopping, and fine dining. In addition, it is within an hour of Portland and the Oregon coast.

Full breakfast is served.

Rates - $$ Map Location - NW

Secluded Bed & Breakfast
19719 N.E. Williamson Road
Newberg, Oregon 97132
(503) 538-2633

The Secluded Bed & Breakfast is a beautiful country home on 10 acres, in the ideal wooded setting for hiking, country walks and wildlife viewing. It's a 10-minute drive to several wineries, located behind the beautiful Red Hills of Dundee, and is convenient to George Fox College, McMinnville, and the Oregon coast.

Room One: Double bed and shared deck, with antiques and collectibles in the room. This room overlooks the yard, including a pond, gnomes and flowers.

Room Two: Extra-large room with queen-sized bed and a private deck. Antiques and stained glass grace this room. The private deck allows you to enjoy a large wooded area with wildlife.

Guest and private bath. Large library.

Secluded Bed & breakfast serves a delectable gourmet breakfast, which varies daily for your pleasure. Your hosts will tempt you with succulent fresh farm fruit from Oregon's famous Willamette Valley.

Your hosts' hobbies include stained-glass working, hunting, violin making, flower arranging, woodworking, gourmet cooking, gardening and birdwatching. They also are involved in the Audubon Society and the Blue Bird Trails nesting project.

Rates - $$ Map Location - NW

The Smith House
415 N. College Street
Newberg, Oregon 97132
(503) 538-1995

Built in 1904, this restored turn-of-century home is a fine example of Victorian architecture. The Smith House is located close to downtown Newberg—just two blocks from George Fox College—in the heart of the Yamhill County wine country.

The Rose Room: Features an early 1900s oak bedroom set with queen-sized bed and matching dresser, plus an oak desk and rocking chair and a bookcase full of reading materials.

The Blue Room: Offers a graceful antique brass queen-sized bed, dressing table, oak dresser, bookcase and rocking chair. Both rooms provide ample closet space for guests, and shared bath.

Treat yourself to the hot tub, porch swing, fresh fruit and flowers, and TV and VCR. Or visit Portland, the Oregon coast, or the area's many wineries.

Full breakfast of juice, fresh-brewed coffee, stash teas, homemade jumbo muffins, fresh fruit, egg specialities, and more, served in the dining room or patio (weather permitting). Fresh-picked homemade raspberries are featured in the summer and are served in jams and syrups year-round.

Rates - $ to $$ Map Location - NW

Springbrook Hazelnut Farm
30295 North Highway 99W
Newberg, Oregon 97132
(503) 538-4606 or 1-800-793-8528

Springbrook Farm is a wonderful find for visitors to Oregon's Yamhill County. Although it is located just 20 miles from the city of Portland, it remains part of a quieter time.

The farm now is a National Historic Register property, but life continues as it always in this beautiful landmark, with its craftsman-style buildings. The matching buildings are nestled among 10 acres of gardens, punctuated by enormous old trees. The grounds are further enhanced by a pool, tennis court and a large pond, complete with canoe and resident blue heron.

Beyond the garden is a 60-acre hazelnut orchard, through which you can walk to the adjoining winery. Beyond the gate, you'll find terrific bicycling opportunities, plus good antique stores, restaurants and wineries.

The main residence has a spectacular entry hall, extending from the covered front porch to the comfortably furnished back porch, which overlooks the lawn and garden. A glassed-in sun porch is filled with plants and wicker furniture. Breakfast is served in the paneled dining room.

Main House: A separate guest floor has wide hallways, a sitting room with garden view and a well-stocked reading room. Two guests rooms share this floor. Both are furnished in wicker, with queen-sized beds. One, with lattice-covered walls, has a view of the pond; the other looks into the branches of a silver maple planted in 1912. A skylight hall bath serves the two rooms.

Carriage House: This hideaway overlooks the pond and garden and is popular with honeymooners and other romantics. It has a fully equipped kitchen, stocked for breakfast. Guests who elect to "eat in" are welcome to help themselves to tomatoes, corn, lettuce and herbs from the garden, in season.

The master bedroom has a queen bed and an adjoining bath with a claw-foot tub. A second queen-sized bed is hidden in one of the couches in the living room.

Rates - $$ Map Location - NW

Spring Creek Llama Ranch and Bed & Breakfast
14700 N.E. Spring Creek Lane
Newberg, Oregon 97132
(503) 538-5717

Spring Creek Llama Ranch is a spacious and contemporary bed & breakfast offering two comfortable rooms with private baths. The Spring Meadows Room, bright and fresh with its minty pastels and animal prints, is at ground level. The Red Cloud Room, with its warm hues and peaceful forest view, offers the cozy comfort of a queen bed. Heat pumps keep indoor temperatures pleasant year-round.

Living and dining areas look out into the deep forest. In the evening, guests may join the family for a bedtime snack.

The family-style breakfast is tailored to your taste and schedule, and includes homebaked treats and seasonal homegrown produce.

Guests may choose to stroll in the woods, visit with the llamas, check for fresh eggs at the hen house, or simply enjoy the soothing tranquillity of forest and field. And if you want to know more about llamas, your hosts will be delighted to answer your questions.

Barn & breakfast is available at an additional charge for traveling llamas, along with parking for a stock trailer. Health requirements must be met. Please ask for details.

Spring Creek Llama Ranch and Bed & Breakfast is in the midst of 24 acres of rolling pasture and woods. While this provides complete seclusion, it also is just one mile from Newberg and offers easy access to Highway 99W.

Within a five-minute drive are wineries, restaurants, antique shops, George Fox College, and Rogers Landing on the Willamette River. Champoeg State Park, home of the famed Champoeg Historical Pageant, is seven miles away. Downtown Portland is 35 minutes; downtown Salem is 45 minutes; and the Oregon coast is 75 minutes away.

Rates - $$ Map Location - NW

NEWPORT, OREGON

Ocean House Bed & Breakfast Inn
4920 N.W. Woody Way
Newport, Oregon 97365
(503) 265-6158 or 265-7779

Overlooking the surf at Agate Beach, Ocean House is home away from home for those who love life's simple pleasures and the varied excitement of coastal living. The windows of the cozy rooms upstairs open toward the sea. Have breakfast at your leisure. It is served in the spacious living room, or out on the sunny porch or decks.

A short private trail leads to the beach and tide pool; the lovely coastal garden is a paradise of birds, flowers, and native shrubs.

If you're lucky and a storm brews, relax by an open fire; enjoy good books, conversation, and a private art gallery.

Outdoor fun may include nearby golfing, fishing, clamming, and surfing. Your host will be happy to help you plan your day.

Rates - $$ Map Location - SW

NORTH BEND, OREGON

The Highlands Bed & Breakfast Inn
608 Ridge Road
North Bend, Oregon 97459
(503) 756-0300

At The Highlands, you will experience one of the best that Oregon has to offer! Situated at a high elevation on six secluded acres, above the coastal wind and fog, it offers a view so breathtaking it's sure to bring out the camcorder!

This spacious home of cedar and glass offers gracious lodging in a relaxed country setting. Cozy quilts, a soapstone wood-burning stove and an eclectic mix of antiques invites you to relax in absolute peace and serenity.

Guests share a Port Orford cedar-paneled family room with wrap-around floor-to-ceiling windows overlooking flower gardens, a gold fish pond, and a spectacular panoramic view of the coastal range!

There's also satellite TV, VCR, CD player, and an excellent small library. Memorable breakfasts (weather permitting) are served on the wrap-around deck.

Adjoining the family room is a complete kitchen with stove, refrigerator, and a microwave for those evenings when you choose to eat in.

The two bedroom—each with its own private adjoining bath—are tastefully decorated in antiques, with an emphasis on comfort. Direct-dial phones and separate heat controls in all rooms assure your comfort. Each room also has a separate entrance and is wheelchair accessible.

A romantic hot-springs spa for two on a private solarium deck offers the perfect end a busy day!

Rates - $$ Map Location - SW

OCEANSIDE, OREGON

Three Capes Bed & Breakfast Inn
1685 Maxwell Mountain Road, P.O. Box 138
Oceanside, Oregon 97134
(503) 842-6126

Nestled on the hillside at Oceanside, this home overlooks the majestic Pacific Ocean. And guests at Three Capes Bed & Breakfast will enjoy garage parking, easy beach access and breakfast served on the upper deck, weather permitting.

Weekday breakfasts include fresh fruit, homemade baked goods, and local cheeses. On weekends, guests are treated to a full breakfast, featuring seafood specialties, Belgian waffles, or omelets.

Each of the two comfortably remodeled guest rooms offers a private bath and spectacular ocean view from Cape Lookout to Maxwell Point.

The Sunny Cape Meares Room: Provides a cozy double bed and three view windows overlooking the beach.

The Cape Lookout Room: Queen bed, private entrance, and a private sitting deck.

Things To Do: Hiking, fishing, crabbing, whale watching, bird watching, and visiting the world-famous cheese factory.

Rates - $$ Map Location - NW

PACIFIC CITY, OREGON

Pacific View Bed & Breakfast Inn
34930 Hillcrest
Pacific City, Oregon 97135
(503) 965-6498

This charming sea captain's home was built on top of the first hill from the ocean, offering panoramic views of Cape Kiwanda, Haystack Rock, the quiet year-round beach community, the Nestucca River, and the Coast Range Mountains.

Watch the whale migration, the spectacular sunsets, or the powerful storms that lash the ocean into a frenzy from the vantage point of the glassed-in "widow's walk," the many picture windows, or the gardens.

Situated on a hill, just a short walk from the ocean, The Pacific View Bed & Breakfast offers easy access by foot, bike, or car to the ocean and dunes. Cape Kiwanda—one of the most photographed coastal areas in the world—is the home of the Dory Fleet.

Stroll along the surf as you beachcomb for treasures from the sea, or climb a dune and race down, picnic on the beach, fly a kite, fish, watch the hang gliders soar from atop the dunes or the dory fishermen launch and beach their boats, or just take it easy on the lawns surrounding the inn.

If you like salmon or steelhead fishing, reserve a room in the fall or winter. Deepsea Dory charters are available in Pacific City, from May through September.

A delicious full breakfast with country heartiness and city sophistication is served daily at Pacific View.

Rates - $$ Map Location - NW

PLEASANT HILL, OREGON

Glendale Resort Bed & Breakfast Inn
85714 Parkway Road
Pleasant Hill, Oregon 97455
(503) 726-2064

Nestled close to the Willamette River and just 20 minutes from downtown Eugene, Glendale Resort is a perfect solution to city stress—whether you're vacationing, traveling on business or just enjoying a quiet weekend.

Glendale Resort is surrounded by life's simple pleasures. Stroll through the nearby filbert orchards, or enjoy a bike ride along the Willamette River. Awaken to the sound of chirping swallows, and surround yourself with 16 acres of rustling trees.

Here you'll find all the amenities of an expensive hotel. Soak away the pressure of your business day with a dip in the heated swimming pool, play a set of tennis, badminton, or pickle ball, or shoot some baskets on the outdoor sport court.

Choose from four rooms in this quiet, country setting. A full, homemade breakfast is included with your stay.

Rates - $$ Map Location - SW

PORTLAND, OREGON

General Hooker's Bed & Breakfast
125 S.W. Hooker
Portland, Oregon 97201
(503) 222-4435

General Hooker's Bed & Breakfast is a blend of Victorian charm, classic decor, quiet convenience, and creature comfort. Custom batique quilts, antiques and rattan grace the light, high-ceilinged rooms, and the library holds a large collection of books and tapes.

The parlor fireplace provides an extra measure of coziness in the winter; and air conditioning/filtration ensures comfort during the hot summers. From the roof deck in this quiet, Historic Conservation District, you can see the lights of Portland. Downtown Portland—described by the *New Yorker Magazine* as a "model of urban development, a city that has returned itself to man, to a pedestrian way of life"— is just a few minutes away.

The Transit Mall, OHSU, Portland State University, the performing-arts center, Riverplace, Waterfront Park, many shops and restaurants all are accessible. The convention center is just a bridge crossing away.

The superb location and flexible breakfast hours make this a favorite of business travelers, who also appreciate the adequate desk space, and easy telephone and fax access. A substantial continental-plus breakfast features fresh-ground coffee or decaf, fruit in season and whole grains, a bonus to the health conscious.

The Rose Room: The master bedroom has the extravagant emperor bed, plus a private skylit bath, a terrific view of Portland's lights and private entry via the roof deck.

The Daisy Room: This sunny room features a large window opening onto the tree-lined street, and a fanciful mirrored canopy over the queen bed. It shares a bath with the Iris Room, but has an in-room sink and vanity.

The Iris Room: This away-from-it-all, cocooning room has a slightly Japanese ambiance. The very comfortable daybed extends to a double bed. It also has a private entry via the roof deck. Shares the bath with Daisy Room but has an in-room sink and vanity.

Note: The Iris and Daisy rooms combine ideally to make the Canopy Suite: Two bedrooms, private bath and entry.

The Dandelion Room: This room features a lower-level, book-lined family room with double bed below and a twin bed above in a loft bed frame. Refrigerator and all amenities of the other rooms are included. Perfect for parents and child, or for two. Shares downstairs bath.

Rates - $$ to $$$ Map Location - NW

Georgian House Bed & Breakfast Inn
1828 N.E. Siskiyou
Portland, Oregon 97212
(503) 281-2250

The Georgian colonial style originated in England in about 1702 and was named after King George. Only three true Georgian colonial homes remain in Portland. This one was built in 1922 by George Schneider, who placed several gold coins in the foundation of the house for good luck.

The Georgian House has recently been restored; it has leaded windows, a wonderful winding staircase to the bedrooms, built-in china cabinets, plus oak floors, sun porch and a fireplace.

East Lake Room: Come enjoy this sunny southern room, with its antique Victorian East Lake double bed and marble-top dresser. It's complimented with french windows, oak floors, an English wardrobe closet and Oriental rugs. From this air-conditioned room, you'll get a pleasant view of the grounds, rose garden and deck. Guests can use the TV and VCR in the sunroom and exercise room. Double bed with shared one and a half baths (tub and shower).

Pettygrove Room: A comfortable country atmosphere makes this room warm and relaxing. The uniqueness of "Old German Pine" beds and a handmade quilt to match the shades of the forest green decor take you a step into the past. This room has a ceiling fan and a view from the front of the house. King bed or two extra-long twins with shared one and a half baths (tub and shower).

Lovejoy Suite: This romantic Honeymoon Suite is light and spacious. It is accented with shades of blue and features an antique queen-sized canopy bed, chaise for child, a sitting room, french windows, oak floors, antique chaise, writing table, TV, and ceiling fan. This gracious room offers a view of all the grounds and is truly a delight. Shared one and a half baths (tub and shower).

Easy access to public transportation, Portland International Airport, train station, bus, and Max Light Rail.

Also close to shopping mall, restaurants, Portland's Old Town, antique shops, museums, waterfront, convention center, hiking, skiing, rafting, and fishing on the Willamette or Clackamas rivers.

Portland special events include the Rose Festival, Art Quake, and a variety of other cultural attractions.

Rates - $ to $$ Map Location - NW

Hartman's Hearth 'A' Bed & Breakfast
2937 N.E. 20th Avenue
Portland, Oregon 97212
(503) 281-2182 or 281-2210

Your hosts make their home in this handsome 1911 arts-and-crafts period house. It's in one of Portland's prettiest and most convenient in-town neighborhoods, marked by stately shade trees and well-groomed yards that burgeon with flowers in the spring. In cooler months, guests succumb to the lure of the hearth, the focal point of the living room.

Throughout the interior, fabrics, colors, and textures mix well with an eclectic collection of antiques, traditional pieces, and contemporary art.

Two guest rooms on the second floor derive their color schemes from subtle floral motifs. The third-floor suite strikes a surprisingly different mood; sleek and sophisticated, it has a muted art-deco look. Mauve and rose tones are used with grey and black in the huge space, which boasts a king-sized canopy bed, a black lacquered deck, and a bathroom with delightfully intricate tilework. Much thought has been given to the aesthetics of decor, lighting, music, and cuisine at Hartman's Hearth; it's a dreamy place to stay.

Full breakfast (special dietary needs accommodated); TV room with VCR; color TV in Room C; fold-out loveseat in Room A; robes provided; sauna; spa; good area for walking or jogging; good public transportation and airport connections.

Rates - $ to $$ Map Location - NW

The Irvington Bed & Breakfast Inn
2025 N.E. 24th Avenue
Portland, Oregon 97212
(503) 282-6409

Located just minutes from downtown and the Lloyd Center, The Irvington is in the lovely historic "Irvington District," which retains all the charm of turn-of-the-century Portland. This Victorian Tudor style manor was built in 1903 by William H. See, whose wife was the sister of "Mary See" of the famous Sees Candy empire.

Enjoy sitting in the hidden study by the fire or ask to stay in the Mrs. See room, were a corner fireplace, antique pine, and a double bed await you.

Two other rooms are available, one with marbleized walls, antique pine, a Chinese silk jacket over the queen bed, and a sleeper sofa. One more bedroom has a private bath.

Two of these guest rooms share a bath but, depending on availability, you may book a private bath.

A full breakfast is served in the dining room amid lovely leaded and beveled-glass windows

Take the bus or vintage trolley to the heart of downtown, or enjoy the area's restaurants and cafés.

Rates - $$ Map Location - NW

Tudor House Bed & Breakfast
2321 N.E. 28th Avenue
Portland, Oregon 97212
(503) 287-9476

Tudor House Bed & Breakfast is located in Dolph Park—just east of Irvington, in an area of fine, large Portland homes. It is elegantly furnished with antique and period pieces in its main rooms.

Of its five guest rooms, three contain private baths and two share baths. One room is an antique suite, popular for getaways and honeymooners; another, on a separate floor, is a family suite—of particular appeal to those traveling with children.

Convenient to the airport, Amtrak station, and the freeway exits, Tudor House is just minutes by car from downtown and the convention center, and is in walking distance of the popular Lloyd Center shopping mall. Bus lines are just four blocks away. And the area restaurants and delis appeal to all tastes and budgets.

In the immediate vicinity is Grant Park, with a public swimming pools, tennis courts, and a distance-measured running and bicycle track.

A full breakfast is served in the dining room. Lighter breakfasts are served by special request.

Rates - $$ to $$$ Map Location - NW

PORT ORFORD, OREGON

Home by the Sea Bed & Breakfast
444 Jackson
P.O. Box 606-B
Port Orford, Oregon 97465-0606

Your hosts built this contemporary wood home on a spit of land overlooking a breathtaking stretch of Oregon coast. The exceptional view can be enjoyed from both bedrooms and from the Sunspace Parlor Room, where guests are free to linger, visit and watch the beach.

From the Home By The Sea, it's a very short walk to restaurants, public beaches, historic Battle Rock Park and the town's unusual harbor, home port of Oregon's only crane-launched commercial fishing fleet. Port Orford is a quiet fishing village with a population of about 1,000. It is a favorite of beachcombers, whale, bird and storm watchers, plus scuba divers and surfers.

Blue Suite: Private bath, ocean view, queen-sized Oregon Myrtlewood bed, and cable TV.

Coral Room: Private bath across the hall, ocean view, queen-sized Myrtlewood bed, and cable TV.

Full breakfast served each morning. Guests have laundry privileges.

Rates - $$ Map Location - SW

SALEM, OREGON

Hampshire House Bed & Breakfast
975 D Street N.E.
Salem, Oregon 97301
(503) 370-7181

Hampshire House is a 1920s craftsman-style private home located at the foot of Capitol Mall. It is within walking distance of downtown Salem, Willamette University and all state buildings, and is close to many fine Oregon wineries as well.

Her you have two guest rooms to choose from. One is decorated with antiques and the other is done in white wicker. Both rooms have double beds, huge closets, color TV, alarm radios and air conditioning.

Guests share a Victorian bath, complete with a claw-foot tub, perfect for soaking.

Your hosts share the living room and dining room with guests. Join them to chat in front of a fire, watch TV or curl up and read.

A tray with coffee or tea is available upon request, anytime of the day. Enjoy it in the living room, in the privacy of your room or on the front porch, weather permitting.

A full or continental breakfast is served in the dining room. The menu is 'Cook's Choice' but will include fresh bread, homemade jam, fresh-ground coffee or tea and fresh juice.

Rates - $ Map Location - NW

SANDY, OREGON

Brookside Bed & Breakfast
45232 S.E. Paha Loop
Sandy, Oregon 97055
(503) 668-4766

Brookside is conveniently located on the Mount Hood Loop to serve the travelers in this recreational area. It is set in a lovely wooded area, and has easy access to Highway 26.

The house was built in 1948, and offers a full view of Mount Hood. A brook flows through the property a short stroll from the house.

Nearby are a candy shop, restaurants, antique shops, hiking, skiing, fishing, sightseeing, and other recreational opportunities. The hosts will be happy to help you find what you're looking for.

Brookside can be ideal for the overflow for weddings, graduations, reunions, and other large gatherings.

A full breakfast is served until 9:30 a.m. Choose lighter fare if you wish. Early-morning serving is offered for those who need an early start.

Brookside is about 10 minutes from fishing streams and a 27-hole golf course, 20 minutes from Ski Bowl, hiking trails at the Mount Hood Area (check Zig Zag Ranger Station for maps), and 30 minutes from Timberline Lodge or downtown Portland.

Rates -$ Map Location - NW

SEAL ROCK, OREGON

Blackberry Inn Bed & Breakfast
6575 N.W. Pacific Coast Highway 101
P.O. Box 188
Seal Rock, Oregon 97376
(503) 563-2259

Blackberry Inn is reminiscent of Oregon's logging history. Originally the site of Orton's Mill, the home was built for the Orton family, which logged timber from the property and processed it at the mill. Time and foliage have erased traces of the operation, but the home retains the charm of those earlier times.

Guest are invited to wander on the beach, explore the tide pools, use their kite or sand toys, relax on the deck or in the hot tub, or treat themselves to body work or a relaxing bubble bath.

Share conversation with fellow guests in a living room made comfortable with a fireplace, small library, color TV, telephone, refrigerator, refreshments, sun deck, and an assortment of games and puzzles.

Irene's Room: A large room with a fluffy goose-down comforter on a queen-sized bed, lace canopy, sitting area, skylight, and a patio door opening onto the deck overlooking the woods. The attached bath has a whirlpool tub and hand-held shower. Breakfast in your room is optional.

Honeymoon Suite: A large, romantic room with goose-down comforter on a king-sized bed, plus sitting area and skylight. Bath in room with antique claw-foot tub and hand-held shower. Breakfast in your room is optional.

Michael's Room: Vine maple decor. Available with king-sized bed or two twins. Private bath.

Jennifer's Room: A sunny room with a queen bed, lace canopy, and private bath.

Besides wonderful beaches, tide pools and spectacular monoliths, Seal Rock has an art gallery, gift shops, a Japanese restaurant, chainsaw art, local arts and crafts, homemade fudge, antiques, food, groceries, and a postal service.

Less than 45 minutes away are the Sea Lion Caves, haunted lighthouse, parks, beaches, covered bridges, fishing, crabbing, old cemeteries, spouting horns, museums, Marine Science Center, and lots of great seafood.

Rates - $$ Map Location - NW

SEASIDE, OREGON

The Custer House Bed & Breakfast
811 First Avenue
Seaside, Oregon 97138
(503) 738-7825

Relax and enjoy hospitality and a wholesome breakfast in a pleasant dining room at the Custer House. Then explore the marvels of Oregon's North Coast. From here, you're just two blocks from the Seaside Convention Center, and four blocks from the ocean and the Turnaround, where you'll find delightful shops and a variety of restaurants.

Room 1: Romantic room with wicker furnishings and queen bed. Large private bath with claw-foot tub.

Room 2: Charming, sunny room with queen bed, daybed and shared bath with shower.

Room 3: Cozy room with queen bed, sitting area with shared bath with shower.

Rates - $$ Map Location - NW

Gilbert Inn Bed & Breakfast
341 Beach Drive
Seaside, Oregon 97138
(503) 738-9770

Upon entering this special Queen Anne Victorian, you are transported into yesteryear. The Gilbert Inn, built in 1892 by Alexander Gilbert, still looks much the same as it did then. The big fireplace in the center of the parlor, the natural fir tongue and groove ceiling and walls throughout the house retain its warmth and charm. The colorful country French print furniture and antiques are truly inviting. And the old party room and side porch have been restored as the setting for hearty breakfasts.

The Gilbert Inn is ideally located in one of the North Coast's most popular towns, Seaside. It's a vacation paradise. Shops, restaurants, and beaches are all within easy walking distance.

The guest accommodations include eight beautiful country French queen-bed rooms and two country suites—The 1880s Suite, built before the main house, and The Garrett, which comprises the entire third floor. All of the accommodations feature thick plush carpeting, period furnishings, down quilts, cozy comforters, and pillows. Family heirlooms help put the emphasis on homey comfort for. All of the rooms feature private baths and color TV.

Rooms: 1880s Suite; Emma's Room; Turret Room; Alexander's Room; The Garrett; Renee's Room; Andrew's Room; Addie's Room; Kimberly's Room; and Matthew's Room.

Rates - $$ Map Location - NW

SHANIKO, OREGON

Shaniko Historic Hotel "A" Bed & Breakfast
Shaniko, Oregon 97057
(503) 489-3441 or 489-3415

The Shaniko Hotel, a two-story brick building with a wooden balcony, was built circa 1900, and opened for business in 1902. "Shaniko" is derived from the Indian pronunciation of the name of one of its early settlers, August Scherneckau, who established a store and stagecoach inn at Cross Hollows in 1879.

When the Columbia Southern Railroad came down from the North in 1900, Cross Hollows moved and became Shaniko. From 1900 to 1911, Shaniko was the largest wool-shipping center in the United States. It also was the site of the last of the range wars between cattlemen and sheepmen.

When the railroad was built along the Deschutes River into Bend, Shaniko's usefulness as a shipping center ended. The railroad continued to run to Shaniko, however, until a flood in the 1950s washed out the track to the north. Shaniko now is a ghost town. From 1955-1977, the hotel was used as a group home for adults. It was auctioned off in October of 1977, and efforts are being made to restore it.

Rates - $$ Map Location - NE

STAYTON, OREGON

Bird & Hat Inn Bed & Breakfast
717 North Third Avenue
Stayton, Oregon 97383
(503) 769-7817

Built in 1907, the Bird & Hat is within walking distance of shopping, movies, and restaurants. It has two rooms, one with a king-sized bed and the other with a double; they share a bath.

The Inn can accommodate nine people, and is centrally located for those visiting the Willamette Valley.

Rates - $$ Map Location - NW

SUMPTER, OREGON

Sumpter Bed & Breakfast Inn
P.O. Box 506
Sumpter, Oregon 97877
1-800-640-3184 or (503) 894-2229

A stay at the Sumpter Bed & Breakfast is like a step back into history. Old-time decor, a warm wood stove in the downstairs sitting room and old-fashioned iron beds make the premises as much a museum as a bed & breakfast.

The two-story building was built in 1900 as a hospital. At that time, Sumpter was a busy mining town, with an estimated population of 3,500 to 5,000.

The inn is popular with skiers, snowmobilers, hikers, fishermen, gold panners, and others.

Four rooms are available, and more will be added in the future. There is no television, and customers say they like it that way.

Rates - $$ Map Location - SE

Gilbert Inn, Seaside, OR

THE DALLES, OREGON

Captain Gray's Guest House
210 West Four Street
The Dalles, Oregon 97058
1-800-448-4729 or 298-8222

Captain Gray's is a small bed & breakfast on a street of restored historical Victorian homes and other B&Bs.

A full breakfast—consisting of muffins, fruit, tea, and coffee, plus a hot entree of eggs, omelets, pancakes, or french toast (the cook's choice)—is served Friday through Monday. There's an open kitchen policy for lunch and dinner. A casual breakfast—consisting of an assortment of muffins, fruit, cereal, yogurt, herbal tea, and fresh-ground coffee—is served Tuesday through Thursday.

Captain Gray's has three air-conditioned rooms, with an assortment of queen and twin beds. The second-floor rooms share a bathroom; there is a common-use full bathroom on the main floor, as well. The bedroom on the main floor has a private bath.

Waxwing Room: One queen, one twin bed furnished with antique spool beds and quilts. This room features a reading table and chairs, where you could enjoy a quiet cup of coffee, tea or lemonade.

Tanglewood Room: One queen bed furnished with an antique bedroom suite and quilt. This charming room overlooks the deck and spa.

Rosebud Room: One queen bed and dark maple dressers. Private bath.

Rates - $ Map Location - NE

Williams House Inn Bed & Breakfast
608 West Sixth Street
The Dalles, Oregon 97058
(503) 296-2889

Located in the Columbia River Gorge, the Williams House is a large and gracious Victorian home occupying its own wooded hilltop. The grounds, separated from the street by a wrought-iron fence, are groomed and green; a natural arboretum extends to Mill Creek on the West.

The interior is furnished with Georgian and Victorian antiques and the Williams' collection of early Chinese objects d'art. Air conditioning provides comfort in summer weather.

Your hosts will be happy to share their broad knowledge of the area, and to advise daytime excursions to landmarks, special events, recreation opportunities and fine restaurants.

Harriet's Room: This is a spacious room with its own furnished balcony overlooking the Klickitat Hills and the Columbia River. The room features a beautiful canopied four-poster double bed, a chaise lounge, and a period writing desk. A modern bathroom with tub and shower is shared with Edward's Room.

Edward's Room: With its period double bed, Edward's Room is predominantly Victorian. It has a north-facing private balcony with chairs and a table. The adjacent bathroom is shared with the Harriet's Room.

Elizabeth's Suite: This suite consists of a private sitting room adjoining a bedroom with a splendid four-poster double bed. The private bathroom, rich in original marble, offers the choice of a convenient shower or a bath in a six-foot-long claw-foot tub. It is furnished with a comfortable hide-a-bed, and can accommodate four people.

All guests are welcome to enjoy a comfortable parlour, where tables are available for games and a warm fire will cheer you in the winter. Each room has a TV.

Breakfast is served either outdoors in the secluded gazebo or inside the spacious dining room. Special needs of traveling business travelers have been anticipated; telephones are available in each room at no extra charge, and you'll find a good desk and reading lamp in each as well.

Rates - $$ Map Location - NE

TILLAMOOK, OREGON

Blue Haven Inn
3025 Gienger Road
Tillamook, Oregon 97141
(503) 842-2265

Blue Haven Inn is located just off Highway 101 at the South end of Tillamook, known as "the land of cheese, trees and ocean breeze." Located on a two-acre park-like setting and surrounded by tall evergreens, the peace and quiet of Blue Haven will help you relax and unwind.

The house was built in 1916 and has been lovingly restored and redecorated. The inn has extensive grounds and gardens, including croquet and lawn-tennis games. Enjoy a relaxing pause on the country porch and swing; visit the library/game room; listen to music from an old radio or antique gramophone; enjoy movies on the VCR; or take your pick from the variety of games and books.

Adjacent to the inn is an "overflow shop," containing items for sale, including antique furniture, glassware, old sewing machines and claw-foot bathtubs.

Individually decorated bedrooms are furnished with antiques, limited-edition collectibles, and all the modern amenities needed for a comfortable evening. Gourmet breakfast is served in the formal dining room.

You will enjoy all seasons in this lush green valley. Eight bountiful rivers and the ocean offer all varieties of fishing, plus clamming and crabbing. The Three Cape Loop connects the valley with spectacular ocean and offshore rock-formation viewing.

Rooms include the Tara (double bed), La Femme (queen bed), and Of the Sea (queen). All with shared bath.

Other things to do: Hiking, touring the cheese factory, antique shopping, train riding, winery touring, kite flying, and hang gliding.

Rates - $ to $$ Map Location - NW

VIDA, OREGON

Heaven's Gate Cottages
50031 McKenzie Highway
Vida, Oregon 97488
(503) 822-3214

Each of Heaven's Gate Cottages is nestled along the shore of the McKenzie River, 36 miles east of Eugene, on Highway 126. These rustic cottages provide grace and charm reminiscent of a gentler era.

All cottages have fully furnished kitchens, fireplaces in the living room, and full bathroom, including tub and shower. They feature windows all along the entire river side, affording an unparalleled view of the whitewater. French doors open from the living room onto a large, spacious deck, directly over the water in the cool, green Willamette National Forest. In addition to a fireplace, each cottage has electric baseboard heat, and a separate kitchen.

The bedroom cottage has a queen-sized bed and double bed in the bedroom, plus a hide-a-bed in the living room. A single cot is available as well.

The studio cottage has a queen-sized bed and a sofa that folds into a double bed.

Trout and steelhead fishing on the McKenzie ranks among the world's finest. Fishing guides, scenic-river guides and whitewater raft trips can easily be arranged for you and your family. A wide variety of hiking trails, lakes, reservoirs, and golf courses are just minutes away. Cafés, restaurants, cocktail bars, food markets, coin laundry, liquor stores, post offices, ranger stations, and antique shops are accessible.

Rates - $$ Map Location - SW

WALDPORT, OREGON

Cliff House Bed & Breakfast
P.O. Box 436
Waldport, Oregon 97394
(503) 563-2506

The Cliff House, a luxuriously restored home with a spectacular ocean view, allows you to escape to a peaceful, relaxed atmosphere and refresh your spirit in a romantic setting

Each room is uniquely decorated with antiques, chandeliers and carpeting, and includes a remote control color TV. Each room also has its own ocean and/or bay view, cedar bath and balcony.

The Great Room, with its vaulted ceiling, accommodates guests for afternoon tea, a roaring fire on cool days, listening to or playing the grand piano, playing games, or simply chatting. Browse through the library and select an interesting book; stroll out onto the 65-foot deck overlooking the ocean and watch the waves crash against the surf below the cliff; take a therapeutic bath in the hot tub or use the binoculars to watch the sea lions sunbathe on the sand. Lounge in a hammock for two; play croquet on the front lawn; or take a leisurely walk and explore the beach.

Enjoy a fresh seafood dinner at one of the fine restaurants in the area; your hosts will be happy to make reservations for you. Then return and fall asleep to the soothing sound of the ocean.

Have breakfast while viewing the ocean in the sun-filled dining room, with china linens and silver service. Breakfast is served at times to accommodate your needs.

The Morning Star: A bright and airy room with a queen-sized, four-poster bed, a balcony on the ocean, an antique wood stove, a private bath with a shower and two four-by-five skylights, two wing-back chairs and a full selection of good books.

The Alsea Room: From here, you'll get panoramic, second-story view of the ocean and bay, with your own private entrance and balcony. King-sized bed, loveseat, desk and chairs, refrigerator, and private bath with shower. Five windows on the ocean.

The Bridal Suite: A step back in time. An exquisite 15th century, powder blue, tufted velvet queen sleigh bed with canopy. This lovely room faces the ocean and the bay. Breakfast is served in the room, where you'll also find a chaise lounge, two overstuffed chairs, a curio cabinet and a complete mirrored bath with an eight-jet Jacuzzi, plus a double vanity and a double shower.

Things to do: Fishing, crabbing, kite flying, clamming, golfing, bike riding, beachcombing, or settling in for a massage.

Rates: $$ Map Location - SW

WELCHES, OREGON

Old Welches Inn
26401 East Welches Road
Welches, Oregon 97067
(503) 622-3754

The Old Welches Inn was built in 1890—in the heart of the Hoodland Recreation Area—by Samuel Welch and his son, Billy. It was operated as the first summer resort and hotel on Mount Hood until the late 1930s, when it was converted to a single-family home. The inn is traditionally styled, reminiscent of the fine homes of the Old South.

Start your day with a full breakfast in the dining room, which overlooks the patio and the Salmon River. Spend your evenings by the fireplace with a selection from the library, or compare your day with new friends.

A complete variety of outdoor, winter activities including cross-country and downhill skiing and mountain climbing are only 15 minutes away, on Mount Hood. Spring and summer will lure the fisherman to the lakes, rivers, and streams, including the Salmon River, which runs right through the property. Hikers and nature lovers can enjoy miles of scenic trails in the mountains and wilderness areas surrounding the inn as well.

Golfers will be in seventh heaven with 27 irresistible holes at Rippling River—the Resort at the Mountain, located conveniently across the road from the Old Welches Inn.

The rooms at Old Welches are named after some of Oregon's wildflowers, all of which grow in the yard. The bedrooms share two full baths.

Trillium Room: The largest of the rooms, this has a queen-sized sleigh bed and projects an aura of the English countryside, with its chintz flower prints and "hunt" scenic paintings. Relax in the over-stuffed chairs and enjoy the view of the golf meadows and Hunchback Mountain.

Sweet Briar: Delicate shades of green, pink, and cream show off the ornate iron double bed in this room. The aroma of cedar from the paneling and chest give you a warm, cozy feeling—as if you're back at grandma's for a visit.

Columbine Room: This room appeals to the sportsman, with the old cannonball-style double bed and a view of the Salmon River. Duck decoys and various paintings combine to make you feel at home.

Luties Cottage: Located adjacent to the inn, this cottage was the first one built—in 1901—for the original summer resort. This cabin and the others were rented during the summers until the late 1930s, when they all became private residences. The cottage overlooks the first hole and second tee of Rippling River's Yellow Course, with Hunchback Mountain looming over Welches Valley. Easy river access for the fisherman is an added bonus. A spacious two-bedroom, one bath, fully equipped kitchen and a charming river rock fireplace in the living room help make for a cozy hideaway.

Rates - $ to $$ Map Location - NE

WEST LINN, OREGON

F.V. Prospector Bed (Bunk) & Breakfast
5035 Prospector Street
West Linn, Oregon 97068
(503) 656-7451

The F.V. Prospector promises a unique overnight experience. Stay aboard the 48-

foot staysail schooner, Prospector, moored in a tranquil setting on the Willamette River between the historic cities of Oregon City and West Linn. It is peaceful and isolated here, yet close to urban amenities—including the Clackamas Town Center, one of Oregon's largest shopping areas, and the I-205 interchange.

Your overnight accommodations feature an impressive upriver view of Willamette Falls, as well as an opportunity to observe the ducks, geese, and blue heron that ply the river. The sailing vessel features a warm, roomy interior with traditional kerosene lamps, as well as electric lighting for evening reading, if you desire.

During fishing season (February-June), enjoy watching the many fishing boats try their luck just outside your door. And you can watch tugs pushing barges up and down the river year-round.

For the fishing buff, the mighty spring Chinook salmon swim is within easy reach of your overnight accommodations. Your host will help you arrange a guided fishing trip on the Willamette or a whitewater trip down the scenic Clackamas River. Or you can simply drop a fishing line off the deck in hopes of hooking a spring Chinook.

Rates - $ to $$ Map Location - NW

WHEELER, OREGON

Nehalem Bay House Bed & Breakfast
117 Rowe Street
P.O. Box 82
Wheeler, Oregon 97147
(503) 368-7153

A Tillamook County historical landmark, Nehalem Bay House has been restored and furnished to reflect the style and elegance of its time. You will find antiques, collections of photographs of 'the old days,' stained glass and Oriental rugs. Choose between two charming garden-view rooms with snug-down comforters and shared bath.

Nestled among fir and alder trees and surrounded by lovely gardens, Nehalem Bay House sits on a hill overlooking picturesque Neah-Kah-Nie Mountain and Nehalem Bay.

Savor the commanding view from the living room. It is a wonderful place to observe activity on the bay—from fishermen clamming on the islands, or pulling a huge Chinook salmon out of the river, to wildlife browsing on Nehalem Bay.

The Manor Room: Elegant mahogany furniture, original art, marble, lace, cranberry glass and velvet. A full bed and comfortable sitting area with a whisper of pink.

The Country Room: Cheerful prints, Oak Barley Twist furniture and masses of flowers grown and dried at Nehalem Bay House. A queen-sized bed with a touch of yellow.

Fishing, crabbing, clamming, beachcombing, fine dining, antiquing, and golfing are moments away. Naturalists and artists find an abundance of captivating subjects. Visit a museum, gallery or winery; sample locally made cheeses, smoked fish or ice cream; or rent a boat, hike or windsurf.

Rates - $$ Map Location - NW

YACHATS, OREGON

The Burd's Nest Inn
664 Yachats River Road, P.O. Box 261
Yachats, Oregon 97498
(503) 547-3683

The Burd's Nest is located in Yachats (pronounced Ya-hots), which is nestled between lush forested mountains and the lapping waves of the Pacific Ocean. The mild climate produces temperatures ranging from 40 to 70 degrees in unspoiled beauty and a friendly atmosphere that make this a favorite destination year-round. Uncrowded beaches and some of the most dramatic surf action during the winter storms are draws as well.

Constructed in 1947 and originally called 'Dream Vista,' The Burd's Nest is located on 1.5 acres, with 200-year-old trees and three creeks gracing the property. It boasts a Spanish decor with a multi-colored roof.

Guests have use of the entire inn and grounds. A color TV with three movies channels is included, and you'll start your day with a gourmet Mexican breakfast.

Eagles Nest: Affords a view of the mountains, ocean, river, and town. This suite with private bath has a brass tub and Mexican tile shower, plus a king-sized bed and French doors that lead to your own private deck.

Robins Nest: Again, you'll get a view of the mountains, ocean, river, and town, plus a king-sized bed with private bath and Mexican tile shower and French doors that lead to a shared deck.

Swallows Nest: View of the mountains, ocean, river, and town. King-sized bed, private bath with claw-foot tub and shower. French doors that lead to shared deck.

Outdoor Activities: Fishing, hiking, beachcombing, hunting, whale and bird watching, picnicking, canoeing, bike riding, and berry picking.

Attractions: Gourmet restaurants, quaint shops, little log church by the sea, smelt run, covered bridges, one-man lumber mill, and pioneer cemetery.

Rates - $$ to $$$ Map Location - SW

Sea Quest Bed & Breakfast
95354 Highway 101
Yachats, Oregon 97498
(503) 547-3782

Relaxation and the hot tub are only the beginning to the pleasures that await you at Sea Quest. Here, all guest rooms are designed for privacy, with generous private bathrooms and hot, bubbling Jacuzzis. Each guest room has its own outside entrance. The large common room has a woodburning stove, TV, VCR, stereo, good books, and plenty of games.

After your night's rest, the morning begins with an alluring and fresh breakfast served on the second floor, with an open view of the ocean, Ten Mile Creek and the forest beyond. The outside deck, encircling all of Sea Quest, brings you just a bit closer to it all.

Sea Quest sits on a slight bluff overlooking the outlet of Ten Mile Creek, and is reached by driving about seven miles south on Highway 101 from the town of Yachats. Another 18 miles takes you to the town of Florence. Between Yachats and Florence are scenic Devils Churn, 800-foot-high Cape Perpetua and its visitors center, famed Sea Lion Caves, parks, campsites, and a grand 15-mile-long ocean beach view.

You may choose to hike to Bray's Point, do tide-pool research, or simply enjoy the feel of salt air, sun and wind in your hair, and sand between your toes.

Rates - $$ to $$$$ Map Location - SW

WASHINGTON

Lynden

Eastsound

Friday Harbor

Lummi Island

Bellingham

Anacortes

Concrete-Birdsview

•Mazma

Forks

Lopez Island

Langley

Port Angeles•

Port Townsend

LaConner

Mount Vernon

Coupsville

Greenbank

•Pateros

Edmonds

Bellevue

Carnation

Bremerton

Seattle

Leavenworth

Belfair

Snoqualmie Falls

Gig Harbor

Bainbridge

Vashon Island

Spokane •

Anderson Island

Westport

Olympia•

Tacoma

Montesano

Eatonville

Centralia

Long Beach

Seaview

Cathlamet

•Naches

•Yakima

•Sunnyside

Clarkston•

Trout Lake•

•Glenwood

White Salmon

ANACORTES, WASHINGTON

Hasty Puddy House
1312 Eighth Street
Anacortes, Washington 98221
(206) 293-5773

The restoration of this 1913 Edwardian home succeeded in highlighting the original charm and elegance of the turn of the century, without sacrificing the comforts of today.

Walk to historic downtown, Cap Sante Marine waterfront, beautiful Causland Park or the Anacortes Community Theater, or just relax in front of a cozy fire and read a good book.

The Hasty Puddy is located in a quiet, beautifully maintained neighborhood, where many of the original Anacortes families flourished at the turn of the century.

Your innkeepers have used antiques and lovely colors, lace curtains, old family photographs and charming wallpaper to bring all the rooms harmony and romantic charm. Private baths with antique accessories have been added to two of the rooms.

Victorian Garden Room: Deep green and roses in this large elegant room with Eastlake oak antiques.

Queen Anne's Lace Room: Soft ivory and lots of lace provide a romantic feeling. Victorian walnut antiques and a king bed.

Robyn's Nest Room: Bright and sunny peach with pine antiques and a queen bed.

Leah's Room: Soft green and apricot in Laura Ashley prints with pine and oak antiques and two twins or a king bed.

A sumptuous home-baked breakfast is served in the dining room each morning.

Anacortes, on Fidalgo Island, beckons you to get away from the hubbub of city life. From here, you have easy access to adventure in every direction—from the North Cascades to the east, Whidbey Island to the south of Deception Pass, the San Juan Islands and Victoria, B.C. to the west and Vancouver, B.C. to the north. Visit the tulip, daffodil, and iris fields during the early spring. Witness the migration of snow geese, swans and other birds that seek sanctuary in area fields and estuaries.

The splendor of the area is unsurpassed. Go boating, fishing, crabbing, hiking, rock climbing, kayaking, golfing, play tennis, or just enjoy the beauty.

Rates - $$ Map Location - NW

ANDERSON ISLAND, WASHINGTON

The Inn at Burg's Landing
8808 Villa Beach Road
Anderson Island, Washington 98303
(206) 844-9185

The Inn at Burg's Landing is a beautiful bed & breakfast on the peaceful shores of Anderson Island, overlooking Puget Sound. During your stay here, tour the island by car, bicycle, or foot. About two miles from the inn is the old one-room schoolhouse built in the 1890s.

A mile farther is the Johnson Farm, now the Anderson Island Historical Society Museum. Other things to do on the island include golf and tennis, or swimming in one of the two freshwater lakes.

The large, wood-heated living room at Burg's Landing affords a spectacular view. In addition, there's an outdoor gazebo, complete with deck and hot tub. Of course, your stay includes a delicious breakfast prepared by your host.

There are three rooms available here—the ground-floor bedroom with a queen-sized bed and private bath, the main-floor bedroom with queen-sized bed and shared bath, and the master suite in the loft, with private bath and hydro-tub for two.

From the large picture window of this rustic log homestead, enjoy the spectacular view of Mount Rainier, the Cascades, and Puget Sound. Watch sailboats glide past the island, or witness a log raft making its way to a mill. Ocean freighters and barges routinely pass on their way to Tacoma and Olympia.

In addition, look for deer browsing in the orchard, or eagles soaring overhead. See a sunset over the Olympic Mountains or a sunrise outlining Mount Rainier, or take a walk on the private beach and collect seashells and agates.

Rates - $$ Map Location - NW

ASHFORD, WASHINGTON

Growly Bear Bed & Breakfast
P.O. Box 103
Ashford, Washington 98304
(206) 569-2339

At the Growly Bear, you'll experience a bit of history and enjoy a mountain stay at a rustic homestead house built in 1890.

Hike in nearby Mount Rainier National Park. Dine at unique restaurants within walking distance of your room. Be lulled to sleep by whispering sounds of Goat Creek, just outside your window. And wake in the morning to the aroma of fresh-baked bread. Indulge in a basket of warm pastries from the Growly Bear Bakery.

Things to do: Fish, hike, swim, sightsee, or just kick back and relax.

Rates - $$ Map Location - SW

BAINBRIDGE, WASHINGTON

The Bombay House
8490 Beck Road N.E.
Bainbridge, Washington 98110
(206) 842-3926 or 1-800-598-3926

The Bombay House bed & breakfast is located on Bainbridge Island, a spectacular 35-minute ferry ride from downtown Seattle. The island is a quiet, semi-rural retreat favored by commuters, novelists, and people seeking simpler lives. It's a great spot for the business traveler or vacationer visiting Seattle as well, and is the gateway to the Kitsap and Olympic peninsulas.

Located in the former mill town of West Blakely—a sleepy unincorporated community about four miles Southwest of Winslow—the house was built in 1907 by a master shipbuilder and sits on a half acre, high on a hillside overlooking "Rich Passage."

The setting is wonderfully reminiscent of the past, with a "widow walk," a rustic, rough-cedar gazebo and masses of unstructured gardens exploding with seasonal color. Watch the ferry pass and see the lights of the Kitsap Peninsula in the distant haze.

The Bombay House is just a few blocks from the beach, a country theater, and fine dining. Nearby, you can also enjoy hiking, walking, tennis, boating, golf, biking, picnicking, shopping, and clam digging.

Crows Nest Room: This room is cozy—but not too small—with a view of the water from the double bed. Shared bath.

The Morning Room: Includes a double and a single bed and overlooks the grounds. Shared bath.

The Captain's Suite: This is the master suite of the house and is quite spacious. It is located on the second level—across the full front of the house—and affords a great water view. It has a claw-foot tub and shower, small refrigerator, game table, queen-sized bed, couch, and a parlor stove.

The King Room: Located downstairs, this room looks out on the grounds and the gazebo. It has a king-sized bed, bathroom facilities, and a tin soaking tub in the room.

The Red Room: This room is on the first floor of the house and has a private bath with a tub and shower right across the hall. It has a queen-sized brass bed and a lovely Victorian sitting area.

Breakfast at the Bombay House includes fresh fruit, juices, and a variety of muffins, including a special fruit bran muffin. Sweet bread, breakfast cakes, pastries, and homemade cereals are included as well. The large country kitchen looks out onto a deck and down the beach.

The inn is comfortably furnished in country antiques and has a wonderful brick open-hearth fireplace where guests can relax year-round.

Rates - $$ to $$$ Map Location - NW

BELLEVUE, WASHINGTON

Bellevue Bed & Breakfast
830 100th Ave. S.E.
Bellevue, Washington 98004
(206) 453-1048

Bellevue Bed & Breakfast features views of the hilltop, mountain and the city of Bellevue. It is located near Lake Washington and Bellevue Square.

Here, your hosts will offer you a private suite or single rooms with a private bath and entrance. And your stay will include a full breakfast, featuring gourmet coffee.

Rates - $ to $$ Map Location - NW

BELFAIR, WASHINGTON

Country Garden Inn
N.E. 2790 Old Belfair Highway
Belfair, Washington 98528
(206) 275-3683

The Country Garden Inn is situated on the Union River, where 21 pristine acres are yours to roam. This inn also sits on one of the Northwest's most popular bicycle touring routes, the old Belfair Highway, and is just minutes from Gold Mountain and Lakeland Village golf courses. Belfair State Park and Twanoh State Park are close by, where you can enjoy swimming, picnicking, and other outdoor activities on the Hood Canal. In addition, Port Orchard is less than 10 miles away, and features a wonderful Farmer's Market and many antique shops.

Here, you'll enjoy the decor of three guest rooms: The Wisteria Room, The Victorian Room, and The Delphinium Room. Each has a private bath and a cozy fireplace.

Country Garden Inn offers shuttle service from the Seattle/Bremerton ferry terminal and from the Bremerton National Airport.

Guests will begin each morning with muffins and coffee, which are placed quietly outside their room. A full breakfast is served later in the morning, and there are a host of options for dinner. Enjoy an intimate dinner for two or plan a special-occasion dinner for as many as 12 people.

Telephones and cable TV are available upon request. A gift shop featuring creative wares from local talent is on the premises. Herbs and flowers are available for sale as well.

"As tradition would demand," the Country Garden Inn serves a high tea on the first Saturday of each month.

Rates - $$ to $$$ Map Location - NW

BELLINGHAM, WASHINGTON

The Castle & Seagoat
1103 15th Street
Bellingham, Washington 98225
(206) 676-0974

The Castle & Seagoat looms high on a hill above Historic Fairhaven. All of its guest rooms in this mansion offer excellent views of Bellingham Bay and the San Juan Islands.

Sultan's Tent: From here, you'll get a panoramic view like no other. Private turret room comes with camel and Arabian nights decor, and features a 400-year-old bed.

Bayview Honeymoon Suite: Affords a spectacular view of the bay, islands and Fairhaven. Cozy fireplace, private veranda, and queen-sized bed and private bath.

King's Balcony: King-sized bed with Romeo and Juliet balcony. Large room with deep hues of purples, blues and gold. Marble-top furniture. Private bath available.

Cupola Oriental: Queen-sized bed in the cupola. This is a red-carpeted royal suite with excellent views of the bay and islands. The Oriental furnishings in here are of museum quality.

The Castle offers Old-World grandeur, extraordinary antiques, a lavish honeymoon suite, private bath and healthful food.

By special advance arrangement, a Thai curried chicken dinner, including seven condiments, salad and dessert, is available.

Seagoat: You don't have to travel far to enjoy this private, clean cottage, right on the beach. Have a crackling fire in the sunken fireplace, take in the spectacular view of Bellingham with the majestic Mount Baker and the Twin Sisters, take a walk on the beach, or hike around nearby Portage Island. This cottage includes three-plus bedrooms furnished with antique bedroom sets and full in-house conveniences.

Here, you will have the feeling of total seclusion, but will be just minutes from stores, restaurants and the Lummi Island Ferry.

Rates - $$ to $$$ Map Location - NW

North Garden Inn
1014 N. Garden
Bellingham, Washington 98224
(206) 671-7828 or 1-800-922-6414

The North Garden Inn is the Robert I. Morse House, built in 1897 and now listed on the National Register of Historic Places. It is located near Western Washington University and is just a short distance from the Canadian border.

Ten guest rooms—with five full baths—offer a beautiful view of Bellingham Bay and the many islands. The inn also boasts two grand pianos, which guests are invited to play.

Nearby activities: Skagit Valley Tulip Festival, kayak races, food and street fairs, Western Washington University Summer Stock Theater, country fairs, boating, fishing, wine tasting, and skiing.

Here, you'll get a Continental breakfast that includes pastries made from flour ground right in the North Garden kitchen.

Rates - $$ Map Location - NW

Schnauzer Crossing Bed & Breakfast
4421 Lakeway Drive
Bellingham, Washington 98226
(206 733-0055 or (206) 734-2808

At Schnauzer Crossing, you can unwind and relax. Enjoy the beauty of tall evergreens, maple, dogwood, birch, and rhododendrons. Stroll in the garden, and pick your fill of raspberries and blueberries. Play tennis, jog, walk or bike the rural Geneva neighborhood.

Hike, climb or ski nearby Mount Baker. Sail, canoe or fish the waters of Lake Whatcom and Bellingham Bay. Tour Western Washington University's outdoor sculpture collection. Shop historic Fairhaven, Bellis Fair, or downtown Bellingham. Take a day trip to Victoria or Vancouver, British Columbia. Ride a ferry. Visit a fish hatchery. Dine on fresh salmon and crab. Curl up with a book on the deck overlooking Lake Whatcom, or snuggle up to a warm fire. Enjoy the hammock, sunshine and songbirds.

The Cottage: Separate from the main house and tucked in among 100-foot cedars, The Cottage offers total privacy. Enjoy the view of the lake from the oversized bedroom, which includes beautiful handmade furniture, a king-sized bed, gas fireplace, skylight, bathroom with Jacuzzi tub and shower, telephone, TV, VCR, and wet bar.

Master Suite: Offers a garden view, king-sized bed, wood fireplace, sitting/child's room, Jacuzzi tub, double shower, TV, VCR, stereo, and telephone.

Queen Room: Partial lake view, queen-sized bed, private bath, and telephone.

Breakfast is an "event" at Schnauzer Crossing. Enjoy homemade quiche, fresh-picked raspberries and blueberries, blueberry bran muffins, tasty fruit parfaits, bagels and fresh-ground coffee.

Rates - $$$ to $$$$ Map Location - NW

BREMERTON, WASHINGTON

Willcox House
2390 Tekiu Road
Bremerton, Washington 98312
(206) 830-4492

Located on a shoreline bluff of Hood Canal, every room in the Willcox House is angled to capture a glorious vista of sparkling water and the Olympic Mountains. In their painstaking restoration of the house, your hosts have preserved the integrity of the original design.

In 1936, at the urging of his wife and her sister, and influenced by the family's former place in San Francisco high society, Colonel Willcox selected architect Lionel Pries to design the residence. Historical accounts describe the home—which ultimately cost more then $250,000 to build—as "the grand entertainment capitol of the Canal region." It once was the private residence of Colonel Julian Willcox and his wife, Constance.

The design includes five marble and copper fireplaces located throughout the home, plus oak parquet floors, polished to perfection, and walnut walls in the formal dining room and great room.

For many guests, however, the library—with views of Hood Canal and the mountains—is a special place. Enjoy it in the winter curled up by the fireside with a good book. In the summer, its sun-washed deck is the only invitation you'll need for an afternoon nap. Also included in the Willcox House is a game room, complete with pool table, darts and board games.

From early spring to late fall, lush gardens provide a striking showcase of blossoming greenery. And, encouraged by special feeding areas and bathing ponds, many species of birds make their homes in the gardens. Occasionally, deer are seen grazing here as well.

During your stay, your hosts will encourage you to take time for a leisurely stroll along one of the forest hiking trails leading from the grounds to the surrounding hillsides or beach.

Constance's Room: King bed, marble art-deco fireplace, fantasy bathroom with tub and large shower.

Julian's Room: King bed, double Jacuzzi tub, shower, English country gentleman's decor.

Clark Gable Room: King bed, private balcony, large, bright room and shower.

Colonel's Room: Antique brass king bed, French decor, large shower with view.

Rose Garden Room: Queen bed, separate view sitting room with sleigh daybed, shower and single Jacuzzi tub.

Breakfast is served at your private table in the view dining room, and lunch is available to multi-night guests. Most dietary restrictions can be accommodated.

Rates - $$$ to $$$$ Map Location - NW

CARNATION, WASHINGTON

Idyl Inn On The River
4548 Tolt River Road
Carnation, Washington 98014
(206) 333-4262

Idyl Inn on the River occupies an exquisite and secluded bend of the Tolt River, on a seven-acre organic hobby farm and gardens. Eastside Seattle is a half-hour drive, with Snoqualmie Falls and Fall City's Herb Farm nearby.

This huge solar villa, luxuriously appointed with antiques, designer wallpaper, and unique furnishings, charms with Old World country elegance. The heated indoor pool, sauna bath, whirlpool, and steam room make for a personal health spa. For cooling down, take a dip in the pristine Tolt River.

The parlor, with complimentary Tea Bar, overlooks the floor-to-ceiling glass of the vaulted pool room and the cascading river beyond. A gourmet kitchen and adjacent dining room and gathering room are available for guest use.

On your walk to the riverside gazebo or the gazebo beside the trout and koi pond, you may see bald eagles, blue herons, osprey or hawks, wild ducks and Canadian honkers.

Come for a personal retreat or reserve the entire villa for groups of as many as nine people. The Continental breakfast varies to include fresh fruit, pastries, cheesecake, muffins, bread and choices of delicatessen cheeses, fresh juice, gourmet coffees and herb teas. Guests on health stays may request fresh squeezed fruit, vegetable or wheat-grass juice.

North Room: Northwest flavor accents the graceful and quaint decor, with firm queen bed and sitting area.

West Room: Offers a view of the Tolt River and duck pond. This is a large gracious room with queen bed, single daybed and sitting area, decorated in an artistic quiet elegance.

Baths: The spacious bathroom has a separate shower and a six-foot Jacuzzi tub and is shared by North and West rooms. An additional bathroom with shower is located near the pool room and sauna.

South Suite: Here, you'll get a breathtaking panoramic view of the river and forests in a lavish suite done up in old-style taste with a firm king four-poster oak bed and two single beds. Elegant throughout, the sitting area is furnished with tapestry sofa and oak writing desk. A private tea bar has refrigerator and coffeemaker and is stocked with gourmet coffees and teas. The private bath has a large steam room and shower.

Rates -$$ to $$$$ Map Location - NW

CATHLAMET, WASHINGTON

Country Keeper Bed & Breakfast Inn
61 Main Street, P.O. Box 35
Cathlamet, Washington 98612
(206) 795-3030 - 1-800-551-1691

Cathlamet is a historic 1846 fishing and logging town, the origin of which dates back to the Hudson's Bay Company. "Cathlamet" is derived from the Indian Tribe that once inhabited the area.

Country Keeper is located on the main street, within walking distance of shops, restaurants, museum, and marina. Built in 1907 as the gracious home of a lumber baron, this elegant house sits on a hill overlooking the historic town of Cathlamet, Puget Island, and the beautiful Columbia River. Designed in the Eastlake style and resplendent with the warm glow of polished wood, the Country Keeper provides a delightful escape. Enjoy a variety of historical and natural sites, as well as activities such as cycling, golf, tennis, fishing, sailing, windsurfing, canoeing, and shopping.

The Rose Room: Spacious room with a view of the Columbia River and the marina from the large bay window. King-sized bed with private bath.

The Monet Room: Large, light airy room overlooking the Columbia River and Puget Island. A double and a twin bed with private bath.

The Garden Room: Large room overlooking the garden and woods behind. Queen-sized bed with shared bath.

The Blue Room: Blue and white lacy charm with a view of secluded woods. Double bed with shared bath.

Breakfast is served in the dinning room, glowing with burnished wood, stained-glass windows and a table set with silver and crystal. Linger over fresh-ground coffee, homebaked muffins, seasonal fruit, and a main course that changes daily.

Rates - $$ Map Location - SW

Little Cape Horn Bed & Breakfast
4 Little Cape Horn
Cathlamet, Washington 98612
(206) 425-7395

Picture windows at Little Cape Horn frame a majestic view of the Columbia River. Seals frolic, gulls soar, cormorants raft on the river, tugboat captains wave or blink their lights, and ships glide by. Pick a warm spot on the deck for star gazing, or watch the stars as you warm by the fire.

After a restful night, the aroma of fresh-brewed coffee and tea helps you greet the new day. A special breakfast will be prepared while you stroll the beach or browse in the gallery/gift shop for a memento of your visit.

This unique home is surrounded with beauty. Waterfalls, tall cedars and firs, fruit and hollow trees, a sandy beach, and a rich history come with the package. Your hosts will tell you of a Scottish nobleman, his Gypsy bride, and buried treasure.

Rates - $$ Map Location - SW

CENTRALIA, WASHINGTON

Candalite Mansion
402 N. Rock
Centralia, Washington 98531
(206) 736-4749

This home was custom-built in 1903 for J.P. Gurrier, a local lumber baron, and is more than 6,500 square feet in size. You'll have six beautiful bedrooms to choose from, with king, regular, or twin beds. All the bedrooms are on the second floor, off a six-foot-wide hall. You'll enjoy either a private bath or share a large bathroom, complete with a six-foot jet bathtub and a shower.

Play a game of pool or ping pong in the third-floor playroom, or choose a book from the library and cuddle up next to the fireplace.

Full breakfast includes a variety of gourmet dishes, homebaked bread, fresh eggs, fresh fruit and other house favorites. Candalite is just six blocks from the Amtrak Train Depot, just more than a half mile from Interstate 5 and factory outlets and two blocks from the city hall and Antique Mall.

Rates - $$ Map Location - SW

CLARKSTON, WASHINGTON

Highland House
707 Highland
Clarkston, Washington 99403
(509) 758-3126

An atmosphere of "ye olde" England welcomes guests to Highland House. This beautiful Colonial house was built in the late 1890s and has many original features. Victorian furniture compliments surroundings, while the lounge and reception area reflect the charm of ancestral England, where high tea can be served in Royal Doulton china.

Bedrooms are complete with vanity wash units or Ensuite. Duvet coverlets adorn the queen- and twin-bedded rooms. In-room courtesy includes coffee or tea trays.

Sample the delights of an English breakfast served in the Huntsmen room, where fine antique furniture is displayed. A traditional evening dinner will be served, upon request, for parties of six or more.

Spend an evening in the Yorkshire room, and play old pub games—darts, dominoes, and shove half penny, to name a few. Or enjoy a drink in the tea garden and savor the evening air, perhaps using the patio barbecue.

Old Consulate Inn, Port Townshend, WA

Highland is situated in a rural area, within easy reach of the Clearwater and Snake rivers. Local amenities include interesting shops with arts and crafts, recreational parks, and picnic and camping sites.

Bedrooms are individually named after famous historical counties. Trace the ancient history of England on maps conveniently placed outside each bedroom.

Suffork, Norfolk and Essex rooms are situated on the ground floor, for those guests who would rather not ascend the staircase to the "Shire" bedrooms.

Rates - $ to $$ Map Location - SE

CONCRETE-BIRDSVIEW, WASHINGTON

Cascade Mountain Inn
3840 Pioneer Lane
Concrete-Birdsview, Washington 98237
(206) 826-4333

Cascade Mountain Inn is in the center of one of the nation's most scenic and primitive mountain areas, the Skagit Valley. Some of the finest steelhead fishing in the world is on the Skagit River, and a fine system of back roads and trails will lead the explorer in you to the unsurpassed beauty of high country meadows, lakes, streams, high peaks and glaciers.

In the evening, you may choose to sit around the fireplace in the living room. In the summertime, weather permitting, there will be campfire outside.

Philippine Room: Includes bamboo, shells and oil paintings by Caesar Buenaventura, a master of the Philippine scene. This room is decorated mainly in shades of yellow, giving it a sunny feel.

American Room: This room has a beautiful Eastlake bed, a "Grandmother's Flower garden" quilt and a collection of Rockwell plates. The soft beige and peach colors give this room a romantic edge.

German Room: Also has a view of Sauk Mountain. The bedroom set, including the feather quilts and pillows, were brought from Germany. Porcelain plates tell the fairy tales of the Brother Grimm. In soft pink, this room reflects German "Gemuetlichkeit."

Scottish Room: Highland dancers, heather and a Scottish soldier adorn the walls. The tartan comforter and the green tones of the room enhance the comfortable setting.

The Studio: The Cascade's Studio has a separate entrance and here, the story of the Hanseatic town of Bremen is told in pictures, tiles, and wall hangings.

Things to Do: Hiking, fishing, river rafting, birdwatching, hang-gliding, bicycling, golfing, and hunting.

Rates - $$ Map Location - NW

COUPEVILLE, WASHINGTON

The Captain Whidbey Inn
2072 West Whidbey Island Inn Road
Coupeville, Washington 98239
(206) 678-4097

The Captain Whidbey Inn is in a scenic setting just three miles from historic Coupeville, one of Washington's oldest towns. The Inn is open year-around, serving breakfast, lunch, and dinner.

Built in 1907 on the wooded shores of Penn Cove, this is one of the last vestiges of the old family-run inn, where warm hospitality, wholesome food, refreshing drink and comfortable lodging are prime considerations.

Today, the inn still retains much of its originality. On the ground floor is a comfortable sitting room with a beach-stone fireplace. A charming dining room and cozy bar overlook the cove. The bar is highlighted by mementos brought from around the world by family and friends.

In addition to the well-stocked library upstairs, you will find antique appointed sleeping rooms, with a bath down the hall. Waterfront cottages with fireplaces and kitchenettes also are available. Overlooking two sleepy lagoons are spacious rooms appointed with turn-of-the-century furnishings and private baths.

Inn rooms, Inn Suite, and Whidbey Suite: Quaint accommodations furnished with antiques. Shared bath down the hall.

Lagoon rooms: Private baths and spacious rooms with verandas overlooking two lagoons and Penn Cove.

Cottages: Cozy little cabins with bedroom, sitting room, fireplace, private bath, and view of Penn Cove.

Cove, Captain's and Rachel's rooms: Attractive one- and two-bedroom houses with fireplaces in the living room, complete kitchens and beautiful views of the surrounding waters.

Enjoy the peaceful waters of Penn Cove aboard the "Cutty Sark," a classic 52-foot ketch. The Captain Whidbey Inn offers a unique opportunity to sail aboard a two-masted sailing vessel reminiscent of the Baltimore Clippers of two centuries ago. Choose a day sail, or a sunset or moonlight cruise from the Captain Whidbey pier, sailing past verdant pastures, sylvan shores and sea farms. Enjoy views of the Cascade and Olympic mountains and the majesty of Mount Baker in the distance. You may see whales, dolphins and porpoises as well as other sea mammals. Bald eagles, great blue heron, and other waterfowl abound in this peaceful haven as well.

Rates - **$$ to $$$$**   Map Location - NW

The Colonel Crockett Farm
1012 South Fort Casey Road
Coupeville, Washington 98239
(206) 678-3711

Step back 135 years into the serenity and comfort of this Victorian farm house, originally the home of Colonel Walter Crockett, Sr. Built in about 1855, the inn is situated on the north shore of Crockett Lake, overlooking Admiralty Bay on Puget Sound, plus Fort Casey, the Keystone Ferry, and the Olympic Mountains. From here, you'll also get sweeping scenic views of the shoreline, coastal cliffs, broad expanses of water, passing freighters, sailboats and ferries, nearby meadows and pastoral farm scenes backed by snowcapped mountains.

Colonel Crockett's surrounding grounds include lilac hedges, century-old trees such as holly, maple redwood, and cedar, a fish pond, wishing well, and many unusual species of plants. Deer browse in the yard; pheasants and quail share the grounds; rabbits make their homes in the hedgerows around the farmhouse and, in the spring, thousands of daffodils bloom in the yard.

Nearby, guests can browse through the small shops of historic Coupeville, hike the spectacular footpaths of Fort Casey State Park, climb the circular staircase of the lighthouse, surf fish from the beach below Admiralty Head, or board the Keystone Ferry and spend the day in Port Townsend. Stretch your legs or picnic on miles of beach or forest footpaths where fox, deer, and raccoon are common sights. Oak Harbor is 15 minutes away, and beautiful Deception Pass is a 30-minute drive. Also within minutes of the inn are fine restaurants for lunch or leisurely dining.

Crockett Room: This is the bridal suite, decorated in blue, cream, and rose. It is furnished with a draped, canopied, four-poster queen-sized bed, Edwardian fainting couch, marble-top washstand, and Belgian field desk. The Victorian bathroom features a lion's head footed tub with private bath.

Alexander Room: This room includes a tiger maple, queen-length double bed and dresser, and is decorated in quiet blue tones. It overlooks meadows to the east, Crockett Lake and Admiralty Bay to the south and has a private bath.

Davis Room: In white and lavender, this room has an antique double bed with a high oak headboard, and looks out to the south and east over freshwater Crockett Lake, ferry landing, and Admiralty Bay. Adjacent to the library, this cozy room also has an English marble-top washstand and a private bath.

Coupe Room: This large, upstairs bed sitting room features twin antique brass beds, marble-top washstand, and a Victorian wicker love seat. It's a light, fresh room of pastel pinks and white, and it looks out on the barn, the fish pond, and wishing well. Private bath.

Ebey Room: A peaceful, large, upstairs bed/sitting room of cream, green and gold. A turn-of-the-century queen length double bed and a daybed can accommodate three guests. Matching dressing table and bureau, caned chairs, and hurricane lamps add to the restful ambiance of this room. Private bath.

Rates - $$ Map Location - NW

The Victorian
602 N. Main, P.O. Box 761
Coupeville, Washington 98239
(206) 678-5305

It has been 100 years since Washington pioneer Jacob Jenne built this Italianate Victorian home in the town of Coupeville, on beautiful Whidbey Island. The house, then at the heart of one of the state's earliest settlements, now is at the center of one of our nation's first historic reserves.

The Victorian Bed & Breakfast provides gracious accommodations throughout the year to Whidbey Island visitors. Guests at the Victorian may choose from either of the charming upstairs bedrooms with private baths and queen bed, or might rather hide away in the guest cottage.

Coupeville's heritage is colorful and alive. Called the City of Sea Captains, for its many seafaring settlers, the town blends its early Indian lore with a unique maritime history and a vigorous pioneer spirit. Visitors are enchanted by its stately Victorian homes, quaint wharf and waterfront shops, and the distinctive character of the surrounding Ebey's Landing National Historic Reserve.

Rates - $$ Map Location - NW

EASTSOUND, WASHINGTON

Turtleback Farm Inn
Rt. 1, Box 650
Eastsound, Washington 98245
(206) 376-4914

Turtleback is a country inn located on Orcas Island, deemed by many to be the loveliest of the islands that dot the San Juan archipelago, in the sparkling waters of Puget Sound.

The inn overlooks 80 acres of forest and farmland in the shadow of Turtleback Mountain. It commands a spectacular view of lush meadows, duck ponds and outbuildings, with Mt. Constitution providing the eastern backdrop.

The inn is centrally located in beautiful Crow Valley—six miles from the ferry landing, 2.4 miles from Eastsound, the Island's principal village, and close to Moran State Park.

Recreational activities in the area include golf, windsurfing, sea kayaking, moped and bicycle rentals, freshwater fishing and swimming, saltwater fishing, cruising and sailing, shopping, and fine dining. Your hosts will be happy to help you plan your activities.

Originally constructed in the late 1800s, the Turtleback was renovated and expanded in 1985. The ongoing work preserves the integrity of the original "Folk National" farmhouse, while incorporating conveniences necessary for the comfort of today's travelers.

The living room boasts a Rumford Fireplace, comfortable seating and a corner game table. The large dining room has a convenient wet bar tucked into one corner. There are seven guest bedrooms, each with its own private bath and furnished with a blend of fine antiques and contemporary pieces.

Breakfast is served in the dining room or on the expansive deck overlooking the valley below. Tables are set with fine bone china, silver, and crisp linen. You'll get fresh fruits and juices, award-winning granola, homebaked breads or pastries and a daily main course featuring farm-fresh eggs and meats in delightful combinations. A wide assortment of teas and coffees are available throughout the day.

At the day's end, guests are offered a glass of sherry, a cheery fire, a game of chess, cards or Scrabble, and good fellowship.

Rates - $$ to $$$ Map Location - NW

EATONVILLE, WASHINGTON

Old Mill House
116 Oak Street, P.O. Box 543
Eatonville, Washington 98328
206) 832-6506

Take the back roads and blue highway to a place where change has come gently. Eatonville, Washington—often called "honest" by its visitors—is still a small town in the best sense of the phrase.

The Old Mill House was built in 1925, at a time of economic optimism, and now is listed on the National Register of Historic Places. It once was the residence of prominent mill baron T.S. Galbraith and, later, his son, John.

Little is left to the imagination as you step through the front door at the Old Mill House. Memorabilia from the 1920s—including magazines and other publications, kitchen tools, vintage music and even an authentic gramophone from 1923—is everywhere. Hats line the upstairs halls, and guests are invited to browse through the closets filled with vintage clothing. Feel free to try some on for size!

Pass the evening in front of the fire in the living room with a borrowed book from the house library, or dress up in vintage costumes and smuggle a bottle into the basement "Speakeasy," where a juke box near the mirrored dance floor plays music of the era.

Isadora Duncan Suite: This suite boasts an art-deco bath with an original seven-head shower and a "his and hers" dressing room. Marbled columns surround the king-sized bed, with airy fabric draped between them.

Will Rogers Room: This simple country look comes complete with a rope for practicing tricks, plus autographed photographs and a wonderful collection of books about and by Will Rogers.

Bessy Smith Room: Here, you'll find a wind-up victrola, a collection of Bessy Smith records, and a steamer trunk filled with glitzy jewelry and costumes.

In the F. Scott Fitzgerald room, you'll find an ongoing novel being penned by its guests.

Fill an afternoon or evening by strolling through the small town of Eatonville. A self-guided historic walking tour is available at the local Chamber of Commerce. Or meander along the banks of the Mashell River, just a stone's throw from the front porch of the Old Mill House.

Things to do: Mount Rainier National Park offers plenty of hiking, skiing, nature viewing, picnicking, and museums. Or visit Northwest Trek Wildlife park, Pioneer Farm Museum, Mount Rainier Scenic Railroad, Alder Lake Recreation Area and other nearby lakes, rivers and streams.

You'll find plenty of trails for day hikes, back roads for sightseeing, wildlife watching, and wild berry and mushroom picking, plus a variety of restaurants and gift and antique shops.

Rates -$ to $$$$ Map Location - SW

EDMONDS, WASHINGTON

Hudgens Haven
9313 190th S.W.
Edmonds, Washington 98020
(206) 776-2202

This bed & breakfast offers a large room, handsomely furnished with Colonial antiques and a queen-sized bed.

Edmonds, directly north of Seattle on Puget Sound, is just 20 minutes from downtown Seattle and offers bus transportation and easy access to Interstate 5.

Formerly a lumber town, Edmonds now has an abundance of excellent restaurants and small shops offering a variety of items to please the most discriminating shoppers.

Your stay at Hudgens Haven will include a tasty Continental breakfast. For an additional charge, your host will prepare a "Hearty Woodman's" breakfast of sausage or bacon and buttermilk pancakes, served with genuine maple syrup.

Rates - $ Map Location - NW

FORKS, WASHINGTON

Miller Tree Inn
P.O. Box 953
Forks, Washington 98331
(206) 374-6806

Come and share a night or two in this great old farmhouse on three park-like acres. Your hosts do their best to provide a European style bed & breakfast, where tradition calls for a warm welcome, hearty breakfast and comfortable lodging.

Weather permitting, you will sleep on crisp, line-dried sheets in one of the bedrooms on the second floor. Four have double beds, one has two twins. The twin room and one of the doubles have half baths, and there are three full baths down the hall.

You might be awakened by the wild rooster that nests in a tree out back, by the besotted frogs who call to their ladies in springtime, or by the aroma of fresh coffee and bacon.

Expect a full breakfast of fresh fruit, cereal and pastries, followed by your choice of entrees.

At Miller Tree, you'll also find a large hot tub on the back deck, lemonade on the lawn, kitchen privileges on request, a laid-back cat, an aging deaf sheltie, TV and books in one living room, and a piano and board games in the other. The ocean beaches are 15 minutes away and the Hoh Rain Forest is about a 30-minute drive.

Much of the winter business here comes from salmon and steelhead fishermen, who enjoy pre-dawn breakfasts in October through May. Your hosts provide facilities to clean and freeze fish and game, as well as ample off-road boat parking, trailer shuttle service, accurate reports on river conditions, and guide referrals.

Thing to do: Discover untamed Pacific beaches, where whales, seals, and seabirds abound; innertube, kayak, or fish the Bogachielm Hoh, Calawash, Sol Duc or Quillayute Rivers; rent a mountain bike locally or bring your own and try out the newly established miles of forest trails.

Tour the Forks Timber or Makah Museums; explore the Hoh Rain Forest and National Park visitor centers; or backpack or walk leisurely on numerous mountain trails, where deer, Roosevelt elk, and bald eagles are often seen.

Forks has several restaurants, offering simple fare to full service.

Rates $ to $$ Map Location - NW

FRIDAY HARBOR, WASHINGTON

Moon & Sixpence
3021 Beaverton Valley Road
Friday Harbor, Washington 98250
(206) 378-4138

Moon & Sixpence is a classic country bed and breakfast in the middle of San Juan Island, with views of Mount Dallas, marshes, meadows, pasture, and pond. This remodeled dairy farm, built in the early 1900s, offers accommodations in the farmhouse or in the outbuildings.

An acre of lawn surrounds the farmhouse, and sheep graze in the pasture beyond. In the weaving studio, wool is dyed, spun, and woven into fabric for the inn. Nearby are walking and hiking trails, seaside picnic sites, and opportunities for whale watching, fishing, boating, or swimming. Or just find a comfortable spot on the deck and do some birdwatching.

Olympic Chamber: With its view of the Olympic mountains towering in the distance, this is the most popular room. It is furnished in antiques, with a brick planter area, and is one of the largest and most comfortable rooms. Queen bed and shared bath.

Navajo Den: A lovely room with Navajo rug, Inuit stone-block prints, Navajo red comforters, and seven different shades of white and grey. Plus a western view of Mount Dallas, the high point on San Juan Island. Twin beds and shared bath.

Island Suite: This is the largest unit, and is worthy of its name. Deacon's bench, bentwood rocker, needlepoint chairs, tiny reading nook with North and East views from a chair, a sofa and primitive paintings make this sitting room and bedroom unit a favorite of many. Queen bed and shared bath.

The Lookout: This post and beam tower, which originally supported the dairy water tank, has its own entry and bath, plus a reading loft. It was built 85 years ago, without the use of nails, and the recent remodeling has left the beams exposed. Choose your view, with windows on all sides. Queen bed and private bath.

The Outpost: A one-room cabin, cozy and quiet, with sofa, desk, and washstand. Tucked in the trees, it's a favorite spot for deer watching. No running water, but just a short walk to the inn. Full bed with shared bath.

Rates - $$ Map Location - NW

Olympic Lights
4531-A Cattle Point Road
Friday Harbor, Washington 98250
(206) 378-3186

This wondrous guest home sits in an open meadow on San Juan Island, overlooking the panorama of the sea and the Olympic Mountains. Walk through open meadows and canopied forests and stroll the spectacular beaches of American Camp, an Historic National Park, just next door. Other activities available on the island include bicycling, golfing, birdwatching, whale watching and, of course, boating and fishing. Olympic Lights also is ideal for small seminars and special occasions.

Come and experience the natural beauty and magic of Olympic Lights. A full breakfast is served, including eggs from the resident hens.

Rates - $$ Map Location - NW

States Inn
2039 West Valley Road
Friday Harbor, Washington 98250
(206) 378-6240

The original States Inn building was an early country school, circa 1910, some two miles from its current location. Following consolidation of the county schools to Friday Harbor, the building was used as a dance hall; the dance floor is still in existence on the first floor of the Inn.

Some 50 years ago, the building was relocated to its current site, where it serves mainly as a ranch house.

The Arizona Suite (Arizona-New Mexico): This three room suite has two bedrooms, plus spacious sitting room and private bath. The rooms boast a tasteful Spanish influence of the early Southwest. Arizona has king and twin beds; New Mexico has a queen bed. This suite offers superb accommodations for families or two couples traveling together. Arizona or New Mexico also may be booked independently, in which case the sitting room and bath are shared.

Rhode Island Room: This offers a cozy New England atmosphere, with a fireplace, a brass full bed and designated full bath adjacent to bedroom.

Wisconsin Room: Queen bed with a private bath. North country charm with a special warmth from the cherry red hardwood floors.

Montana Room: Full bed with a private bath. Overlooks the nearby ranch and pastures, and offers a touch of the Western feeling, with modern comforts.

South Carolina Room: Think peach! Twin beds with a private bath. A bright, airy room overlooking a small stream and pasture.

Louisiana Room: White wicker and eyelet truly give the feeling of Southern charm, comfort and grace. Queen bed and private bath.

California Room: King bed with private bath and powder room. This spacious room has a spectacular view across the valley and ponds to nearby hills. Comfortable sitting area with romantic lighting.

Washington Room: Full bed with private bath. A quiet room featuring tasteful decor of the Northwest. This room is located near the entrance for ease of access. The bath is handicapped accessible.

States Inn accommodations also are available for business conferences, seminars, wedding receptions and special family gatherings.

Rates - $$ to $$$$ Map Location - NW

Trumpeter Inn
420 Trumpeter Way
Friday Harbor, Washington 98250
(206) 378-3884 or 1-800-826-7926

Situated among the rolling hills of the fertile San Juan Valley, Trumpeter Inn is a pastoral estate surrounded by acres of meadows. It enjoys a panoramic view of the entire valley and, in the distance, False Bay and the snowcapped Olympic Mountains.

Named for the magnificent Trumpeter Swans that grace the nearby marshlands in the winter, this inn is a perfect retreat for those wishing to enjoy the gentle beauty and repose of the San Juans.

Accommodations at the Trumpeter Inn include comfortably furnished guest rooms, individually temperature controlled, each with a private bath. King- and queen-sized beds are freshly made with crisp sheets and luxurious down comforters. Enjoy a hearty breakfast served in the dining room, in the family-style kitchen, or on the deck.

Relax and enjoy the warmth of the Trumpeter Inn. Watch the pastel hues of sunrise and sunset. Hear fine music, the soft bleating of sheep, the distant mooing of cows and honking of geese. Marvel at the sight of rare wildlife. Enjoy the fragrance of baking bread, cut flowers and freshly mowed grass and hay.

San Juan and the surrounding islands are located in a "banana belt" so they experience less rain and more warm weather than the nearby mainland, making it an ideal vacation spot anytime of the year.

Rates - $$ Map Location - NW

Westwind Bed & Breakfast
4909-H Hannah Highlands Road
Friday Harbor, Washington 98250
(206) 378-5283

The Westwind Bed & Breakfast commands one of the most magnificent views in all of the San Juan Islands. Situated on five acres of pastoral beauty, the location hosts miniature horses, deer, eagles, and colorful waterfowl.

The Master Suite offers serene tranquility for the mind and spirit. It includes a large bedroom and bathroom, living room with fireplace, kitchen, dining room and den.

French doors open to private decks overlooking the breathtaking panorama of the Olympic Mountains and the Straits of Juan de Fuca, home of the Orca whales.

Breakfast is highlighted with fresh strawberries, herbs and flowers from the extensive gardens.

This private paradise is for one couple or a family of up to four people.

Rates - $$ to $$$ Map Location - NW

Wharfside Bed & Breakfast
P.O. Box 1212
Slip K-13 Port of Friday Harbor
Friday Harbor, Washington 98250
(206) 378-5661

Wharfside Bed & Breakfast, aboard the 60-foot traditional sailing vessel, Jacquelyn, is the original floating Bed & Breakfast on the West Coast. Although moored at the Friday Harbor Port Dock, cruising charters also may be arranged. An especially popular voyage is the 'High Sea & Tea' cruise to Victoria, British Columbia. The ship is open year-round at the port's K-Dock, just a short walk to the ferry, shops and restaurants.

Jacquelyn offers two private guest staterooms, plus the elegantly appointed main salon. The ship affords guests the best in Victorian charm and modern comfort. Its nautical ambience appeals to old salts and landlubbers alike!

Aft Stateroom: Graceful Victorian curves, velvet elegance and gleaming hardwood floors conjure visions of Captain Nemo in this romantic low-beamed Captain's cabin. Queen bed, velvet settee, stern windows, private head and sink, and a separate entrance from the deck. Shared shower/tub in the main head.

Forward Stateroom: The double bed, with down comforter, adds a bit of length for taller guests. Two additional seaman-sized berths give children a taste of life at sea, while ports afford views of harbor activity. Adjacent to salon and main head.

In addition to the woodburning fireplace in the salon, the rooms are equipped with electric heaters.

Use the Wharfside as home base to explore the many attractions of the: Abundant wildlife, nature walks, beachcombing, kayaking, sailing, bicycling, tennis and golf. Visit the world's only whale watching park and museum. Learn about the 'Pig War' between the United States and Britain at two National Historic Parks. Or, simply relax on deck and enjoy harbor life, take a tour in the ship's rowing gig, or book a sportfishing charter with Captain Clyde on the 32-foot 'Nordi'.

A sumptuous array of breakfast specialities are prepared in the galley each morning. Special diets can be accommodated, with advance notice.

Inn Rates - $$ Cruise - $$$$ Map Location - NW

GIG HARBOR, WASHINGTON

The Davenport Bed & Breakfast
7501 Artondale Drive
Gig Harbor, Washington 98335
(206) 851-8527

The Davenport has a room with a private bath and French doors onto the deck, which looks out over six acres of pasture and the golf course. Other rooms look out over the front lawn. The bath is across the hall.

A three-course breakfast is served in the dining room or, on warmer days, on the deck. The Davenport is wheelchair accessible.

Things to do: Gig Harbor Country and Golf Club is a half mile away; Tacoma Industrial Airport is four miles away; and the public boat dock is three miles away.

Rates - $$ Map Location - NW

GLENWOOD, WASHINGTON

Flying L Ranch
25 Flying L Lane
Glenwood, Washington 98619
(509) 364-3488

Located on the sunny eastern slope of the Cascade Range, the Flying L Ranch is nestled in the ponderosa pines and meadowland of the Glenwood Valley, at the base of Mount Adams. Built as a fly-in home in 1945, the ranch opened for guests in 1960. The 160-acre retreat reflects the adventures that are part of the inn's history. Experience the tranquility and beauty of a nature preserve, or enjoy a quiet walk or cross-country ski on the two-mile loop trail system, where you usually will see deer and grouse and where wildflowers bloom from May through September.

The relaxing atmosphere and varied facilities—including a spacious lodge—are ideal for retreats, club outings, seminars, reunions and other group functions. The inn can comfortably accommodate 32 guests in 13 units, most with private baths and showers.

Full breakfasts are served family-style in the ranch cookhouse. Dinners for groups can be arranged, with advance reservations, or you may cook your own meals in one of the three common kitchens.

Things to do: Road touring, mountain biking, whitewater rafting, kayaking, fishing, hiking, climbing, huckleberry picking, and museum and winery touring.

Rates - $ to $$ Map Location - SW

GREENBANK, WASHINGTON

Guest House Cottage Bed & Breakfast
3366 South Highway 525
Greenbank, Washington 98253
(206) 678-3115

The central location of Guest House makes it an ideal vacation or weekend destination —or a stop on the way to Victoria or Vancouver, B.C. The Keystone Ferry,
just 20 minutes away, is the gateway to Port Townsend, the Olympic Mountains and
rainforests, and Pacific Ocean beaches. Whidbey Island is in the northwest corner of
Washington State, between the Olympic and Cascade Mountain ranges in Puget
Sound. It is the largest island in the contiguous United States, and is home to the
world's largest loganberry farm. Greenbank Farms vineyards and tasting room are
just a mile north of the Guest House.

Wildlife abounds here—from a croaking frog to soaring eagles, roaming deer,
rabbits and other small woodland creatures. Six storybook cottages in woodsy seclusion with a wildlife pond or a luxurious log lodge for two make the perfect setting for
a peaceful retreat or memorable honeymoon.

While all the cottages have the niceties of a small home, including TV, VCR,
movies, electric heat, petite kitchens, hot tubs, fireplaces, books and magazines, each
is totally different and individually decorated with country antiques, warmth and
imagination. Outdoor swimming pool, spa, and exercise room are available to all guests.

The Kentucky & Emma Jane's Tennessee cottages are set on a gently wooded
slope and surrounded by trees. They include river rock fireplaces, Swedish finish
floors, king-sized feather beds and Jacuzzi bathtubs for two.

Hansel & Gretel is an authentic log cabin with cement chinking and all the comforts of home. Stained-glass and crisscross paned windows make this rustic cabin in the
woods a real gingerbread house! A low-ceilinged loft with a double and twin bed is
bordered by log railing and reached by short ship's ladder. Fireplace and Jacuzzi for two.

Carriage House has stained-glass arched entry door, two skylights, and a picture
window overlooking a wooded hillside. A used-brick fireplace and Jacuzzi for two
creates warmth and intimacy. And a beautiful brass queen feather bed with comforter and dust ruffle promises sweet dreams.

Farm Guest Cottage includes a sunny setting bordered by woods and fruit trees.
An oversize deck encourages outdoor lounging and barbecuing. Indoors, you'll find
a fireplace, knotty pine walls, stained-glass windows and warm surroundings. Snuggle
in a queen-sized feather bed, or kick back and soak in the Jacuzzi.

The Lodge, a spacious custom log home, is truly a delight to the senses. This one-
of-a-kind home is yours alone, and every nook and cranny is a discovery. Soak in the

jetted tub or enjoy the large bedroom hot tub and watch the stars through a ceiling glass. Cuddle by the warm flames of the big stone fireplace before you snooze in the king-sized bed.

Grandma Benson's Farmhouse, a 1920s original, combines the comforts of olden days with the best of the new. Pretty wallpapers, queen and double feather beds, a brick fireplace and TV/VCR watching offer the comforts of home. Pool, hot tub, barbecue and picnic table in the back yard.

Rates - $$$ to $$$$ Map Location - SW

LA CONNER, WASHINGTON

Heather House 'A' Bed & Breakfast
505 Maple Avenue
La Conner, Washington 98257
(206) 466-4675

Easy to find, impossible to forget, Heather House is on the east edge of La Conner, with a vista of farmland, the Cascades and Mount Baker. It's an easy walk to downtown and the waterfront.

Walk past the rose hedge and down the brick pathway to the lovely Cape Cod house, built in 1979. It's an exact replica of a turn-of-the-century home in Marblehead, Mass. The oak floors, wainscoting and mantles give the house warmth and comfort.

Your hosts made Heather House their home for several years before moving into a cottage next door. The charming house now is used exclusively for bed & breakfast guests, who will be pampered by the caring hosts. The house includes three bedrooms and two baths. One bath has a tub and shower; the other has a shower stall.

The Blue Room: This was the guest room when the owners lived in the house. It has a double bed and a great view.

The Rose Room: Formerly, the hosts' master bedroom. It has a queen bed and a spectacular view of the farmland, Cascades and Mount Baker.

The Fireplace Room: This room was the den. It has a queen bed, a sofa and a woodburning fireplace.

Terry robes, over-sized bath towels and blow dryers are offered in each room. Candy, coffee, homemade cookies, tea and snacks are available at all times.

You'll start the new day with a breakfast of fresh ground coffee or tea, juices, fresh fruit with the hosts' famous sour-cream sauce, fresh-baked scones with homemade jams and muffins.

Rates - $$ Map Location -NW

Rainbow Inn
1075 Chilberg Road, P.O. Box 15
La Conner, Washington 98257
(206) 466-4578

Solid and unpretentious as the dairy farmer for whom it was built, this lovingly restored, turn-of-the-century farmhouse provides a luxurious retreat.

Make yourself at home in one of eight spacious guest bedrooms, each impeccably maintained and furnished with charming period pieces, queen-sized beds and antique-patterned wallpaper. Both private and shared bathrooms are available, some with showers and some with claw-foot tubs. Gather in the main floor parlor around a unique woodburning ceramic fireplace. And enjoy the privacy of the hot tub on the back deck, with a sweeping view of the rich Skagit Valley and Mount Baker.

Set apart in the solitude of Skagit Valley farmland, the Rainbow Inn is a half mile east of historic La Conner, where quaint shops, galleries, fine restaurants, antique stores and a museum await you. You'll also find miles of level roads to tour on bicycle. Watch boats navigate through diked sloughs. Or set up an easel or tripod and capture the scenic splendor.

In springtime, miles of surrounding fields blossom with tulips and daffodils, and April features the renowned Skagit Valley Tulip festival. Summer offers local cruising and fishing charters.

Harvest time brings bountiful local produce and brilliant foliage; watch for snow geese and swans. In winter, great skiing is just a couple of hours away.

The Rose Room: Located on the main floor and named for its turn-of-the-century rose chandelier. Private bath features a sunken Jacuzzi tub.

The Violet Room: Large, sunny second-floor room with ornamental woodburning stove. Opens onto a semi-private deck at the front of the house with a view of a neighboring Victorian farmhouse, farm fields and the Olympic Range. Private bath with shower.

The Heather Room: This second-floor room also opens onto a semi-private deck at the front of the house. It has a separate, large, private "captain's bathroom" down the hall with claw-foot tub and shower.

The Tulip Room: Named after the Skagit Valley Tulip Festival in April, this popular second-floor room is shaded in the summer by a 100-year-old chestnut tree. Private bath with shower.

The Daisy Room: Large second-floor room with views to the east of pastures, Mount Baker and the Cascade Range. Private bath with claw-foot tub in room.

The Belle Room: Third-floor room with queen and double bed. Great for friends and family traveling together. View to the east of the farmlands, Mount Baker and the Cascade Range. Shares full bath with claw-foot tub and shower.

The Sadie Room: Elegant, restful room on the third floor. Shaded in the summer by the chestnut tree. Shares bath with Belle and Ginger rooms.

The Ginger Room: Cozy third-floor room with a window seat for enjoying the view of the farmlands. Shares bath with Belle and Sadie rooms.

Awaken to savor a leisurely, full-course gourmet breakfast. You'll be served on the sunny, French windowed front porch or amidst the casual country antiques that grace the dining room.

Your hosts delight in preparing fresh local fruits, fresh-baked breads and muffins, plus a variety of egg and griddle dishes.

Rates - $$ Map Location - NW

LANGLEY, WASHINGTON

Eagles Nest Inn
3236 E. Saratoga Road
Langley, Washington 98260
(206) 321-5331

High on a hill away from the road, the Eagles Nest Inn is a beautiful home that was born after several years of planning. Located just one and a half miles from the quaint seaside village of Langley, the inn offers breathtaking views of Saratoga Passage, Camano Island and Mount Baker.

Sit back with a good book, relax in the spa, go canoeing, or stroll leisurely on the beach or in the forest. For those who like to browse, Langley abounds with unique shops and restaurants.

The library is located on the third level, and has a large sunny window seat that overlooks the south deck and provides a refreshing view of the forest. Your hosts boast an ever-growing book library and several hundred video selections. Each of the four rooms has a TV and a VCR.

Eagles Nest Room: This room sits high atop the house with a majestic view of Saratoga Passage and Mount Baker. Relax on the private deck with a cup of coffee and nestle in with nature at its best. With a private bath, queen bed and a 360-degree view, this room is a favorite among guests.

Saratoga Room: From inside the room or from the private balcony, this room gives a sweeping view of Saratoga Passage, Camano Island and Mount Baker. It's a perfect place to sit back and experience the beautiful sights, country sounds and fresh air of Puget Sound. The Saratoga Room has a private bath and king-sized bed.

Forest Room: From the large bay window, look out on Saratoga Passage through the tall trees. With its own private entry—in addition to the inside entry—the Forest

Room offers as much privacy as you desire. A skylight brings the outdoors into the room, where you'll find a private bath, king-sized bed and a twin bed.

Garden Room: Enjoy the newest and largest room, decorated in a garden motif. The Garden Room is located on the first level of the house and looks out over the east garden area. With a private bath, queen bed and queen sleeper couch in a large sitting area, this room will accommodate four.

Breakfast is served each morning in the family room or, weather permitting, on one of the lower decks. The menu is delightfully different each day, and coffee and tea is available at the hospitality bar. A bottomless cookie jar is filled with homemade chocolate-chip cookies.

Rates - $$ to $$$ Map Location - NW

Log Castle Bed & Breakfast
3273 E. Saratoga Road
Langley, Washington 98260
(206) 321-5483

Log Castle Bed & Breakfast is a charming country inn that provides gracious accommodations for travelers. It is located on Whidbey Island, a mile and a half from Langley, on a secluded beach facing Mount Baker and the beautiful snowcapped Cascade Mountains.

Relax before a large stone fireplace after a walk on a secluded beach. Listen to the sounds of gulls as you watch for bald eagles and sea lions. Take a stroll through quiet woods, where some of the oldest trees on the island still grow.

The guest rooms are named after your hosts' daughters. All have private baths.

The Gayle Room: A cozy room with French doors opening to a porch facing the beach, mountains and morning sun.

The Marta Suite: Complete with a sun porch and hanging swing, this room looks over the water to the Cascade Mountains.

The Lea Room: This eight-sided turret has two large windows overlooking Saratoga Passage to Camano Island and beyond.

The Ann Room: Perhaps the favorite is this third-story turret and its five large windows, which offer a panoramic view of the water, beach, mountains and pasture.

The quaint village of Langley is only a short walk on the beach. Canoes are available for your use, as is a rowboat if you care to fish for perch, cod and sole.

Homemade bread and warm cinnamon rolls direct from the oven are included in the full breakfast, which is served on the big round log table.

Rates - $$ Map Location - NW

LEAVENWORTH, WASHINGTON

Bavarian Meadows 'A' Bed & Breakfast
11097 Eagle Creek Road
Leavenworth, Washington 98826
(509) 548-4449

In the European country theme, this uniquely decorated guest facility is situated just three miles from the Bavarian village in one of Leavenworth's most beautiful meadows.

Enjoy the sounds of silence, nearby Eagle Creek and the forest wildlife. Relax in a chaise lounge or at the patio table on the covered decks and enjoy the view of the nearby mountains. Each of the three country-styled queen bedrooms has a private full bath. The detached upstairs apartment suite has two queen beds and private entry.

Kitchen and laundry-room privileges are offered. Non-alcoholic refreshments are always available. No TV.

The hot tub is available year-round. Relax in the tub and gaze at the stars or count the satellites orbiting overhead. Juice and sparkling cider is served at the hot tub. There also is a chipmunk crossing at the hot-tub deck, so don't be surprised if you're greeted there by a few furry friends.

During your stay at Bavarian Meadows, browse through the many European styled shops this Bavarian village offers. Enjoy cross-country skiing at the well-groomed tracks in the Leavenworth area or ski the meadow just off the covered decks. Bavarian Meadows is situated between two of the state's most popular alpine ski areas, Mission and Steven's passes.

Whitewater rafting is popular on the lower Wenatchee River. Two nearby ranches offer horseback riding, hay rides, and sleigh rides. Play golf at the beautiful 18-hole Leavenworth Golf Course, which is bordered by the Wenatchee River and the Icicle Ridge. Enjoy hiking, berry picking, river and lake fishing. A fully equipped picnic basket will be prepared for guests who want to experience a mountain picnic.

Guests are greeted each morning with a coffee-and-juice tray. Everything is made from scratch for the full country-style breakfasts—including Belgian waffles and dutch honey, raspberry-almond pull-a-parts, muesli, bratwurst, farm fresh eggs, yogurt fruit smoothies, seasonal fresh fruit, breakfast quiche, and various other specialties.

Rates - $$ Map Location - NW

Run Of The River
9308 East Leavenworth Road , P. O. Box 285
Leavenworth, Washington 98826
(509) 548-7171

Run of the River promotes itself as the Northwest's only bed & breakfast exclusively for non-smokers. It features natural log lodging and picture windows exposing a spectacular Icicle River and Cascade panorama. Leavenworth offers a host of activities year-round, and your hosts are happy to assist with any arrangements.

Summer bursts forth in the Icicle Valley with deep blue skies and sun-splashed days. Whether it's a raft trip down the Wenatchee, a hike in the Cascades, a bicycle adventure on country roads or a leisurely stroll along the river or in the Bavarian Village, you can depend on the warm summer sun. In the evening, view a sunset from the decks and watch quietly as deer drift down to drink from the river.

Fall brings crisp evenings and colorful foliage. The bird refuge is a special treat, ablaze with yellow, orange and red. And fall is the season to grab some of Washington's finest at local fruit stands; apples and pears are a tasty treat for friends back home.

Winter features soft, fluffy snow as guests tune up their skis in anticipation of downhill and cross-country adventure. Steven's Pass and Mission Ridge are both 35 miles from Run of the River. Cross-country trails start right across the river on the golf course. Afterward, scurry back for a hot drink, then ease on down to the hot tub and dream.

Spring swoops into Leavenworth on the wings of returning ducks, geese and heron. And wildflowers display their fanfare, announcing the joys of the season.

Tumwater Suite: Ideal for a honeymoon, anniversary or that special celebration, this suite is the finest. Luxuriously spacious, it features a Jacuzzi, two wood stoves, a loft and a private deck. Riverside with private bath.

Rose Room: Offers river, meadow and mountain views. The suite's private hot tub helps to create a distinctive atmosphere. Riverside, second level and private bath.

River Room: The large windows in this room allow bold views of the Icicle River in both directions. Views of Tumwater and Icicle Canyon are spellbinding as well. Riverside, second level and private bath.

The Meadows: Wake up and smell the coffee! The Meadows is the first to see the morning sun. The south-facing picture window overlooks the meadow, where you'll see deer and a host of ducks and geese. Second level; large private bath.

The Pinnacles: A sun-splashed deck with an inviting log swinging bench tickles the senses outside. A river-rock enclosed woodstove and Jacuzzi warms the soul inside.

Things to do: Ohme Gardens, horseback riding, wildflower tours, birdwatching, Waterville and Winthrop tours, Wenatchee and Cashmere Pioneer Museum, whitewater rafting, fishing, hiking in Icicle Valley, bicycling, tennis and golfing.

Rates - $$ to $$$ Map Location - NW

LONG BEACH, WASHINGTON

Scandinavian Gardens Inn
Route 1, Box 36
Long Beach, Washington 98631
(206) 642-8877

This luxury inn is a quiet and romantic getaway. Immaculately clean, it is decorated with a Scandinavian theme—using bright, cheery colors and both contemporary and antique furnishings. For reading and relaxing, cozy up to the fireplace in the living room. A social room offers a view of the colorful floral gardens. An indoor deluxe hot-springs spa, a cedar-lined sauna and exercise equipment are in the recreation room.

The old Scandinavian custom of removing shoes at the entrance allows guests the comfort of slippers, socks or bare feet on the inn's carpeted floors.

Swedish Suite: This two-room honeymoon suite is decorated in soft pinks and light blues. Both rooms have dormer windows; there is a comfortable sofa and refrigerator in the day room and a garden tub for two with a skylight behind louvered doors off the day room. The private bathroom has a large pink shower and a skylight. Queen-sized teakwood bed set, antique vanity and additional half bathroom in bedroom. The hide-a-bed sofa in the day room can accommodate an additional one to two guests.

Finnish Room: In teal and red with a dormer-window area containing a decorated storage trunk. Antique vanity, queen-sized pine bed, and a tub/shower combination bathroom with a skylight.

Icelandic Room: Accented in plums and greens with an antique armoire and loveseat, and queen-sized pine bed. Tub/shower combination bathroom with rosemaling on wall cabinet doors.

Danish Room: With dark blues and cinnamon tones, this room is decorated with a "hearts-and-nautical" emphasis, queen-sized pine bed, antique vanity, and a bathroom with shower only.

Norwegian Room: This room is done up with greens and golds, Norwegian wall artifacts, an antique vanity, and queen-sized pine bed. The tub/shower combination bathroom across the hall from the bedroom is for the use of the Norwegian room guests only.

Things to do: Beachcombing, fishing, horseback riding, clamming, visiting museums and art galleries, kayaking, canoeing, driving on the beach, surfing, windsurfing, flying a kite, playing volleyball and sunbathing.

Rates - **$$**   Map Location - SW

LOPEZ ISLAND, WASHINGTON

Aleck Bay Inn
Aleck Bay Road
Route 1, Box 1920
Lopez Island, Washington 98261
(206) 468-3535

The Aleck Bay Inn provides facilities for vacationers, business travelers, honeymooners, or for weekend getaways, weddings, family gatherings and the like.
The inn is located on the south end of Lopez Island and is accessible by ferry, air or boat. It's a seven-acre facility bounded by beaches and offshore islands accessible by boat for picnics. Or just relax in seclusion to revitalize your life. Aleck Bay is truly an artist's paradise.
Rooms contain small fireplaces, queen-sized beds, floral linens, telephones, and TV. Two of the accommodations have private bathrooms with Jacuzzi tubs. The Inn is handicapped accessible.
A 600-square-foot meeting room is available for business meetings, weddings, and such. When not functioning as a meeting room, guests use it as a music and play room, with its large TV, table tennis, billiards, piano and guitar. You can view Aleck Bay while sitting at a game table stocked with the most popular games.
Other activities include bicycling, canoeing, kayaking, golfing, hiking, badminton, volleyball, croquet, hot tubbing, or walking on the beach and watching wildlife—including deer, pheasants, sea otters, seals, eagles, fish, rabbits, and whales.
Refreshment are available at all times. A full breakfast, afternoon tea, and evening snacks are served.

Rates - $$ to $$$ Map Location - NW

MacKaye Harbor Inn
Route 1, Box 1940
Lopez Island, Washington 98261
(206) 468-2253

MacKaye Harbor Inn was originally built in 1927, and has always been pervaded by hospitality. Its sandy beach was the site of many island picnics, and your hosts keep Norwegian cookies in the entry to welcome passers-by.
In the 1960s, the home was purchased and converted to a restaurant and pub. In 1985, it was completely restored and decorated to its earlier charm as one of Lopez

Island's most grand and gracious homes. The inn now offers five beautiful guestrooms, each with furnishings reminiscent of the past.

The Captain's Suite: Here, you'll get views the harbor through large leaded-glass windows. A queen-sized brass bed, cozy down comforter and private bath make this room fit for any captain.

The Harbor Suite: Overlooks the bay, and has a fireplace and a private sun deck. It is furnished with a beautiful antique Italian bedroom set of golden oak and marble.

The Blue Room: This room is a favorite of many. Small, cozy and romantic, you may view the ocean from the bed in this Norwegian style room.

The Rose Room: With its white wrought-iron beds (a double and a daybed), this room is perfect for a party of four. Warm rose-colored fabric and wall covering make this Victorian room charming.

The Flower Room: Boasts a beautiful king-sized brass bed. A flower motif in rose and mint green brightens this room overlooking the lawns.

Enjoy a lovely view of the harbor from the spacious waterfront parlor. Use the various recreational equipment or simply walk the quarter-mile sandy beach and return to the inn for a snack.

A exceptional and bountiful breakfast is served daily. Special dietary needs and schedules are considered with notice.

Rates - **\$\$** to **\$\$\$**   Map Location - NW

LUMMI ISLAND, WASHINGTON

The Willows Inn
2579 West Shore Drive
Lummi Island, Washington 98262
(206) 758-2620

Situated near Bellingham, Lummi is the most northeastern San Juan island. It is accessible by a small car ferry that departs Gooseberry Point hourly, taking a mere six minutes for its scenic cruise. This wooded island is graced with tranquil beaches and 18 miles of quiet country roads ideal for biking, birdwatching and hiking.

Relax in front of a crackling fire in the spacious living room, sip a sherry, enjoy idle conversation, or just curl up with a good book. Enjoy the panoramic marine view from the veranda, or witness spectacular sunsets over the Gulf Islands. Treat yourself to a candlelight dinner in the intimate dining room, and enjoy the tradition and elegance of fine dining through the pleasures of fresh regional cuisine and Northwest wines.

The two downstairs rooms—"Hillside" and "Rose"—each has an antique double bed, private bath and private entrance. The two upstairs dormer rooms are "view" rooms and share a bath at the foot of the stairs. "Sunrise and "Sunset" are each furnished with a king-sized bed that can be converted to two singles.

"Piece of Cake," the honeymoon cottage, has a double bed, antique claw-foot tub, sitting area, kitchen area, and private deck—with a spectacular view of the islands.

Scottish "Highland Home", a spacious, two-bedroom guest house, has a fully appointed kitchen, living room with open fireplace, TV/VCR/stereo, and a terrific view from the comfortable loveseats or private deck. The "Thistle" and "Heather" each has a queen bed, open skylight and private bath—"Thistle" with a whirlpool tub and "Heather" with a double shower. "Highland Home" can be made accessible to handicapped.

A three-course breakfast is served in the dining room. Wake-up coffee or tea, with hot Irish soda bread, is delivered to your room.

Rates - $$ to $$$$ Map Location - NW

LYNDEN, WASHINGTON

Century House
401 South B.C. Avenue
Lynden, Washington 98264
(206) 354-2439

Come feel the quiet, peaceful Victorian elegance of this beautifully restored century-old home. Nestled deep in the rich Nooksack River valley, you will enjoy a breathtaking view of Mount Baker and the picturesque Cascade Mountain Range. Situated on more than 35 acres of riverfront property, Century House Bed & Breakfast features the old farmstead atmosphere.

You will appreciate this beautifully landscaped estate at the edge of town in the quaint Dutch village of Lynden.

This Victorian homestead was established in 1888 by R.O. Blonden. It was thought to have been built as the town hotel for travelers along the flourishing Nooksack River. In 1905, however, this once-thriving dream site evolved into the DeValois family farmstead.

As this home celebrated its century mark, your hosts re-ignited the dream by purchasing the home and beginning the restoration process in 1988. Now fully reinstated, you will find this 12-room Victorian farm home set off with antiques of its previous glory. Relax in its formal dining room and breakfast room, front sitting room and parlor. Enjoy its piano, fireplace, curved staircase, bay windows, balcony, chandeliers and claw-foot tubs.

Century Tower Suite: This spacious suite on the third floor features a romantic atmosphere with views of the river valley and Cascade Mountains. You will enjoy complete privacy, as well as a full-sized, extra-long bed, attached private bath, window front sitting room, vanity and TV.

Garden View Room: Overlooking the garden and valley, you will find yourself on the second floor with a spacious shared bath across the hall. This red floral room is filled with antique furniture, full-sized, extra-long bed and mirrored dresser.

Rose Room: This room is on the second floor, overlooking the quiet north lawn. It includes a full-sized antique bed and shared bath. If you like soft colors and quiet atmosphere, you'll love this room.

Rates - $$ Map Location - NW

MAZAMA, WASHINGTON

North Cascades Basecamp
255 Lost River Road
Mazama, Washington 98833
(509) 996-2334

This small, family-style lodge offers relaxing accommodations in a secluded setting at the upper end of the beautiful Methow Valley, away from the hustle and bustle of town. Lodge facilities include six rooms, all with shared baths. Three of the rooms have double beds; two have double beds and bunk beds; and one has a double bed in a loft and two twin beds below. The lodge also includes a children's playroom, library, cozy living room, and a dining room in which meals are eaten together around a big table.

Right outside the door are a hot tub, patios, lawn, and a big sand-box play area. A housekeeping cabin with sleeping facilities for six also is available.

Stroll along trails and enjoy quiet cedar groves and an isolated river frontage on the Methow River. On hot days, cool off with a splash in the beaver ponds and fish in the stocked trout pond or the many side streams that flow into the Methow River. The North Cadscades Basecamp is just minutes from major trailheads in the Pasayten Wilderness, the North Cascades National Park, and the Pacific Crest Trail. Other recreational opportunities include bicycling, river running, swimming, and horseback riding.

Your hosts offer bed & breakfast or full board. Breakfast is a hearty meal such as waffles and sausages or eggs, muffins, oatmeal and fruit. With full board, you get a delicious dinner in the evening, a hearty breakfast and fixings for a packed lunch.

Rates - $$ Map Location - NW

Century House Bed & Breakfast, Lynden, WA

MONTESANO, WASHINGTON

The Abel House Bed & Breakfast Inn
117 Fleet Street South
Montesano, Washington 98563
(206) 249-6002 or 1-800-235-ABEL

The Abel House was built in 1908 and has nine bedrooms on three of the four floors, leaving the main floor as a common area. There you will find a comfortable living room and a well-stocked library, each boasting a box-beamed ceiling and a unique fireplace.

The entry, staircase and dining room feature the original natural wood, with an authentic Tiffany chandelier in the latter. There is a game room on the upper floor, and three lower floors are serviced by an elevator.

William H. Abel, for whom the house was built, was born in Sussex, England in 1870 and moved to 'Monte' in 1892., where he became one of Washington's most distinguished defense and trial attorneys. His great love for books led to the naming of Montesano's public library in his honor. Both the Abels and the subsequent owners raised large families in the house before it was transformed into a bed and breakfast.

An energetic hike will take you to idyllic Lake Sylvia for fishing, boating and swimming. A short drive will take you to the famed Tall Ships project, where you can board the Lady Washington.

Or try Westport's sport fishing, Ocean Shore's beaches, or the Olympic National Park Rain Forests. From the northern edge of the Olympic Peninsula, Victoria, British Columbia is a pleasant ferry cruise away.

Breakfast and tea may be served in the garden, the Country English dining room, or the privacy of your own room, as you prefer. Greet your morning with coffee and juice in bed, followed by a gourmet breakfast with fresh-ground coffee or tea and chilled seasonal fruit. Special dietary needs can be accommodated.

Rates - $$ Map Location - SW

MOUNT VERNON, WASHINGTON

The White Swan Guest House
1388 Moore Road
Mount Vernon, Washington 98273
(206) 445-6805

This 1890s Victorian farmhouse has three inviting bedrooms, with queen- and king-sized beds and two full baths to share.

There's a woodstove in the parlor, wicker chairs on the back porch, piles of books and magazines to browse through, and a platter of homemade chocolate chip cookies waiting on the sideboard.

The "Garden Cottage" under the trees is the perfect romantic hideaway, or a great place for a family of up to four people. It has a private bath, kitchen and sun deck.

Enjoy the English style gardens, fruit trees, acres of surrounding farmland and country roads. Bring your bicycle, or rent one in La Conner, just six miles down the road.

La Conner is a delightful fishing village, full of interesting art galleries, gift shops, a waterfront restaurant and antique stores. The inn is located just an hour north of Seattle, 90 miles from Vancouver, B.C. and 25 minutes from the San Juan Ferries.

A filling country Continental breakfast is served every morning in the sunny yellow dining room.

Rates - $$ to $$$ Map Location - NW

NACHES, WASHINGTON

The Cozy Cat Bed & Breakfast
12604 Highway 410
Naches, Washington 98937
(509) 658-2953

The Cozy Cat is a delightful country home on scenic Chinook Pass, where the pine trees reach out to greet the desert foothills of the Yakima Valley.

The inn, which is about 32 miles from the city of Yakima, has two bedrooms with private baths. One unit has a flair for burgundy, a queen-sized brass bed, plus a powder room and a tub/shower. The Mini Suite has a Southwestern theme with queen-sized bed, a lavish bathroom with brass fixtures and a new angle shower. An adjoining TV room has knotty pine walls and a day bed.

The living room, with fireplace, is at the disposal of guests, along with a small coffee room equipped with a coffee pot for early birds.

Breakfasts are Continental, but vary day to day. You'll get muffins, sweet rolls, cereal, fruit, juice, and coffee.

Rates - $$ Map Location - SW

OLYMPIA, WASHINGTON

Puget View Guesthouse
7924 61st N.E.
Olympia, Washington 98506
(206) 459-1676

Come and celebrate the charm and romance of a two-room waterfront cottage suite in an idyllic Northwest setting. Enjoy a panoramic view of Puget Sound that still makes even the residents pause every for a moment of reflection now and again.

Part of the secret to enjoying Puget View to its fullest is staying long enough to discover the simple pleasures that make it more than just a place to stay—it's a memory that will stay with you.

On winter days, you can curl up in the cottage, relax with a specialty tea, your favorite book or a challenging round of cribbage.

Keep cozy with cocoa and slippers—and flannel sheets. Awaken to the sounds of shorebirds or the playful barking of a sea lion. At your cottage, you may even get a visit from neighborhood raccoons.

Take a morning walk on the beach and add a few sand dollars or agates to your collection. Scuba dive at the underwater park just offshore, spend an afternoon exploring the wooded trails of nearby Tolmie State Park, or set off with a field book and binoculars for a look at the resident heron, migratory brant and rare bald eagles. Bring your own kayak or canoe, or your hosts will help you make arrangements.

Gusty spring days are perfect for kite flying, while the warmer months bring out the boats, from cruisers to schooners. Enjoy sightseeing, oystering, or an evening cookout at the beach-side campfire or barbecue on your deck.

Your hosts at Puget View will pamper you with an elegant breakfast prepared just for you and delivered to your cottage door.

Rates - **$$**   Map Location - NW

PATEROS, WASHINGTON

Amy's Manor
P.O. Box 411
Pateros, Washington 98846
(509) 923-2334

Amy's Manor is a stately home nestled in the foothills of the Cascade Mountains overlooking the Methow River. It has been in your host's family since 1928 and is decorated and furnished to offer the character and comforts of days gone by.

Set on 170 acres, Amy's Manor includes a tennis court and a place for a barbecue. Or maybe you'd rather pack a picnic lunch and go for a hike to pick wildflowers. Or try some fishing or swimming in one of the nearby lakes or rivers.

In the winter, the Pateros area, blanketed with snow, provides for cross-country skiing. Afterward, you can curl up in front of the stone fireplace and read a book or sip hot chocolate.

The Manor also is available for weddings, receptions, meetings, family reunions, church gatherings, retreats and other special occasions.

This small farm also is home to goats, ducks, chickens, rabbits and cows. You may wake to the sound of the rooster crowing and the smell of fresh country air drifting through your open window.

After a homemade breakfast, relax in a hammock or stroll to the edge of the large tree-covered yard to view the beautiful Methow River and savor the peace and quiet.

Rates - **$$**   Map Location - NE

PORT ANGELES, WASHINGTON

Glen Mar By The Sea
318 North Eunice
Port Angeles, Washington 98362
(206) 457-6110

As you relax by the fireplace in the spacious living room at Glen Mar, you can look out at the Port Angeles Harbor, the magnificent Olympic Peninsula and the lights of Victoria across the Strait of Juan de Fuca. Or pamper yourself with a cup of tea or coffee, served from an antique tea cart on 19th century china, in the comfort and privacy of your own room.

Glen Mar by the Sea offers two bedrooms and a suite, one with a double bed and two with queen-sized beds. Upper rooms feature private baths and a spectacular view of water or mountains.

The Hideaway is the most secluded room, and features a king-sized bed and luxurious private bath. Sink into the whirlpool tub for two, and experience total relaxation.

Glen Mar is within walking distance of ferries, buses, shopping and restaurants.

A large breakfast featuring egg dishes, fresh-fruit specialties and other delicacies is served in the dining room or on the patio overlooking the water.

Rates - $$ Map Location - NW

PORT TOWNSEND, WASHINGTON

Ann Starrett Mansion
744 Clay Street
Port Townsend, Washington 98368
(206) 385-3205 or 1-800-321-0644

Situated on a bluff overlooking the mountains and Puget Sound sits the lovingly restored Starrett Mansion. Reflecting the heart and soul of historic Port Townsend, this priceless gem was built by a wealthy contractor—George Starrett—as a wedding present to his wife, in 1889.

The Mansion is internationally renowned for its classic Victorian architecture, frescoed ceiling, and free-hanging, three-tiered spiral staircase, which leads to one of the most unusual domed ceilings in North America.

The eight-sided dome is actually a glorified solar calendar with frescoes that depict the four seasons and four virtues in the eight panels. Small dormer windows are situated on the roof of the tower so that the sun shines on a ruby red glass causing a red beam to point toward the appropriate seasonal panel on the first day of each new season. The scantily clad nymph in the winter panel caused a minor scandal among Victorian ladies.

The inside of the mansion is just as detailed as the outside, with elaborate molding that features carved lions, doves and ferns. Relax amid a dozen beautiful rooms finished with antiques painstakingly collected to recreate the Victorian period of 100 years ago.

Gable Suite: Puget Sound's sparkling waters and majestic Cascadian peaks will take your breath away while nestling into this love nest high atop the mansion. It features a private bath with hot tub.

The Master Suite: Get a view of Mount Rainier, the Olympic Mountains and Port Townsend Bay from the sitting alcove of this large exquisite room with private bath.

Ann's Parlor: View Puget Sound shipping lanes, Mount Baker and the Cascade Mountains from the balcony of this splendid room, which was Ann Starrett's private hideaway. Private bath.

The Drawing Room: From this magnificent suite, view the snowcapped volcanoes from Mount Rainier to Mount Baker, Port Townsend Bay and Puget Sound. Watch the ships go by, and bathe in the antique tin tub adorned with cherubs. Private bath.

The Nursery: Ann and George's only child—Morris Starrett—grew up in this room. It offers a partial view of mountains, water and historic uptown Port Townsend. Detached private bath.

Nanny's Room: Next to the nursery, this room views Mount Baker, Cascade Mountains and Puget Sound. Private bath.

The Carriage Room: Brick walls, carriage doors and a sleigh bed adorn this cozy room, which offers views of the garden. Private bath.

The Garden Suite: A romantic hideaway with brick walls , a charming alcove and garden view. Private bath with claw-foot tub and shower.

The Amana Room: Five of the seven walls are brick. Features include antiques from Iowa's Amana Colonies. Private entrance.

Monika's Room: Wicker furnishings and brick work highlight this cozy room.

Parakeet Bill Guest House: Cozy and private one-bedroom cottage next door to the Starrett House.

A full breakfast is served in the dining room, or in the privacy of your room.

Rates - $$ to $$$ Map Location - NW

Heritage House
305 Pierce Street
Port Townsend, Washington 98368
(206) 385-6800

Heritage House, a stately Italinate, was built, circa 1870, by famed wooden boat builder John Fuge. Early owners included Francis Pettygrove, who helped found and then named Portland, Oregon. In 1984, the house was restored and opened to the public as a Victorian bed & breakfast and now is listed on the National Register of Historic Places.

Each room of Heritage House is distinctly furnished with a variety of Victorian antiques, some museum quality, some original to the house. Period paper covers the walls.

Heritage House sits on a bluff and provides its guests with a commanding view of the bay and the snowcapped Olympic Mountains beyond. The grand old buildings and shops of historic Port Townsend are within easy walking distance. At nearby Fort Worden, where "An Officer and a Gentlemen" was filmed, visitors stroll the beach and, in season, attend a variety of musical and theatrical events. The Olympic National Forest is a short drive away.

Lily Suite: From the beautifully appointed Victorian sitting room to the hand-carved, four-poster bed in the bedroom, you'll find the Lily Suite the perfect setting for your own personal celebration. French doors open to the balcony. Private bath.

Lilac Room: This room affords a view of the Olympic Mountains and the bay, combined with the warmth of old walnut. Private bath.

Peach Room: Mark Twain, we're told, had a bed like this high Victorian, but it's doubtful that he had anything like the Peach Blossom's tin and oak claw-foot tub that folds away like a Murphy bed. Private bath and sitting area with a gorgeous view.

Susan Room: Memories of grandma's house will be rekindled when you step into this sunny yellow room. Hall bath.

Morning Glory Room: An unknown artist—whose initials are on the bed—used morning glories on a pastel background, a winter scene and a volcano (Mount St. Helens?) to decorate this three-piece Victorian bedroom set. Hall bath. View of the bay and Port Townsend.

Rose Room: Two turn-of-the-century beds from England make this large main-floor room a real delight. Original wainscoting. Private bath. Bay view.

Breakfast at Heritage House is a delight. Crystal and Royal Albert "Old Country Rose" china grace the ornate oak dining table. The air is perfumed with the aroma of fresh-brewed coffee and homebaked pastry.

Rates - $$ to $$$ Map Location - NW

Holly Hill House
611 Polk
Port Townsend, Washington 98368
(206) 385-5619 or 1-800-435-1454

The Robert C. Hill house, built in 1872, has been beautifully maintained. It is famous for its stippled woodwork and authentic Victorian plantings—including the huge Camperdown elm (the upside down tree) and towering Holly trees. Now a bed and breakfast, the Holly Hill House is in the uptown portion of historic Port Townsend. Fort Worden and Centrum are convenient.

Holly Hill House includes three guest rooms in the main house and two guest rooms in the Carriage House. Four rooms are graciously furnished with queen-sized beds, and Colonel's Suite has a king-sized bed.

Billie's Room: Overlooks the Admiralty Inlet, Mount Baker and the Cascades. Queen-size bed with private bath.

Lizette's Room: With its rounded corners, this room overlooks the gardens. Queen-sized and twin beds. Private bath.

Skyview Room: Features a huge overhead skylight, queen-sized bed and private bath.

The Colonel's Room: Picture window overlooks Admiralty Inlet and Mount Baker. King-sized bed, queen sleeper sofa and private bath.

A delicious full breakfast is served daily in the dining room.

Rates - **$$** to **$$$$**   Map Location - NW

The James House
1238 Washington Street
Port Townsend, Washington 98368
(206) 385-1238

A grand Victorian mansion, built by Francis James in 1889, was to become the first bed & breakfast guest house in the Northwest.

The James House continues today with its fine tradition of warmth and hospitality. It reflects Mr. James' love of fine woods and his interest in the shipping and commerce of early Port Townsend. He built this home on the bluff for his wife, Mary. It provides sweeping views of Port Townsend, the Olympic and Cascade Mountain Range, and the waters of Puget Sound.

The spacious rooms of the James House are furnished with period antiques, and the main floor features two parlors with fireplaces. Guests gather for breakfast either in the formal dining room, also with a fireplace, or around the big oak kitchen table next to the wood cookstove.

James House is on the National Register of Historic Places within Port Townsend's National Historic District. A night in this fine old mansion is a reminder of an era when the bay was filled with sailing ships and downtown streets were bustling with activity.

A short pleasant walk takes you to the downtown district, which today is filled with fine restaurants, a variety of interesting shops, an excellent museum, and an exciting waterfront.

Other short jaunts take you to miles of beaches, delightful parks, or to the uptown district, originally established to provide ladies more sedate shopping than the bawdy waterfront.

Alcove Room: This room is furnished in oak with an antique queen brass bed. It has a delightful view from the alcove, and shares a shower/bath.

Oriental Room: Heirloom antique carved Oriental furnishings grace this room, which offers an outstanding view of the bay, Mount Baker and the ferry landing. Shares a shower/bath.

Bay Room: Features a cozy bay window with a view of the bay, Mount Rainier and the Olympic Mountains. Furnished in Eastlake period antiques, including the queen bed. Shares a shower/bath.

Olympic View Room: This bright, cheery room has a westerly view of the bay, Olympic Mountains and rooftops. The antique oak furnishings include a queen bed. Includes an in-room sink and a shared shower/bath.

Bridal Suite: From here, you'll get unsurpassed bay and mountain views from an elegantly furnished bedroom with an adjoining bay-windowed sitting room and private balcony. It has a private bath with claw-foot tub, and boasts an in-room fireplace with an ornate antique mantle.

Chintz Room: Furnished in antique carved oak, this room affords a wonderful view of the bay, Mount Rainier and the Olympics. Shares an adjoining shower/bath.

Blue Room: Offers a westerly view of the bay and Olympics. Furnished with an original James family cherry bedroom suite, including feather mattress. Shares adjoining shower/tub.

Mary's Room: Get a view of the bay and mountains across the garden from this room, which has a wicker desk, rocker and an ornate iron bed with feather mattress. Shared shower/bath.

Hide-Away Room: Windows on three sides lets the warm afternoon sun into this quiet, secluded room. It shares a shower/bath.

Cascade Garden Suite: Features two bedrooms, fireplace and private bath with claw-foot tub. This cozy suite has brick walls, antique and wicker furnishings, and views across the lawn and garden to the water.

Olympic Garden Suite: This two-bedroom suite boasts an antique parlor stove and private bath. The spacious suite has brick walls, brass, oak, and maple furnishings and a view across the lawn and garden to the water.

Gardener's Cottage: A double and a twin bed and private bath included. Furnished with wicker and oak, this charming room has a private patio that offers wonderful garden, mountain and water views.

Rates - $$ to $$$ Map Location - NW

Lizzie's
731 Pierce
Port Townsend, Washington 98368
(206) 385-4168

Lizzie's is a Victorian bed & breakfast, where you will find quiet relaxation in two parlors with fireplaces, leather sofas, a collection of books, and a grand piano meant for use, not ornament.

Part of the charm of Lizzie's is Port Townsend itself, an historic and fabled seaport. The grand old buildings within walking distance are only part of your adventure. Miles of beaches, a busy fishing port, and Fort Worden State Park are just minutes away. In addition, you'll want to check out the town's wonderful array of shops.

Lizzie's Room: Romantic half-canopy queen bed, fireplace and bay window sitting area. Private bath with claw-foot tub.

Sarah's Room: Bay window overlooking the water and mountains, two double beds and a shared bath.

Daisy's Room: Daisy signed her name on the wall in 1894! Art Nouveau king-sized bed and a view of the sunrise over the bay. Shared bath.

Jessie's Room: Queen-sized bed, half bath, and sunrise at the bay window.

Georgia's Room: 1840 furnishings, and a cooling century-old plum tree outside your window. Double bed and private bath.

Hope's Room: 1880s collection with charm. Pick plums from your window. Double bed.

Sharon's Room: Mid-Victorian hardwoods with a shower bath tucked under the servant's stair. Double bed.

Patricia's Room: French antiques lend an elegant ambiance to this room with queen bed and private bath.

Enjoy breakfast in the grand old kitchen around the 11-foot oak table.

Rates - $$ Map Location - NW

Old Consulate Inn
313 Walker
Port Townsend, Washington 98368
(206) 385-6753

This mansion was the official residence and office of the German consul from 1908 to 1911. A perfect example of Queen Anne Victorian, it sits high on the bluff commanding spectacular views of the bay, Mount Rainier and the Olympics. Built in 1889 by Senator F.W. Hastings—the son of founding father Loren

B. Hastings—the mansion is one of the most photographed Victorians in the Pacific Northwest.

"The Red Victorian on the Hill," as the mansion is known, has kept its original color over the years. Trimmed in white, with black and greens accents, it looks now as it must have looked more than 100 years ago. It is graced with white lawn chairs amidst flowering beds and birch trees, plus inviting porch swings.

The main floor offers room to read or just daydream by one of two fireplaces. In the formal parlor, the grand piano and antique organ are tuned and meant to be played. Gaze at the beauty of Port Townsend Bay from the tower nook. Or read in comfort in the study/library. The aroma of fresh-roasted coffee announces breakfast, which is a multi-course affair, served in the formal dining room.

Play a leisurely game of billiards in the garden level game room or relax by the fire in the beautiful woodstove and enjoy your favorite movie on the VCR.

Above the grand-oak staircase, each private room and suite is uniquely furnished in fine antiques, family memorabilia, and custom bed linens, comforters and wallcoverings.

Master Anniversary Suite: This exquisite suite encompasses the entire water-view side of the second floor. A sitting alcove, king-sized canopied four-poster carved rice bed, and an antique woodburning fireplace are in the bed chamber. The two-level bathroom, with claw-foot soaking tub, Victorian pedestal sink, matching commode and raised shower section complete this luxury getaway for two.

Parkside: This room includes Victorian lavender wallcovering, three large white lace curtained windows and expansive views of the park and historic courthouse. This king-bed room with private bath is the perfect romantic retreat.

Garden View: Watch beautiful sunsets from the double-view windows in this large room of roses. King wicker bed and rocker, Victorian walnut furnishings and private bath help provide quiet relaxation.

Alcove Mini Suite: Features high-backed antique oak queen bed, unique views of the Olympics and Kah Tai Lagoon, angled ceilings, very large private bath with claw-foot soaking tub and European shower. The private entry foyer off the main hallway offers an unusual view of the bay.

Tower Honeymoon Suite: Five curved-glass windows encircle the turret sitting room. View the Admiralty Inlet and the Olympics from wicker rockers or the moonlight on the bay from the half-moon window above the pillow of your oversized king bed. Relax in soothing bubbles in your claw-footed bed chamber bathtub.

Harbor View: Another half-moon window graces this room of angled ceilings. Water view from the king brass bed with chiffon half-canopy. Victorian fainting couch and private bath with roomside Victorian marble sink are included.

Village Room: This large L-shaped room has king white iron/brass bed and a matching daybed that converts to accommodate two additional guests. The private bath also includes a roomside Victorian marble sink.

Gabled Room: This charming retreat, tucked into the front gable, boasts an unusual high-peaked ceiling and king-sized brass bed. Soothing tones of champagne, pink and pale green. Bathroom with private detached shower.

Rates - $$ to $$$$ Map Location - NW

Quimper Inn
1306 Franklin Street
Port Townsend, Washington 98368
(206) 385-1060

Built by Henry Morgan in 1888, this simple two-story Georgian style house was remodeled by Harry Barthrop and his wife, Gertrude. They purchased the home, February 4, 1904, and immediately began remodeling.

They added the third floor with gables and dormers, completely changing the look from the front. They also enlarged the windows and added bay windows on both sides of the house. Furthermore, they changed the interior, including the addition of closets, new details and woodwork that survive to this day. During its lifetime, the house was used as a boarding house, living quarters for nurses at a clinic on Jefferson Street and, in the 1950s and 1960s, was used only as a warehouse for furniture storage.

In 1976, it became the "Quimper Inn" after its restoration. Through two owners, it was operated as a unique bed & breakfast. In the late 1980s, the Quimper was closed and the wonderful building again became a home. At that time, some much-needed restoration was completed and, at the end of 1989, its current hosts fell under the spell of the house, made it their home for a year and a half, then once again put up the "Quimper Inn" sign.

Harry and Gertie's Suite: Named for the Barthrops, this suite include two rooms, separated by pocket doors and bay windows facing the Olympic Mountains. It affords a view of Port Townsend Bay and Admiralty Inlet as well as Jefferson County's 100-year-old clock tower. Period decor, queen bed, writing desk, wing-backs, sofa and private bathroom with walk-in shower.

Michele's Room: This is a bay-windowed room with a luxurious view of the tip of Marrowstone Island, Admiralty Inlet and the Cascades. Large private bath has a six-foot claw-foot tub, pedestal sink, wicker furniture and is beautifully ornamented with Victorian-era lighting fixtures and medallions. The brass queen bed is nestled into the bay windows.

The Library: This is the only guest room on the first floor, and includes a queen bed amongst books and memorabilia. Private bathroom with "maids" claw-foot tub and Victorian shower ring.

Christopher's Room: The best view in the Quimper is from this room on the front corner of the house. It features twin beds that make a grand, large bed when pushed together. Victorian fixtures, Eastlake furniture, built-in shelves, large vintage windows and the morning sun to greet you. This room shares a large bathroom with John's Room.

John's Room: Cozy and secluded, John's Room has a double bed and lovely garden views to keep you company. A charming water-closet sink is hidden in the built-in cabinets, and you'll have enough closet space for a long stay.

Rates to $$ to $$$ Map Location - NW

Ravenscroft Inn
533 Quincy Street
Port Townsend, Washington 98368
(206) 385-2784

The Ravenscroft Inn is located high on a bluff at the tip of the Olympic Peninsula. Built in 1987, it is a replica of an historic Charleston Single House. Guests choose from nine well-appointed, spacious guest rooms, all with private baths.

Various rooms include fireplaces, soaking tubs, verandas and fabulous water and mountain views. The elegant great room is where guests gather each morning for a multi-course gourmet breakfast, accompanied by Ravenscroft's own fresh-ground coffee and a morning concert by your host.

Mount Rainier Suite: Queen bed, panoramic view and two-person soaking tub in room.

Mount Baker Room: Queen bed, panoramic views and private bath.

Fireside Room: Fireplace, queen bed, bay and mountain views and French doors that open to Piazza.

Bay Room: King (duel twins) bed, view of Mount Baker, Admiralty Inlet and French doors that open to Piazza.

Wicker Room: Queen bed, mountain and bay views and French doors.

Windsor Room: Sleeps four people in king plus trundle twin beds. Offers view of historic homes, and includes a very spacious sitting area.

The Study: Queen bed and fireplace, at garden level. Quiet and secluded.

Quincy Room: Queen bed, garden level, quiet and secluded.

Rates - $$ to $$$$ Map Location - NW

SEATTLE, WASHINGTON

Chelsea Station
4915 Linden Avenue North
Seattle, Washington 98103
(206) 547-6077

From the moment you enter the Chelsea Station, you'll experience warm feelings and old memories of grandma's house—lace curtains, crocheted doilies and antique furniture included. This elegant 1920 Colonial home is located near the south entrance of the Woodland Park Zoo, in a peaceful wooded setting.

Chelsea Station's neighborhood welcomes strollers. On nearby Shilshole Bay, walk along the docks at the marina or visit the Chittenden Locks in Ballard, after enjoying a traditional Northwest dinner at one of several fine restaurants. Greenlake is within walking distance, and you'll find a three-mile running trail around the lake. Try roller skating, swimming, boating, tennis, biking, golf and picnics.

Chelsea Station has five guest rooms, including two suites. All have private baths.

A soothing hot tub is located in the Carriage House for private use. A bottomless cookie jar fulfills midnight cravings and mid-afternoon munchies. Feel free to use the kitchen, with refrigerator for cold-beverage storage, to prepare snacks. A guest telephone is located in the parlor, and the inn has a complete library with resource materials for planning sightseeing, shopping, entertainment and restaurants. Your innkeepers will help you plan your itinerary.

Included in your stay: A full breakfast with special treats including family-recipe muffins, banana french toast with butterscotch maple syrup, cheese-baked eggs, ginger pancakes with lemon sauce and hot fresh-ground coffee.

Chelsea Station is five minutes from downtown Seattle, the Seattle Center, Washington State Ferries and all major transportation systems. SeaTac International Airport is 25 minutes away. Several Metro bus routes are within walking distance.

Rates - $$ to $$$ Map Location - NW

Gaslight Inn
1727 15th Avenue
Seattle, Washington 98122
(206) 325-3654

Built in 1906, the Gaslight Inn was the private residence of the Dwight Christianson family until the current owners bought it in 1983. In the process of refurbishing and restoring the home, they brought out its original turn-of-the-century ambiance, charm, and warmth, while keeping in mind conveniences and style of contemporary travelers. The living room has a large oak fireplace, and the library offers a TV, VCR and game table for your entertainment.

Gaslight's nine comfortable and unique guest rooms are furnished with double- or queen-sized beds, refrigerator, and TV. Additional features include private bath, phone service and kitchenette in some rooms. A Continental breakfast is provided in the dining room or in the privacy of your room.

The Gaslight Inn is conveniently located in the heart of the city, just a few blocks from the bustle of Broadway, with its popular night clubs, restaurants, theaters and fine shops.

Through the late spring and summer months, you can relax and unwind after a busy day, with a glass of wine at poolside. The private in-ground heated pool includes several decks and sauna at the back of the inn. Here, you can swim, sunbathe, and chat with other guests.

Rates - $$ Map Location - NW

Prince of Wales Bed & Breakfast
133 13th Avenue East
Seattle, Washington 98102
(206) 325-9692

The Prince of Wales, a charming turn-of-the-century bed & breakfast on Seattle's Capitol Hill, is well located for business travelers and tourists alike, with easy access from Route I-5. Walk to the Washington State Convention and Trade Center or take a short bus ride to the Seattle Center, Seattle Trade Center, the University of Washington, or downtown Seattle.

The Prince of Wales boasts four guest rooms, three of which have great views of the city skyline, Puget Sound and the Olympic Mountains. Start your day here with a hearty homecooked breakfast in the dining room.

Double Room: One double bed and semi-private bath.

Twin Room: Two twin beds, semi-private bath, view of Puget Sound and Olympic Mountains.

Suite: Queen bed, sitting room, private bath with shower and great view of city skyline, water and mountains. This room pampers two or accommodates three.

Attic Room: Queen bed, sitting area, private bath with claw-foot tub, hand-held shower, private deck, plus panoramic view of Seattle's skyline, Puget Sound and Olympic Mountains.

Rates - $$ Map Location - NW

SEAVIEW, WASHINGTON

The Shelburne Inn
4415 Pacific Way, P.O. Box 250
Seaview, Washington 98644
(206) 642-2442

The Shelburne Inn was established as a retreat for Portlanders, and has operated continuously since 1896. Charles Beaver named the home and boarding house he built after a grand hotel in Dublin, Ireland. In 1911, a team of horses was used to pull The Shelburne across the street to join it to another building. In those early days, travelers ventured up the Columbia River to Astoria on the stearnwheeler, T.J. Potter. From Astoria, they ferried to Megler and then traversed the Long Beach Peninsula via the narrow gauge Clamshell Railroad. The Shelburne Station was one of the main stops, dropping off summer residents and visitors to the inn.

The Shelburne is surrounded by stunning scenery. The peninsula is an unspoiled, 28-mile stretch of wild Pacific Sea Coast—the longest, continuous beach in the United States. It is a natural paradise, complete with bird sanctuaries, lighthouses, and panoramic vistas. Willapa Bay, just east of the Inn, is a haven for waterfowl, and Ilwaco's nearby docks provide access to unsurpassed sport fishing.

The Shelburne Inn houses 15 antique-filled guest rooms, all with private baths and most with a private deck.

Savor the inn's country breakfast, served family-style at the large oak table in the lobby. The menu changes each morning to reflect what is fresh and in season. Herbs from the garden enhance many of the dishes. Typical fare might include your host's own Italian sausage omelette, scrambled eggs with smoked salmon, or razor clam fritters, accompanied by homemade pastries, fresh fruit, juice, and tea or fresh-ground coffee. Delicious low-fat or vegetarian dishes often are featured—or can be made upon request. Guests of the Honeymoon/Anniversary Suite may dine in their room.

Rates - $$ to $$$$ Map Location - SW

SNOQUALMIE FALLS, WASHINGTON

The Old Honey Farm Country Inn
8910 384th Ave. S.E.
Snoqualmie Falls, Washington 98065
(206) 888-9399

At the Old Honey Farm, you'll enjoy one of Snoqualmie Valley's most beautiful pastoral settings, with a full view of Mount Si and the Cascades. This country inn is 25 miles from Seattle or Snoqualmie Pass, and just minutes to Snoqualmie Falls, golfing, historic train ride, Snoqualmie Winery and outdoor recreation.

The inn features 10 rooms with private baths. One is a luxury room with a queen-sized bed, fireplace, Jacuzzi tub and reclining loveseat. All other rooms have a queen-sized bed and private bath. There are no telephones or TVs in the rooms.

Old Honey Farm is furnished with antiques and collectibles and is decorated in country style. A cozy gathering area with a fireplace, as well as an outside deck, are available for your enjoyment.

The inn is open to the public for breakfast, lunch and dinner. Brunch is offered on Saturdays and Sundays. Service bar and wine cellar are available.

Rates - $$ to $$$ Map Location - NW

SPOKANE, WASHINGTON

Fotheringham House
2128 West Second Avenue
Spokane, Washington 99204
(509) 838-4363

This lovely Victorian home features hand-carved woodwork, tin ceilings and an open, carved staircase. The first mayor of incorporated Spokane built the Fotheringham House in 1891. Located in historic Browne's Addition—which is on the National Historic Register—the house faces Spokane's oldest park and is across the street from one of the city's finest restaurants, The Patsy Clark Mansion. Dine in the mansion, picnic in the park, enjoy downtown Spokane, or just relax in the elegance of this home.

Downtown Spokane is less than a mile away, with a bus stop one-half block from the back door of the Fotheringham. In the winter, enjoy a cheerful fire in the main room; in the summer, relax on the curved veranda and enjoy a view of the park or take a stroll along the tree-lined streets of this historic area.

The spacious bedrooms of the Fotheringham House feature Victorian decor, queen-sized beds, and air conditioning. From your room, you may have a view of The Patsy Clark Mansion or the oldest park in Spokane.

Things to do: Take walking tours, visit museums and library, stroll to the old drug store, complete with a soda fountain, fish, or ski Mount Spokane.

Breakfast features Four Seasons fresh-ground coffee or tea, homemade whole-wheat croissants and muffins, fruit or juice. Weekly rates are available.

Rates - $$ to $$$ Map Location - NE

Hillside House
1729 E. 18th
Spokane, Washington 99203
(509) 534-1426, weekdays
(509) 535-1893, nights

This charming house offers country decor and modern-day comfort on the beautiful South Hill of Spokane. The original house was built in the early 1930s and was the inspiration for the current structure, which features fine amenities, including wall-to-wall glass in the living room.

Downtown Spokane is three miles away; you can drive or take a bus, which stops one block away, to visit fine specialty shops, restaurants, museums and galleries. Lincoln Park is just a short walk away, and offers opportunity for a stroll above the city.

Blue Room: Decorated in blue, this room has a double bed with quilt coverlet, a cozy feel and a hillside view. Its bath is just across the hall.

Lace Room: Two twin lace-draped beds distinguish this romantic room. This is the largest guest room and has a TV, ice-cream table and chair, and recliner.

Wake up to the aroma of hot coffee and a hearty breakfast served in the dining room and on the sun deck.

Rates - $ Map Location - NE

Marianna Stoltz House
427 East Indiana
Spokane, Washington 99207
(509) 483-4316

The Marianna Stoltz House is a classic American four-square home situated on a lovely tree-lined street near Gonzaga University. Built in 1908, this stately residence displays top craftsmanship of the day and is listed on the Spokane Register of Historic Homes.

Guests enjoy exclusive use of the elegant parlor, dining room and sitting room, all furnished with Oriental rugs and authentic period pieces. Enjoy the warmth and charm of beautifully maintained fir woodwork, high ceilings and leaded glass throughout these rooms.

On the second floor, choose from four distinctively tasteful bedrooms with king, queen or single beds and private or shared baths. Old family quilts and lace curtains create a comfy but romantic atmosphere.

Awaken to a generous and sumptuous breakfast that may include specialties such as Stoltz House Strada, puffy Dutch pancakes with homemade apple syrup or peach melba parfait, prepared fresh each morning. Juice, coffee or tea, and muffins or home-made granola complete this superb meal.

Your hosts can recommend delightful neighborhood cafés and restaurants or provide information about local tours, concerts, cultural and social events.

Things to do: Skiing, swimming, fishing, strolling through the many parks, shopping, going to the Civic Theater or Spokane Opera House, Spokane Convention Center, or Riverfront Park.

Rates - $$ to $$$ Map Location - NE

SUNNYSIDE, WASHINGTON

Sunnyside Inn
800 E. Edison Avenue
Sunnyside, Washington 98944
(509) 839-5557 or 1-800-221-4195

Sunnyside Inn offers accommodations that are a cut above common experience. Here, you'll find yourself amid more than 20 of Washington's finest wineries. Visit these wineries, or the area's farms, orchards and historical sites.

Each of the eight rooms at Sunnyside are tastefully decorated in a warm country style, and all have their own private bath, plus color TV, phone, and daily maid service. Seven of the rooms feature double Jacuzzi tubs. The eighth room features the original fixtures from this historical 1919 home.

A full breakfast is served daily in the dining area and includes homebaked muffins, pastries and fresh specialties selected from the abundant harvest of the Yakima Valley.

Rates - $$ to $$$ Map Location - SW

TACOMA, WASHINGTON

Adventure Traudel's Haus
15313 17th Ave. Ct. E.
Tacoma, Washington 98445
(206) 535-4422

Traudel's Haus blends Old World German hospitality and comfort with the modern excitement and unmatched natural beauty of the Great Pacific Northwest. The gardens and lush year-round greenery make it seem remote from city life, but it's all just a moment away.

Traudel's Haus is the perfect place to unwind after a long day of traveling and sightseeing. Antiques, old clocks and handmade lace lend an atmosphere of unhurried relaxation. The charming German hostess will see to it that your stay here is the highlight of your trip.

Traudel's Haus features all the comforts of home, including color TV, fireplace, private full bath, complimentary newspaper, and Continental or full-course breakfast.

Things to do: Boating, scuba diving, fishing, hiking, touring, museums and skiing.

Rates - $ to $$ Map Location - NW

Keenan House
2610 N. Warner
Tacoma, Washington 98407
(206) 752-0702

Enjoy the friendly, personal hospitality of an English type bed & breakfast inn on your next visit to Tacoma, Washington.

The Country and Keenan houses are located seven blocks from the University of Puget Sound, 10 minutes by car from Point Defiance Park and Vashon Island ferry, and and hour and a half from Paradise Resort on Mount Rainier. They are just off Highway 16, your route to Victoria, and near I-5, your route to Vancouver. They are five minutes away from Commencement Bay and a fine selection of excellent restaurants.

Single or double rooms available. Long-term rental available at the Country House.

The Keenan House and Country House offer you clean, attractively decorated rooms and a complimentary full breakfast, featuring fresh-baked bread and rolls.

Rates - $$ Map Location - NW

TROUT LAKE, WASHINGTON

Mio Amore Pensione
P.O. Box 208
Trout Lake, Washington 98650
(509) 395-2264

This Inn sits on six acres at the foot of majestic Mount Adams, beside Trout Lake Creek. Take a leisurely stroll along the creek, fish, or soak in the spa. In addition, Pandora's Box Gift Shop is always open.

Camping and hiking enthusiasts will find unlimited access to the Gifford Pinchot National Forests. And nature lovers will enjoy investigating the waterfalls and Ice Caves near Trout Lake and Beacon Rock State Park. Cross-country skiers take to the vast Mount Adams Wilderness area, and photographers flock to Mount Adams, which rises to an impressive height of 12,326 feet.

In the summer and fall, try nature floats or whitewater raft trips. The leisurely, "first-timer" floats depart mid-morning and explore a beautiful river and wilderness.

Vesta (Goddess of the Home): Built in 1894, this "rustic getaway" sits on Trout Lake Creek. The cozy room has a double bed in the loft, two twin beds on the first level and a woodstove to keep you warm.

Bacchus (God of Wine): This is a serene room with artifacts of wine-growing and wine-tasting throughout the world. It overlooks the Trout Lake grazing area, and has a double bed and shared bath.

Ceres (Goddess of Agriculture): Another delightfully distinctive and warm room overlooking the garden and corral, this one features a queen-sized rattan bed and shared bath.

Venus (Goddess of Love and Beauty): This is a romantically warm and inviting room with a queen-sized brass bed, private bath, sitting room, and views of Mount Adams and Trout Lake Creek. A bottle of complimentary champagne awaits your arrival.

A generous breakfast includes homemade muffins, cakes, tortes, breads, fruit, juices, coffee or tea, plus an added surprise to make your breakfast a little different. Wine or a gourmet picnic lunch also is available.

Rates - $$ to $$$ Map Location - SW

VASHON ISLAND, WASHINGTON

All Season Lodging
12717 S.W. Bachelor Road
Vashon Island, Washington 98070
(206) 463-3498

Treat yourself to waterfront elegance in this romantic cottage overlooking the lights of Tacoma and the splendor of Mount Rainier.

Located on the south end of beautiful Vashon Island, this inn offers a complete kitchen, TV, fireplace and a large sun deck.

Things to do: Walk on the beach, storm watch, sunbathe, or just relax.

Rates - $$ Map Location - NW

Crown & Sceptre Bed & Breakfast
20611 87th Ave. S.W.
Vashon Island, Washington 98070

The Crown & Sceptre Bed & Breakfast is a spacious, one-bedroom apartment in the loft of a traditionally styled barn. Separate from the primary residence, it offers complete privacy and is fully equipped with everything you need to make your stay comfortable—including a microwave and VCR.

The Crown & Sceptre is located mid-island, close to the popular Sound Food Restaurant. It is just a short walk to the beach and Tramp Harbor fishing pier. Fishing gear and bicycles are available, free of charge.

The Crown & Sceptre also is the home of the London Taxi, offering Vashon's only limousine service. Picnics and island tours are available by appointment.

The complete kitchen will be stocked with fresh eggs, courtesy of resident chickens, plus fresh-baked pastries from Bob's Bakery, and juices and jams made here on the island. Even the coffee is locally roasted—by Stewart Brothers.

Day trips from the Inn: Ski or hike the spectacular Mount Rainier, ferry to Victoria or Vancouver, B.C., fish or golf, or visit parks, rainforests and historic landmarks.

Rates - $$ Map Location - NW

WESTPORT, WASHINGTON

Glenacres Inn
222 N. Montesano, P.O. Box 1246
Westport, Washington 98595
(206) 268-9391

Ben Armstrong and his wife, Minnie Ross Smith, built what is now Glenacres Inn for themselves and their seven children at about the turn of the century. In 1923, Paul and Evelyn Guilford bought the house and lived there for about 20 years.

Glen and Clarine Edwards purchased the property in 1943, planning to raise Easter lilies. But the market was flooded by inexpensive imports from Japan. So the Edwards turned the house into a motel, naming it "Glenacres" and adding several cottages.

In 1962, Bobby Kennedy's family stayed at Glenacres during a Department of Fisheries fact-finding trip. The current owners have completed an extensive renovation and restoration program, returning the house to its early days of grace and elegance.

Secluded among stately evergreens on eight wooded acres, the inn offers a choice of eight bedrooms, all with private baths. The formal rooms in the main house are furnished with brass beds, quilted comforters, and lace curtains. A sitting room adjacent to the dining room provides comfortable seating and a place to relax. Photographs and other memorabilia from the past compliment the antiques that grace the rooms. For a more informal atmosphere, you may prefer the rooms that open onto a large deck. Centered on the deck is a gazebo-covered hot tub.

Nestled among the trees surrounding Glenacres are four cottages of varying size, which accommodate families and groups from four to 14. All contain completely furnished kitchens, and two also offer patios with fish- and clam-cleaning facilities, as well as picnic tables. The larger cottages are ideal for family reunions or other gathering.

Complete breakfasts that reflect the area harvest are served in the dining room.

Things to do: Fishing, clam digging, horseback riding, beachcombing, crabbing, bird and whale watching, bicycling, surfing and touring the Cranberry Coast.

Rates - $ to $$$$ Map Location - SW

WHITE SALMON, WASHINGTON

Llama Ranch Bed & Breakfast
1980 Highway 141
White Salmon, Washington 98672
(509) 395-2786

Enjoy a relaxing stay at this unique llama ranch, where you'll discover that llamas come in various sizes, colors and lengths of wool. Besides intriguing body language, their verbal language is humming, chortling and bugling. Their curiosity excels at all times. They are highly intelligent, but are selective eaters.

Things to do: Horseback riding, whitewater rafting, windsurfing, fishing, hunting, hiking, cross-country skiing, snowmobiling, biking, cave exploring and huckleberry picking. Of course, all-day llama treks also are available.

Rates - $ to $$ Map Location - SW

Orchard Hill Inn
199 Oak Ridge Road
White Salmon, Washington 98672
(509) 493-3024

Orchard Hill is secluded homestead, surrounded by forests, orchards, fields and vineyards that attract migratory birds and wildlife. Choose from a six-bed cabin for groups, or spacious gabled double or family rooms with shared baths. Explore the 1,000-book library at the only Inn in the Gorge with whitewater access.

At Orchard Hill, you'll also find miles of trails for mountain biking, whitewater frontage for fishing, and access to swimming, rafting and kayaking. Enjoy horseshoes, badminton, frisbee, golf, volleyball, croquet, gorge bowling, darts, windsurfing, skiing, Stonehenge, Mount St. Helens, Ice Caves, Maryhill Museum, Lava Beds, or waterfalls of the Columbia Gorge National Scenic Area. Then pamper sore muscles and tired spirits in the whirlpool back at the inn.

The Caldwell Room: This is a large, sunny room with one double and one single bed from Grandma Caldwell's bedroom set. The beds are covered with handcrafted antique quilts, and the room offers a beautiful view of the southern sky.

Thuringia Room: Modeled after the alpine huts of Europe and authentically trimmed by a German master carpenter, this six-person cabin includes two sets of bunks and a queen-sized bed. Full bath, meeting room and wood heat also included.

The Blue Room: This room is popular with families for its double bed and set of bunk beds dressed with Early American blue woven comforters. From here, you can view the forested slopes of the White Salmon Valley or look into the two-story treehouse.

The Calico Room: This romantic double bedroom overlooks the circular orchard and pitch & chip golf course. The gabled window is the perfect spot to watch for deer and coyote.

Delicious wholesome sideboard breakfast includes fresh breads, cheeses, spreads, yogurts, homegrown fruit and fresh-ground coffee.

Rates - $ to $$ Map Location - SW

YAKIMA, WASHINGTON

Birchfield Manor
2018 Birchfield Road
Yakima, Washington 98901
(509) 452-1960

The Birchfield Manor was built by Yakima sheep rancher Thomas Smith in 1910. The two-and-a-half story home has 23 rooms. From the crystal chandeliers and cherished antiques to the winding staircase that leads to the mansion's other 20 rooms, this is truly a Victorian jewel in the Yakima desert.

The Inn has five generous rooms with queen- or king-sized beds, and modern bathrooms with tub or shower. In the winter, enjoy the indoor hot tub and, when the weather warms, take a dip in the swimming pool and stroll through the flower-filled grounds.

Jenny's Room: This small, light and airy room faces east and welcomes the morning sun. Queen bed and bath with shower.

Anne's Room: Brass queen bed and corner window seat. Bathroom with shower.

Victoria's Room: Brass queen bed with bay window and reading nook. Bathroom with shower.

Allison's Room: Brass queen bed and cozy sitting area, spacious bathroom with built-in bathtub.

Elizabeth's Room: This is the largest, most formal room. It includes a king-sized bed with separate dressing room, and bathroom with shower. A daybed in the dressing room can accommodate an additional person.

Rates - $$ Map Location - SW

BETTER
Bed &
Breakfast
Inns

IDAHO

ASHTON, IDAHO

Jessen's R.V. Park Bed & Breakfast
P.O. Box 11
Ashton, Idaho 83420
(208) 652-3356

This is an old three-story Victorian home with stream, patio, gazebo and nice walking area. Victorian and French furniture helps provide the great homey atmosphere. Three large bedrooms with large baths. Full or Continental breakfast.
Things to do: Fishing, waterskiing, snow skiing, hunting, hiking, snowmobiling, or visiting national parks.

Rates - $ Map Location - NE

BOISE, IDAHO

Idaho Heritage Inn
109 West Idaho
Boise, Idaho 83702
(208) 342-8066

The Idaho Heritage Inn was built in 1904 for one of Boise's early merchants, Henry Falk. It remained in the Falk family until 1943, when it was purchased by Gov. Chase A. Clark. The home was used by Clark's daughter, Bethine, and her husband, Sen. Frank Church, as their Idaho residence during Church's tenure in the Senate. The home remained in the Clark/Church family until 1987, when it was purchased and lovingly restored by its current owners. It now is listed on the National Register of Historic Places.

Located in Boise's historic Warm Springs District, this inn enjoys the convenience of natural geothermal water throughout the year. It is surrounded by other distinguished turn-of-the-century homes, but also is within walking distance of downtown, Eighth Street Marketplace, and Old Boise, all of which offer excellent restaurants, shops and theatres. The Idaho Heritage Inn also is less than a mile from Boise State University, near the greenbelt by the sparkling Boise River, where wild geese and ducks make their home year-round.

Skiers delight in the excellent facilities at Bogus Basin Ski Area, a mere 19 miles from the inn, in tree-covered mountains overlooking Boise. From here, you also have easy access to surrounding mountain ranges, with abundant trout fishing, quaint old mining towns, and unsurpassed camping and hiking opportunities.

All of the rooms at the Idaho Heritage Inn have private baths, period furniture, and crisp linens. Spacious main-floor common rooms include a large entry hall, formal dining room, living room and sunroom, featuring diamond-paned French doors, oak flooring, Oriental carpets and plentiful, comfortable seating.

Governor's Suite: This stately room features a queen-sized bed, private bath with tub, walk-in shower and enclosed sun porch.

Senator's Room: Awaken in this cheerful room overlooking Idaho Street and featuring a private bath with tub and shower.

Judge's Chamber: This extra-large room features Victorian furnishings, private bath and private access to the covered veranda.

Mayor's Study: A delightful room with its own covered veranda and private bath. Definitely bright and cozy!

Executive Suite: This spacious retreat has two queen-sized beds, a cozy sitting area, breakfast nook, skylight, private bath and cable TV.

Enjoy a complimentary breakfast of fresh-squeezed juice, choice of beverages, fresh fruit in season, and oven-warmed bread and muffins served with homemade jams and preserves, and delivered to your room.

Rates - $$ Map Location - C

Victoria's White House
10325 W. Victory
Boise, Idaho 83709
(208) 362-0507

Built in 1980, Victoria's is a plantation-like estate that combines modern conveniences with antique heritage. The inn consists of a 1906 solid quarter sawn oak stairway, saved from an Idaho courthouse and assembled piece by piece to preserve its original beauty and history. Victoria's also boasts a solid wood mantel fireplace, Strauss crystal, solid pewter chandeliers and oak floors.

The Inn provides two rooms with private bath. A full breakfast is served each morning.

Victoria's is close to the Center of the Birds of Prey, five minutes from the airport, and 15 minutes from downtown Boise and Basin ski slopes.

Rates - $ to $$ Map Location - SW

CALDWELL, IDAHO

The Manning House Bed & Breakfast
1803 South Tenth Avenue
Caldwell, Idaho 83605
(208) 459-7899

This bed and breakfast was built in 1906—by a Mr. Manning—near a shallow lake that has since been drained and turned into a golf course.

Caldwell is an agricultural town from the early days. Crops here include vegetables, sugar beets, apples, cherries, peaches, and grapes. You'll find several wineries in the area.

Guest bedrooms are upstairs and share a large bathroom, which has a tub and shower.

Full breakfast: cereal or yogurt and granola, fruit, juice, eggs or waffles and sausage.

Fish the Snake and Boise rivers, visit the vineyards, wineries, fruit stands and cheese factory, or Boise, which is a half hour away. Ride a bicycle built for two, croquet and enjoy the hot tub for two.

Rates - $ Map Location - SW

CASCADE, IDAHO

Warm Lake Lodge
P.O. Box 450
Cascade, Idaho 83611
(208) 257-2221 or (208) 734-2387

Warm Lake Lodge was established as a hunting and fishing lodge in the early 1900s. Today, it maintains the tradition of homecooked meals and friendly hospitality.

The lodge has two bed & breakfast rooms and 10 cabins. Breakfast for two is included with the bed & breakfast rooms, and there's a full restaurant, which prepares homecooked meals.

Things to do: Fishing, hunting, boating, hiking and horseback riding.

Rates - $ to $$ Map Location - SW

COEUR D' ALENE, IDAHO

Anderson's Country Cabin
E. 6495 Sunnyside Road
Coeur d'Alene, Idaho 83814
(208) 667-2988

At Anderson's Country Cabin, you'll experience a hint of life in the Old West, yet enjoy the luxury and comforts of modern times.

Choose from two upstairs suites in the beautifully restored 1930s main log home or the private log cabin, known as the Bunk House. All are furnished with restored antiques, Western and Indian art, and have beautiful hand-stitched quilts on queen-sized beds, plus full private baths.

The private cabin also has a loft with extra sleeping accommodations, a kitchen with an authentic wood cookstove, and a large covered front porch, where you can sit and watch the sunset and enjoy the cool evening breeze.

A full breakfast served in the main log-house dining room features hardy home cooking, baked specialties and fresh fruit, in season.

Things to do: Boating, fishing, hunting, golfing, hiking, biking and skiing.

Rates - $$ Map Location - NW

The Blackwell House
820 Sherman Avenue
Coeur d'Alene, Idaho 83814
(208) 664-0656

Located on Coeur d'Alene's main street, this stately home was built in 1904 by F.A. Blackwell, as a wedding gift to his son Russell and Russell's bride, Pauline Kelly. The house has seen numerous owners over the years, and eventually sat vacant until the current owners bought it in 1983 and restored it.

Today, each guest room in the Blackwell House has a charm and warmth designed to make you feel at home. Relax in the elegance of the master suite, with its private bath and curved bay window overlooking main street.

Other suites have private baths and sitting areas, one with a fireplace. The main floor of the home includes the music room, living room with fireplace and dining room.

Breakfast is served in the bright and airy morning room, with its lovely French doors overlooking the patio and lawn. A roaring fire greets guests on chilly mornings.

Coeur d'Alene, the "City by the lake," offers a variety of sports and leisure within walking distance of the Blackwell House. Stroll the "Worlds Longest Floating Boardwalk," hike the nature trails of Tubbs Hill, picnic in the park or tour the lake and St. Joe River by boat. Canoe, paddleboat and bicycle rentals are available for the more adventurous visitors. Winter sports include snowmobiling, cross-country and downhill skiing. You'll also discover a variety of shops, boutiques and restaurants nearby.

Rates - $$ to $$$ Map Location - NW

Cricket On The Hearth
1521 Lakeside Avenue
Coeur d'Alene, Idaho 83814
(208) 664-6926

Cricket On The Hearth is a 1920s cottage-style home with dormer windows on the second floor, and enclosed patio used for breakfast during the summer months, plus two fireplaces, and a beautiful front porch with swing.

Miss Kitty's Room: Gunsmoke's Miss Kitty would have found this Victorian room with antique brass bed and claw-foot tub a delight. Scarlet and lace accent this "naughty-but-nice" room to set the mood for romance. A private deck with swing awaits two lovers. Private bath.

Lilac Room: The abundant lilacs in Coeur d'Alene were the inspiration for this room, furnished with white wicker furniture, a queen-sized bed and color true to its namesake. If you take a deep breath, you may even get a refreshing scent of lilac. Private bath.

Navajo Room: Guests in this first-floor room step back in time to experience the life in a Navajo pueblo. The queen bed and furnishings are hand-crafted with Southwestern art and native American artifacts—combining soft colors with rough textures. Private bath.

Pine Room: The dormer windows of this large room offers a view of the stately pine tree that graces the front lawn. The theme is carried out by the impressive queen-sized bed and furnishings for lounging or for an extra guest. Shared bath.

Tulip Room: This upstairs dormer room is alive with the beauty and simplicity of pink tulips. The unique natural pine bed, woodwork and textured walls are reminiscent of a cozy country cottage. Shared bath.

Things to do: Fishing, hunting, boating, canoeing, hiking, rafting, skiing, snowmobiling and golfing.

Rates - $ to $$ Map Location - NW

Gregory's McFarland House
601 Foster Avenue
Coeur d'Alene, Idaho 83814
(208) 667-1232

The McFarland House was built in 1905 by Mr. Landt for R.E. McFarland, who was attorney general of Idaho during the late 1800s. At the time it was built, there were four houses on the block and the area was wooded. This was the McFarland home for more than 65 years.

Included in the guest house today are three rooms with king-sized bed, one room with queen-sized bed and one room with either two twins or a king-sized bed. All have private bath with tub and shower.

This a vacation paradise for sun lovers, fishermen, hunters, birdwatchers, golfers, tennis players, horsemen, skiers, hikers and photographers.

Rates - **$$ to $$$**   Map Location - NW

Katie's Wild Rose Inn
E. 5150 Coeur d'Alene Lake Drive
Coeur d'Alene, Idaho 83814
(208) 765-9474 or 1-800-328-WISH

Surrounded by pine trees and overlooking beautiful Coeur d'Alene Lake, Katie's Wild Rose Inn welcomes all who enjoy a cozy, warm atmosphere. The home features a spacious living and dining area, as well as a family room with a pool table.

Katie's Rose Suite: Queen bed with private bath and Jacuzzi.

Red Rose Room: Double bed with private bath.

Irish Rose Room: Double bed with shared bath.

Primrose Room: Double bed with shared bath.

Breakfast is served beside huge windows or on the cedar deck. The rose motif abounds throughout the light and airy rooms, and wild rose bushes edge the property.

Katie's is within 600 feet of a public dock and swimming area. Tennis courts, ball parks, hiking trails of Tubbs Hill, City Park, the "World's Longest Floating Boardwalk," and the downtown shopping area are all within four miles. Enjoy boat rides, swimming, waterskiing, biking, and horseback riding in the summer or skiing and snowmobiling in the winter.

Rates - **$$**   Map Location - NW

Someday House Bed & Breakfast
790 Kidd Island Road
Coeur d'Alene, Idaho 83814
(208) 664-6666

Someday House is a place where dreams take flight. This sophisticated home, decorated with simple country charm, was designed and built by the innkeeper's husband. More than 20 years ago, he packed his youngest daughter to the summit of the mountain, where the house now commands a 180-degree view of Lake Coeur d'Alene, the city and the surrounding mountains and prairie. Surveying the magnificence he told his daughter: "Someday I'll build a house here." Hence came the name of the current bed and breakfast.

Five cozy rooms await guests. The Hideaway and the Lookout are large rooms with king-sized beds, sitting areas, outside entrances and private baths. Open the French doors of the Hideaway and step onto the patio or relax in the Jacuzzi tub right in the room. From the second story deck of the Lookout, enjoy the spectacular view of the lake and the surrounding area.

The Master Suite has a queen-sized bed and private bath with shower and Jacuzzi tub. The bathroom is spacious, with a skylight to brighten your mornings. If you choose, there is ample space to enjoy breakfast in your room, where full-length mirrors reflect the lovely floral decor and the beautiful evening sunsets.

The Sewing Room, charmingly decorated in blue and yellow, has a full-sized bed and shared bath. Also included are an antique sewing cabinet and night table, plus white ruffled curtains that frame the morning sun as it rises through the stately evergreen forest.

Cindy's room, with it's full-sized red iron bed, bright floral accents, white eyelet comforter, round-top trunk and antique wash stand, brings back memories of grandma's house. A roll-top writing desk is the icing on the cake. The bath is shared.

The beach is just a mile down the hill from the Someday House. Or, if you choose to spend the day shopping and sightseeing, Coeur d'Alene shopping and dining are just 15 minutes away by car.

Throughout the seasons, Coeur d'Alene's cultural community offers concerts, plays, and other art events. Several museums and points of interest also are in the area. Recreational activities include fishing, boating and golfing in the summer and snowmobiling and skiing in the winter.

Have breakfast—breads and fruits or a full breakfast—on the patio overlooking the lake or in the dining room with the same incredible view. Your meal will be accented with homemade jam and hand-painted china.

Rates - $$ Map Location - NW

The Warwick Inn
303 Military Drive
Coeur d'Alene, Idaho 83814
(208) 764-6565

The Warwick Inn is a beautifully restored early 1900s home on the Old Fort Grounds of Fort Sherman. Nestled among the tall, ancient pines and just steps from the lake, this lovely inn is ideally located and adjacent to the park—with its cultural center on one side and the college grounds on the other. The Warwick Inn is an award-winner, having received the 1990 Chamber of Commerce Award for Excellence in Lodging in Coeur d'Alene.

Coeur d'Alene Lake has been designated as one of the 10 most beautiful lakes in the world. Coeur d'Alene is located at the junction of Idaho's two main highways, Interstate 90 and U.S. 95. The city is about 35 miles east of Spokane and 100 miles south of the Canadian border, on the north shore of Lake Coeur d'Alene.

The Warwick Inn is small but discriminating. The decor is warm and gracious, with a country French/Victorian charm. The inn has a library stocked with plenty of interesting books and current magazines. Your hosts also provide fluffy towels and guests robes for your use, and complimentary refreshments are served in the evening.

Guest rooms are named after your hosts' grandmothers. Two rooms share one large bath, while the other offers a private bath.

Emma's Room is beautifully done in French blue and cranberry, trimmed with fluffy white lace. The old double sleigh bed is comfortable and promotes snuggling. A sitting area located in a cozy alcove is perfect for quiet moments with a book or for just listening to the whispering of the pines outside.

Edy's Room is a spacious and cheerful suite done in buttercup yellow, with a comfortable queen-sized bed. The large sitting area offers a view of the lake and a large seating alcove that will accommodate a sleeping adult as well.

Drucie's Suite is elegantly done with designer fabric and sheets, and features a beautiful bay window with a sparkling lake view. Here, you will sleep in a king-sized pewter iron bed that is more than 100 years old. The decor is refreshingly rich in floral colors and lace. The spacious private bath is adjacent with a tub for soaking, a shower and double pullman sinks.

The Coeur d'Alene area has four distinct seasons—crisp winter, gentle spring, warm sunny summer and resplendent autumn—with a variety of recreation to suit. Try golf, tennis, roller skating, swimming, waterskiing, hiking, boating, or fishing. Or shoot off to one of the gun clubs or head to the public beach. Major ski areas are within 60 miles of the city, including Mount Spokane, Schweitzer and the new Silver Mountain, with the world's longest gondola ride. Transportation is available to all ski areas.

Begin your day at The Warwick with a delicious breakfast served in the cheerful garden room or outdoors on the patio. Choose a light breakfast of juice, yogurt, fresh fruit and fresh baked bread or muffins or a full breakfast that may include waffles, pancakes, egg dishes or breakfast meats.

Rates - $$ to $$$ Map Location - NW

COOLIN, IDAHO

Old Northern Inn
P.O. Box 177
Coolin, Idaho 83848
(208) 443-2426

The Old Northern Inn originally was built as a hotel shortly after the turn of the century, and operated in conjunction with the Great Northern Railroad. It provides a magnificent waterfront setting, and includes a large deck with comfortable lounge chairs overlooking the lake.

The Inn also boasts a huge fireplace, antique furnishings throughout, and outdoor dining.

Coolin, Idaho is at the south end of 20-mile-long Priest Lake, which connects to Upper Priest Lake, a national preserve bordering Canada, via a picturesque thoroughfare.

The Twin Island One: Queen-sized bed with private bath.

The Twin Island Two: Queen-sized bed with private bath.

The Papoose: Queen-sized bed with private bath.

The Kalispell Suite: Two rooms, queen-sized bed, couch (hide-a-bed), with private bath and beautiful lake view.

The Bartoo Suite: Two rooms, queen-sized bed, couch (hide-a-bed), with private bath and beautiful lake view.

All rooms are furnished with luxurious Polo bath towels and robes, and European goose-down comforters.

Breakfast specialties include huckleberry hot cakes and fresh-baked muffins. Afternoon refreshments include a wine and cheese bar. In the evening, coffee, tea and cookies are served.

Recreational opportunities near the Old Northern Inn include hiking, boating, waterskiing, swimming, and fishing for world-record trout. The inn also has a volleyball court and marina for boating, as well as a swimming and sunbathing beach.

Rates - $$ Map Location - NW

DRIGGS, IDAHO

Pines Motel & Guest Haus
105 S. Main, P.O. Box 117
Driggs, Idaho 83422
(208) 354-2774

Located on land homesteaded by Leland Monroe Driggs in 1900, the Pines Motel originally was a two-story log cabin. William Ethelbert bought the cabin—with more than an acre of ground—for $525 in September 1907. Ethelbert's daughter, Wanona, was born in the cabin in 1910.

In the late 1930s and early 1940s, after she married, Wanona and her husband, George Flowers, enlarged the cabin to its current size. The Flowers bought the home in July 1941, and eventually began to rent rooms on a nightly basis. They also opened a café in what is now the living room, and called the establishment the Pinecrest Motel. Charles and Rosemary Frantz bought the motel in July, 1972 and ran it as such for nearly 20 years until their daughter, Nancy, and her husband, John Neilson, bought them out in June, 1991.

The inn has eight rooms—two with shared bath and six with private bath. Three rooms have two double beds, two have queen-sized beds, and two have king-sized beds. One suite has a queen and three double beds.

Full breakfast is included with rooms with shared bath. There is an additional breakfast charge for people 13 and older in rooms with private bath; children eat for half price.

Things to do: Fishing, and hunting for deer, elk, duck, geese and upland game birds.

Rates - $ to $$$ Map Location - SE

ELK CITY, IDAHO

Canterbury House Inn
501 Elk Creek Road, P.O. Box 276
Elk City, Idaho 83525
(208) 842-2366

Situated on six acres in a lovely rural setting, Canterbury House Inn has a splendid view across open countryside, woodlands and mountains. The Old English decorating includes antique furniture, wood beams, mullioned windows and three log-burning fireplaces. Local legend adds a resident ghost.

Canterbury House Inn is located just three quarters of a mile from the small

Pines Motel & Guest Haus, Driggs, ID

town of Elk City. Situated in the heart of he finest outdoor recreation in the state, this is a peaceful retreat.

The accommodations include two attractively furnished bedrooms, a private bath and the Canterbury Pub reception room. A full country breakfast is served in the English Pub atmosphere. Special diets can be accommodated with advance notice. A refrigerator, barbecue and laundry facilities are available to guests.

Things to do: Touring old mining towns and wilderness areas, fishing, hunting, hiking, horseback riding, photography and mountain biking.

Rates - $ Map Location - NW

FISH HAVEN, IDAHO

Bear Lake Bed & Breakfast
500 Loveland Lane
Fish Haven, Idaho 83287
(208) 945-2688

The Bear Lake Bed & Breakfast is a beautiful log home designed, cut down, hand-peeled and built by its owner. One room has a king-sized waterbed, fireplace and private bath. Three rooms have king- or queen-sized beds and shared bath. Full country breakfast is served.

Things to do: Fishing, hunting, skiing, snowmobiling and photography.

Rates - $ to $$ Map Location - SE

HARRISON, IDAHO

Peg's Bed 'n Breakfast Place
202 Garfield Ave., P.O. Box 144
Harrison, Idaho 83833-0144
(208) 689-3525

The 1905 historical home on one acre of landscaped grounds is located in the turn-of-the-century Timber town of Harrison, overlooking Lake Coeur d'Alene.

Enjoy the common room with phone, TV, books, magazines, puzzles and games, as you sit back and relax the easy chairs.

Bedroom one sleeps four; bedroom two sleeps three; bedroom three sleeps two.

Lumberjack breakfast provided, and lunches packed for fishermen, hunters, picnics and hikers.

Things to do: Boating, photography, fishing, hunting, hiking and skiing.

Rates - $ to $$ Map Location - NW

IRWIN, IDAHO

McBride's Bed & Breakfast
P.O. Box 166
Irwin, Idaho 83428
(208) 483-4221

This bed & breakfast differs somewhat from others because the guest room is not in the main house, but in a house beside the log home. The guest facility affords complete privacy in a 900-square-foot unit with refrigerator, coffee pot, TV, private bathroom, plus a king, queen and two twin beds.

McBride's has a beautiful yard and offers use of the barbecue grill. Or you may choose to visit the area's five cafés and restaurants. There are also country and western lounges for live entertainment. Your chances of seeing the bald eagles that nest across the river from the inn are excellent.

This bed & breakfast is located in a high mountain valley, about 15 miles long and five to six miles wide. The elevation is 6,000 feet.

Summers here are beautiful, with elk, deer, and moose in abundance. Winter has a lot to offer as well; you'll find groomed snowmobile trails, and Grand Targhee Ski and Summer Resort is just 45 miles away. The cross-country skiing is excellent as well. Palisades Lake is the site for plenty of ice fishing, as well as a fishing derby in February. The Snake River is world-famous for its fishing as well. Sign up for a guided fishing trip or just a boat ride. Or test your skill at big-game and waterfowl hunting.

Hiking enthusiasts will be thrilled by the hundreds of trails in the area, as will those who enjoy horseback riding. One of the most beautiful hikes is the Upper and Lower Palisades Lakes. The Upper is a seven-mile hike and the Lower is about five miles. No motorized vehicles are allowed so it is a quiet, beautiful hike.

From McBride's, it's an easy one-day drive to Grand Teton and Yellowstone national parks and back. And just 30 minutes over the hill in Victor is the famous Pierre's Playhouse, which presents a nightly barbecue and melodrama. A 45-mile drive from McBride's will take you to Jackson Hole, Wyoming, or take the short seven-mile trip to Palisades Reservoir.

A full country breakfast is served daily at McBride's.

Rates - $ to $$ Map Location - SE

KOOSKIA, IDAHO

Bear Hollow Bed 'n' Breakfast
HC 75 Box 16
Kooskia, Idaho 83539
(208) 926-7146 or 1-800-831-3713

At Bear Hollow, you'll enjoy a homey atmosphere and country comfort, where each of the gracious rooms overlooks the Middlefork of the Clearwater River.

Whether you choose to go fishing, take a dip in a crystal clear river, hunt for deer, elk, bear or a wildlife photograph, shop for handmade gifts, or just relax on one of the porches, Bear Hollow is the place to be.

Located on the "Wild and Scenic" Middlefork of the Clearwater River on U.S. Highway 12—six miles east of Kooskia, Idaho—Bear Hollow rests at the foot of the Selway-Bitterroot Wilderness. At an elevation of just 1,140 feet, weather is nearly always pleasant. Enjoy the area's natural hot springs, or go hiking, whitewater rafting, innertubing, canoeing, kayaking, horseback riding, swimming, fishing, hunting or wildlife photographing. Follow the Lewis and Clark Trail and make your own delightful discoveries of a majestic country the nature intended it to be.

Your hosts will help you book guided hunting and fishing trips with any of the many licensed outfitters in the area. Back at the inn, relax in a hot tub, gaze at the Milky Way, try your skill at a game of pool, or enjoy conversation with your hosts.

The Cub's Den: Twin bed and common bath.

Mama Bear's Suite: California king bed, daybed with trundle and private bath.

Papa Bear's Suite: Luxurious and spacious, for special occasions. King-sized bed and private bath.

Awaken to a morning filled with the sounds of nature. Perhaps catch a glimpse of a deer, eagle, or osprey as your hosts serve you a complete country breakfast.

Rates - $$ Map Location - NW

LEWISTON, IDAHO

Carriage House Bed & Breakfast
611 Fifth Street
Lewiston, Idaho 83501
(208) 746-4506

The Carriage House is a cozy two-bedroom guest house that offers a feeling of old country-style comfort. Located in a quiet historical neighborhood, this bed & breakfast is just a short walk from Lewis and Clark State College, several parks, the Civic Theater, and St. Joseph Regional Medical Center. Downtown Lewiston is nearby as well, as is recreational access to the Snake and Clearwater rivers, including a pleasant walking path along the river levee.

The Carriage House reflects the charm of a European Country Inn. The elegance of delicate lace is enhanced by the scents of imported potpourri, soaps and lotions. The cozy sitting room is tastefully appointed with lovely antiques to carry you back to another era. Experience the relaxing warmth of an indoor spa that opens onto a private courtyard. Guest rooms are furnished with comfortable queen-sized Victorian beds, fluffy comforters, bath or half-bath, individually controlled heat and air conditioning, and direct-dial telephones.

The gift shop, Nancy Nook, is the old country kitchen. Although not used for cooking, it does include a refrigerator for guests. Coffee, tea and cookies are available any time of the day.

The Victoria Room is a quaint room with a half-bath. Its sun porch, which is furnished in white wicker, opens for a summer breeze and a Continental breakfast.

The Landau Room is highlighted by a cathedral ceiling and etched windows. It includes a full bath with a Roman tub, and is elegantly furnished.

A full breakfast is served in the dining room of the main house, or you may have a Continental breakfast in your room.

Rates - $$ Map Location - NW

McCALL, IDAHO

1920 House Bed & Breakfast
143 East Lake Street , P.O. Box 1716
McCall, Idaho 83638
(208) 634-4661

1920 House is a beautifully restored historic home, centrally located in a popular year-round resort by Payette Lake, just minutes from Brundage Ski Resort. Relax and enjoy being pampered—your hosts take great pleasure in customizing your stay as much as possible!

The guest sitting room at 1920 features lake and Brundage Mountain views, plus games, tea kettle and snacks. You'll find fireplaces in the living room and library, and a private yard and patio opened during the summer.

Richter-Traller Room: Large windows overlook downtown McCall and are perfect for watching a Rocky Mountain Sunrise. Decor with a Southwest flavor features a custom four-poster bed made of Western red cedar as a tribute to the father of one of your hosts, Lowell Traller. Paintings by both Lowell and his wife, Margaret Richter-Traller, are some of the only things left from a life filled with adventures throughout the Southwest and Mexico.

Barrie-Shikrallah Room: English antiques handed down from the mother of one of your hosts, Doris Barrie-Shikrallah, set a mood in this room that invites intimate talks or curling up with a good book. Tucked into the south-facing gable, this cozy room has windows in three directions, bringing in tree-filtered light. Dad's antique skis, snowshoes and skates, the tiny piano and fragile cocoa cup from Doris' childhood, their wedding picture and hope chest are all reflected in the old, triple-mirrored dressing table.

McLeod-Shikrallah Room: The truly unique look in this popular room stems from the dynamic combination of Scot and Arab. When Mary McLeod of Prince Edward Isle married Naseeb Habib Shikrallah of Beirut, they brought together the powerful influences of diverse backgrounds. Mary's family tartan of rich green, blue and black, shot through with red and yellow, provides the dramatic backdrop for Naseeb's brass and ebony furniture. With it's western exposure and partial view of the lake, this room is a favorite for couples looking for a romantic setting.

Breakfast time varies based on guest preference. As it is cooked to order from a variety of choices, guests can linger over coffee in their room, then eat when they feel like it.

Things to do: Hiking, fishing, hunting, skiing, boating, biking, or taking a car tour of the area.

Rates - $$ Map Location - NW

The Chateau
1300 Warren Wagon Road
McCall, Idaho 83638
(208) 634-4196

This is a 90-year-old Cape Cod, established in 1991. It has four bedrooms, all with pedestal sinks; two have private baths and two have a shared bath. Each room has a feather bed and down comforters, and a hot tub is available for guest use.

Breakfast may consist of omelets, French toast, eggs Benedict, huckleberry and pecan waffles and pancakes. Bread and muffins are baked daily.

Things to do: Fishing, hunting, boating, waterskiing.

Rates - $$ to $$$ Map Location - NW

MOSCOW, IDAHO

Beau's Butte Bed & Breakfast
702 Public Avenue
Moscow, Idaho 83843
(208) 882-4061

Beau's Butte Bed & Breakfast is on the north edge of Moscow, just seven blocks off Highway 95. Visitors enjoy a sweeping view of Moscow Mountain and the rolling hills of the Palouse Country.

The Inn is convenient to downtown Moscow and the University of Idaho; Pullman and Washington State are just eight miles away. Some of the best forests, lakes and streams in the United States offer outdoor recreation nearby.

The four acres of land surrounding this country inn provide privacy and quiet. Pheasants, hawks, owls, rabbits and other wildlife may be seen from the back deck.

Guests enjoy a complimentary beverage served on the deck or in front of a crackling fire. Stroll through the yard and inspect the latest garden project or unwind in the hot tub.

Locally handcrafted treasures and wildlife art are featured throughout the house. Games, magazines, TV and puzzles are available in the living room.

Cinnamon Bear Room: A cozy room with redwood ceiling, plush carpet, and king-sized waterbed; bath is shared. Guests enjoy the garden views, rose-scented potpourri and sunbeams through the stained-glass window.

The Rainbow Mints Room: Decorated in soft pastels, this room overlooks the solarium and rose garden. It has a king-sized brass bed, hardwood floors with rag rugs and a private bath. "Gram's" handmade quilt extends a special welcome to guests.

Breakfast won't disappoint. A whiff of spiced-apple Dutch babies, German sausage, and sour cream twists will lead you to the kitchen. Choose a mug from the cook's collection and help yourself to fresh-ground coffee while breakfast is being prepared. The family-style meal often includes garden-fresh fruits, berries and famous Idaho potatoes.

Things to do: Go hiking, biking, visit museums and the Camas Winery, or take a scenic drive.

Rates - $$ Map Location - NW

OAKLEY, IDAHO

Poulton's Bed & Breakfast Inn
200 East Main Street
Oakley, Idaho 83346
(208) 862-3649 or 1-800-484-9685

Oakley, Idaho is in south-central Idaho near the Utah and Nevada borders. It is nestled between the mountains in a lovely valley that is home to farmers and ranchers whose families have lived here for generations.

Oakley residents are proud of their rich heritage. The town features pioneer architecture in historic homes and buildings constructed during Oakley's prosperous years, 1880-1912.

The Inn is a three-story Georgian style home built in 1903. It has four bedrooms, two with private baths and two with a shared bath.

Breakfast includes homemade bread, muffins, "Goldenrod" (old family recipe), jams, fruit juices, herb teas and coffee.

Rates - $ Map Location - SE

Heritage Inn, Salmon, ID

SALMON, IDAHO

Heritage Inn
510 Lena Street
Salmon, Idaho 83467
(208) 756-3174

The Inn is an historical brick building, built in 1885 by Idaho's first governor, George L. Shoup. Surrounded by trees, flowers and gardens, the decor is Victorian, with large windows in all rooms.

One cottage has a private bath; two large rooms have queen-sized beds; one has a double bed; one has a single bed; one has two beds. Five rooms share two large bathrooms, one for the men and one for the ladies.

Continental breakfast plus homemade muffins, juices, fruits, breakfast casseroles, teas, and coffee.

The city of Salmon is located near The River Of No Return. For recreation, try your hand at fishing, whitewater rafting, hiking, golfing, swimming and touring the area's ghost towns.

Rates - **$$**   Map Location - NE

SANDPOINT, IDAHO

Angel Of The Lake
410 Railroad Avenue
Sandpoint, Idaho 83864
(208) 263-0816

About 100 years ago, Sandpoint's first mayor built himself a beautiful home. Now, the Angel Of The Lake is a very special guest house that takes you back in time.. Enjoy a peaceful waterfront setting on beautiful Lake Pend Oreille, or take a short walk to downtown Sandpoint, the Cedar Street Bridge or the City Beach.

The house offers four classic motion-picture theme rooms. Choose from "Gone with the Wind," with its oversized antique tub and Mediterranean feeling, "Casablanca," with its plants and lace canopy, the rustic "African Queen," with its mosquito netting and artifacts, or "Blazing Saddles," with its Old West hotel ambiance.

Enjoy a full gourmet breakfast and try the hot tub under the stars. Summer activities include fishing, sailing, waterskiing, swimming, golfing and hiking. In the winter, visit Schweitzer for skiing, snowmobiling, sleigh riding, ice fishing or ice skating.

Rates - **$$**   Map Location - NW

SHOSHONE, IDAHO

Governor's Mansion
315 Greenwood, P.O. Box 326
Shoshone, Idaho 83352
(208) 886-2858

This private mansion was built by Frank R. Gooding, governor of Idaho from 1901-1905, and is on the list of National Historic Sites. Frank Gooding was one of several brothers known as "Sheep Barons" in the heyday of Idaho's sheep industry.

Now an authentic bed & breakfast, the Governor's Mansion offers good cooking in a comfortable home atmosphere.

One room with private bath and five rooms with shared bath.

Full country breakfast included.

Shoshone is within easy traveling distance to Sun Valley, Ketchum, Craters of the Moon, Balance Rock, The Ice Caves, Shoshone Falls, Stanley Basin, Red Fish Lake, and the Magic Valley Antique Trail. This region is famous for its trout fishing, and big-game and migratory bird hunting.

Rate - **$ to $$**   Map Location - SW

SUN VALLEY, IDAHO

Idaho Country Inn
P.O. Box 2355
Sun Valley, Idaho 83353
(208) 726-1019

The Idaho Country Inn is in world-famous Sun Valley, founded by Mountain Pioneers and Averill Harriman. This newly constructed inn is mountain-lodge style, made of logs and river rocks.

Spacious rooms with private baths. King- and queen-sized beds, remote-control TV, refrigerators, telephones and fantastic views.

Enjoy whitewater rafting, fishing, hunting, hiking, skiing, tennis, and golfing.

Rates - **$$$ to $$$$**   Map Location - SE

The River Street Inn
P.O. Box 182
Sun Valley, Idaho 83353
(208) 726-3611

The world-famous ski resort of Sun Valley is a mile from Ketchum, Bald Mountain, and the ski lifts are just four blocks from this inn. Ketchum is an old mining and sheep shipping town with a Western flavor. Historic sights, shops and galleries abound.

Architectural features such as nooks, asymmetrical lines on different levels, beveled edges and moldings make for a rich, elegant look. The inn has nine rooms, all with spacious baths—eight with Japanese soaking tubs and one with regular tub.

Full breakfast with a choice of hot entrees, such as Magic Omelet or lemon ricotta pancakes and raspberry butter.

Enjoy skiing, skating, horseback riding, tennis, golfing, fishing, bike riding, balloon riding, whitewater rafting, and touring spectacular mountains, creeks and the Sawtooth National Recreational Area.

Rates - **$$$ to $$$$**   Map Location - SE

BETTER
Bed
& Breakfast
Inns

MONTANA

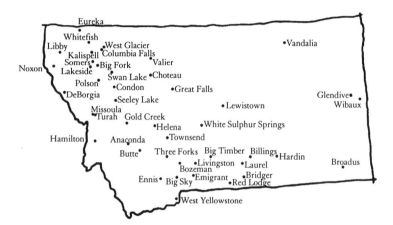

ANACONDA, MONTANA

Hickory Suites Bed & Breakfast
522 Hickory Street
Anaconda, Montana 59711
(406) 563-6422

Hickory Suites was built in 1893 for Zenas Evans, the father-in-law of Montana's copper magnate, Marcus Daly. The two-story Victorian mansion still retains original carved ceilings, molding and woodwork. The inn has two suites, one with a king-sized bed and the other with a queen-sized bed. Both have private baths, phones and cable TV. Breakfast might include apple walnut French toast, muffins, fresh fruit, granola, yogurt, coffee, tea, juice and breakfast meats.

Things to do: Fishing, hunting, skiing, hiking, rafting, boating, horseback riding, golfing, wildlife viewing and photography.

Rates - $$ Map Location - SW

Pintler Inn
Georgetown Lake, P.O. Box 217
Anaconda, Montana 59711
(406) 563-6546

The Pintler Inn is new, with a country-Western theme and a 360-degree view overlooking Georgetown Lake and the Pintler Mountains. It has four guest rooms, three with private baths and one with a shared bath. Breakfast included.

While you're here, enjoy skiing, fishing, hunting, boating, canoeing and golfing. You also may want to discover the history behind Anaconda, which has many historical buildings, including the courthouse and the Washoe Theater.

Rates - $$ Map Location - SW

BIGFORK, MONTANA

Burggraf's Countrylane Bed & Breakfast
Rainbow Drive on Swan Lake
Bigfork, Montana 59911
(406) 837-4608, (406) 837-2468 or 1-800-525-3344

Bigfork is a quaint town with wonderful restaurants and art galleries, as well as a summer playhouse.

You will relax in a true 5,000-square-foot log home overlooking a panoramic view of the Rocky Mountains that is reflected in the expanse of Swan Lake. Walk through acres of tall trees, listen to the many species of birds, sunbathe by the lake at the picnic area or take a dip in the water.

The master suite has a king-sized bed, spacious room with private bath. The Jacuzzi/whirlpool suite has a king-sized bed, Jacuzzi/whirlpool tub or walk-in shower and private bath. Two additional guest rooms have queen-sized beds and private baths, and another has a twin bed and private bath.

Full country breakfast features all you can eat, and trays of fresh fruit and hors d'oeuvres are served daily.

Guests enjoy swimming, fishing, canoeing, hiking, boating, and lawn croquet. Burggraf's is just minutes from Flathead Lake and an hour from Glacier National Park.

Rates - $$ Map Location - NW

Cherry Way Inn
P.O. Box 1255
Bigfork, Montana 59911
(406) 837-6803

The Cherry Way Inn Bed & Breakfast, located in the quiet hamlet of Woods Bay, is one of the latest attractions overlooking Flathead Lake. Just five miles south of the historic town of Bigfork, this inn has a unique history of its own.

It was built as a saloon and house of ill repute during the early 1930s. Accommodating the working man along east lake shore, the Cherry Way Inn was the talk of the area.

The five bedrooms are done in a charming rustic style, with emphasis on comfort and relaxation. Four have queen beds and one has twin beds. The large living area is complete with pool table and lending library; and the original bar still exists.

Your stay begins with a social hour, at which fresh fruit, cheese, and complimentary wine are served.

Breakfast includes homemade bread, pastries, fresh fruit and a hearty entree.

While you're in the area, try fishing, rafting, sailing, swimming or playing golf on one of the six challenging courses. You won't want to miss strolling through the historic town of Bigfork, where you'll find galleries, novelty shops, restaurants and the summer playhouse. Most activities are within walking distance or 10 minutes from the Cherry Way Inn, and none are more than 45 minutes away.

Rates - $ Map Location - NW

Jubilee Orchards Lake Resort
Sylvan Drive
Bigfork, Montana 59911
(406) 837-4256

Jubilee Orchards is a custom home with 200 feet of private beach on Flathead Lake. The lower level has large picture windows, a large recreation room with a stone fireplace, and a complete kitchen. Patios, decks and picnic tables allow you to enjoy the lake while you dine.

An extensive library will fill your quiet moments, and your hosts will help make arrangements for your explorations of the area—including dining and theatre outings.

The inn has three rooms, all with private baths, private entrances, patios and access to the kitchen and large recreation room.

To your hearty breakfast, add homemade rolls, muffins, jams, crepes, waffles, pancakes, cereal and fresh fruit, or start your day with lighter fare, as you choose.

The recreational opportunities are endless—including fishing, boating, canoeing, wildlife viewing, waterskiing, photography and hiking. Visit Glacier National Park or golf in Bigfork, home of the No. 2 nationally rated public golf course, Eagle Bend.

Rates - $$ Map Location - NW

O' Duach' ain Country Inn
675 Ferndale Drive
Bigfork, Montana 59911
(406) 837-6851

O' Duach' ain is a gracious three-level, authentic log home, set on five beautiful acres in Ferndale, five miles from Bigfork Village, Montana.

Suites are in a separate log building, and there's an outdoor hot tub and spa. Large balconies enhance the spectacular view, and two rock fireplaces provide cozy warmth. O' Duach' ain means peaceful, discreet, luxurious solitude for travelers and vacationers.

The charming home, decorated with eclectic furniture, artifacts and artistry, provides a lodge atmosphere, lovely rooms, bath, relaxation and game area, conversation and entertainment center, and access to boating, fishing, swimming, walking and trail riding. Winter lends a glorious snow blanket for alpine and Nordic skiing.

The grounds feature a pond, wildflowers, exotic birds, wild game, waterfowl, a pristine landscape, horses and a miniature donkey.

While you're here, visit Glacier National Park, Flathead Lake, National Bison Range, Historic Jesuit Mission, Bob Marshall Wilderness, Swan Lake, Big Mountain Ski Area, Bigfork Summer Theatre, Jewel Basin, Elk Glen Farm, and four world-class restaurants.

Rates - $$ Map Location - NW

Schwartz Bed & Breakfast
890 McCaffery Road
Bigfork, Montana 59911
(406) 837-5463

Schwartz Bed & Breakfast is located near Flathead Lake and Glacier National Park. The area also has four great golf courses, restaurants and many resident artists and galleries.

The inn has two bedrooms, a living room and one shared bath. One bedroom has a double bed and shared bath, and the other is a suite with a double bed.

Full breakfast with fresh fruit and homemade baked goods.

Enjoy fishing, whitewater rafting, hunting, photography, wildlife viewing, and the National Bison Range.

Rates - $ to $$ Map Location - NW

BIG SKY, MONTANA

Rainbow Ranch Lodge
P.O. Box 160336
Big Sky, Montana 59716
(406) 995-4132

Originally a 160-acre dude ranch, the Rainbow Ranch Lodge was built in 1957 on five and a half acres of Gallatin River frontage.

Located five miles south of Big Sky and 11 miles from the remote northwest corner of Yellowstone Park, Rainbow Ranch abounds with the rustic charm and breathtaking beauty of the Montana Rockies.

With the fantastic Gallatin National Forest as its back yard, the all-season waterfront lodge is Big Sky's only bed & breakfast. The gracious and experienced staff will help you make the right choices for your recreational fun and sporting activities. And you are just minutes from fine dining, elegant shops and great outdoor activities.

The lodge has 12 bedrooms, each with a private bath. Enjoy the sun deck and outdoor spa. Relax in the sun-drenched lounge with fireplace and regional library.

Full breakfast buffet includes beverage.

Enjoy blue-ribbon trout fishing, horseback riding, hiking, whitewater rafting and mountain biking. Information available about day rides or pack trips.

Rates - $ to $$ Map Location - SW

BIG TIMBER, MONTANA

The Grand Bed & Breakfast
P.O. Box 1242
Big Timber, Montana 59011
(406) 932- 4459

Built in 1890 and now listed in the National Register of Historic Places, the original dignity of The Grand recently was restored.

Preceded by an established tradition of fine dining, The Grand Bed & Breakfast offers original hotel rooms, dressed in their Victorian best—high ceilings, sunlit rooms with period furnishings, and modern conveniences. It's all set in the sociable travel atmosphere of the era, with delightfully cozy sitting rooms, where you may take breakfast, as you might in the comfort of your own home.

The Grand has seven rooms, two with private baths and five with shared baths.

Enjoy the breathtaking beauty of the Crazy Mountains, head up south for a day of hiking, fishing and horseback riding in the Boulder River Valley, or sit on the bank of the Yellowstone River or one of the blue-ribbon trout streams and watch for the deer, antelope, fox and coyote. Don't forget to bring your camera and plenty of film!

Rates - $$ Map Location - SE

BILLINGS, MONTANA

The Josephine Bed & Breakfast
514 N. 29th Street
Billings, Montana 59101
(406) 248-5898

This lovely, historic home is comfortably elegant. The porch, with it's swing and quaint seating, is the ideal place for breakfast or just relaxing. Charming picket fences, shade trees and flowers add to the delightful ambiance. Each room is individually decorated with antiques, collectibles and old photographs.

The Josephine Bed & Breakfast has four rooms, one with a private bath and three with a shared bath. Full breakfast is included.

Things to do: Fishing, rafting, hiking, rodeo, photography, tennis and golf, skiing, museums, galleries, theaters and shopping. You're just an hour from Little Bighorn Battlefield, and Yellowstone National Park is just three hours away via scenic Beartooth Pass.

Rates - $ to $$ Map Location - SE

Pinehill Place Bed & Breakfast
4424 Pinehill Drive
Billings, Montana 59101
(406) 252-0313 or (406) 252-2288

Pinehill Place has a two-bedroom cabin with bath and shower.
Breakfast included.

Close to Yellowstone Park, Little Bighorn Battlefield, plus fishing, hunting, skiing and rafting.

Rates - $ to $$ Map Location - SE

BOZEMAN, MONTANA

Bergfeld Bed & Breakfast Home
8515 Sypes Canyon Road
Bozeman, Montana 59715
(406) 586-7778

Bergfeld (German for mountain field) sits on sunny Montana acreage, where guests enjoy a sweeping 360-degree view of five mountain ranges and the Gallatin River Valley.

Deer and other wildlife frequent the property, and a national-forest trail just up the road, past the neighbor's farm of llamas, goats and other critters. The Sypes Canyon Trail is a refreshing step into a wilderness of aspen slopes and pine forest.

Relax in the hot tub after the day's activities, or lounge in the comfortable living room. An array of interesting books and magazines are at arm's reach.

All rooms have private bathrooms and mountain views.

Cottonwood Room: Pine furnishings, Montana sporting theme. Queen bed and queen sleeper.

Spruce Room: Handmade queen bed, pine and wicker decor. Great sunset views. Nature lover's theme.

Lodgepole Room: Log queen bed and antique furnishings. Country charm with a vaulted ceiling.

Willow Room: Studio apartment with full kitchen. Western motif.

Start your day off right with a hearty breakfast at the Wagon Wheel table. Watch the sun rise over the Bridger Mountains, while you enjoy piping hot coffee, fresh juices, warm pastries and special egg dishes.

Yellowstone National Park, the Gallatin National Forest, and six blue ribbon trout streams are all less than an hour away; Bridger Bowl and Big Sky ski areas are even closer. Cross-country skiing is available at nearby prepared trails, and your hosts can arrange for guided tours, fishing, hunting and other excursions.

Rates - $$ Map Location - SW

Miller of Montana Bed & Breakfast Inn
1002 Zacharia Lane
Bozeman, Montana 59715
(406) 763-4102

Miller of Montana is a Cape Cod style home on 20 acres, with a beautiful view of Montana's landscape from every window!

The inn is 12 miles south of Bozeman, en route to West Yellowstone, and is two miles from the Gallatin Gateway.

The Rose Room, on the main floor, has a queen bed with lace half canopy, antiques, shared bath, and a great view.

The Blue Room has a double bed with antique white wicker headboard, white wicker chairs and table, shared bath, and a spectacular view of Spanish Peaks from its second-floor window.

The Green Room, upstairs, has two antique single beds, antique mirrored dresser, dormer and gabled ceiling, and shared bath.

The Peach Suite has a queen-sized antique bed, large dresser decorated in peach-colored, dried-flower wreaths and other crafts, dormer and gabled ceiling with private shower/bath. It is upstairs.

Enjoy breakfast in the sunlit breakfast room, formal dining room, or your room.

Miller of Montana is close to Big Sky Ski Resort, Bridger Bowl Ski Resort, Yellowstone National Park, Montana State University, and the Museum of the Rockies, plus fishing, hiking, and biking opportunities.

Rates - $$ Map Location - SW

Our Neck O' the Woods
603 West Babcock
Bozeman, Montana 59715
(406) 587-2621 or (406) 58R-BNB1

Centrally located in the Cooper Park Historic District, this 50-year-old inn is within minutes of the Museum of the Rockies, Montana State University, city parks, churches, unique shops in historic downtown Bozeman, and fine cuisine, not to mention local theaters, the Bozeman Symphony, Intermountain Opera and Montana Ballet Company.

You're also just a short drive from Yellowstone National Park, Lewis and Clark Caverns, Big Sky Summer and Winter Resort, Lone Mountain Summer and Winter Guest Ranch and Bridger Bowl Alpine Area. Fishing, hunting, rafting, wildlife viewing and photography opportunities are nearby as well.

The Inn has two bedrooms, one with a shared bath and the other with a private bath.

Breakfast is full or Continental.

Rates - $$ to $$$ Map Location - SW

Silver Forest Inn
15325 Bridger Canyon Road
Bozeman, Montana 59715
(406) 586-1882

The Silver Forest Inn is nestled among the pines at the base of the spectacular Bridger Range in South Central Montana. It is just minutes from excellent alpine ski slopes and cross-country trails. The fully restored, historic log-hewn inn features five charming, country-style guest rooms, plus hot tubs, delicious breakfasts, and warm Western hospitality.

Relax by the fire and enjoy the panoramic view of the Bridgers through the living room and turret windows, or join in any of the exciting year-round activities your hosts have available for you. Enjoy fishing, hunting, horsepacking, mountain biking, hiking, skiing and photography.

McKinney Room: A dusty rose suite with a touch of romantic charm. Queen bed with tub and shower.

Forest Room: A rustic room rich with wood and handwoven rugs. Two queen beds, tub, shower and closet.

Amber Room: A warm room with sporting motif. Queen bed, closet and shared bath.

Turret Room: Intimate log-hewn room with a panoramic view of the Bridger Mountains. Queen bed and shared bath.

Bridger View Room: Secluded room with mountain and forest views. Queen bed, and private bath and entrance.

Rates - $$ Map Location - SW

Torch & Toes Bed & Breakfast
309 South Third Avenue
Bozeman, Montana 59715
(406) 586-7285

The Torch & Toes has four guest rooms, all with private baths. A full breakfast is served daily.

Bozeman was founded in the 1860s, during the Montana Gold Rush and became a mercantile center and agricultural center because the land that surrounds it is flat and fertile.

This area is a fisherman's dream come true. Enjoy the hiking, hunting, skiing, museums and old ghost towns as well.

Rates - $$ Map Location - SW

Voss Inn Bed & Breakfast
319 S. Willson
Bozeman, Montana 59715
(406) 587-0982

The Voss Inn, a Victorian home restored in 1984, originally was built by a prominent businessman as a private residence in 1883. It has six guest rooms, all with private baths.

Full breakfast and afternoon tea served.

Enjoy the blue-ribbon trout fishing, wildlife viewing, hiking, skiing and your innkeeper's own photographic tours.

Rates - $$ Map Location - SW

BRIDGER, MONTANA

Circle of Friends Bed & Breakfast
Rt. 1 Box 1250
Bridger, Montana 59014
(406) 662-3264

Circle of Friends is a three-bedroom bed & breakfast on 24 acres in the Clark's Fork Valley. It's just a two-hour drive from Yellowstone Park via the scenic Beartooth Highway and is an hour from Red Lodge Ski Area, Yellowstone Dam, Bighorn Canyon National Recreation area, Pryor Mountains, and Cody, Wyoming. This is truly the heart of the finest recreation in the Northwest.

Bridger sits in a beautiful irrigated valley. To the east are Pryor Mountains, home of more than 100 free-roaming mustangs, plus fossil hunting and backcountry riding opportunities. West of this farming community rises the rugged Beartooth Range. A drive from Red Lodge to Cooke City offers sky-top views of peaks, glaciers, lakes and plateaus—69 miles drive of unforgettable beauty. Bridger is a rich farming community; the irrigated soil grows alfalfa, pinto beans, malt barley and sugar beets. This is a small town of fewer than 1,000 people who work hard, smile often and are friendly to guests.

The Circle of Friends Bed & Breakfast has three bedrooms—one large bedroom with private bath, and two others with a shared bath.

A full breakfast is served; special attention is given to individual needs. Homemade waffles, sourdough pancakes and quiche are among the specialties.

Rates - $ Map Location - SE

BROADUS, MONTANA

Oakwood Lodge
South Pumpkin Creek Road
Broadus, Montana 59317
(406) 427-5475

Oakwood Lodge was built, in 1990, out of solid-oak logs attached to the existing home by hard working friends, neighbors and family. The lodge's three guest rooms are clean, spacious and each has a private bath. The Duck Room has a comfy queen bed, while the Sunset Room has two single beds and the country Blue Room has an antique double bed.

In the lodge's Great Room, gather 'round the cozy stove on a chilly evening, watch video or TV or just visit with friends in the sitting area. In the dining area, hearty country breakfasts are served, family-style. A gift shop of local craftsmen's wares is part of the lodge as well. A quiet reading area and library with lots of local history is located in the loft, and a large bunkhouse suitable for families, with private half bath, shower, refrigerator, table and chairs, also is available.

Enjoy hiking, fishing, hunting, skiing, photography, hay rides, wildlife viewing and rock hounding.

Rates - $ Map Location - SE

BUTTE, MONTANA

Copper King Mansion
219 West Granite Street
Butte, Montana 59701
(406) 782-7580

The Copper King Mansion has been owned, operated, and occupied by the Cote family for four generations. Recognizing the historical value of the mansion, the family has endeavored to keep the home in its original state.

Solely funded by tours, bed and breakfast guests, and catered events, preservation of the W.A. Clark Mansion continues to this day. It originally was built in 1884 as the home of Montana Sen. William Andrews Clark.

Here, you'll step back in time more than 100 years to visit the home of a man who truly appreciated quality and master craftsmanship and had an exquisite sense of beauty.

His foresight in using the best techniques and materials of his day has made it possible for the mansion to survive to this day.

Master Suite: Sleep in the same rooms that Sen. Clark used. The suite includes the master bedroom and a private bath. It features sycamore woodwork, a burled walnut bed and matching dresser. The sitting room is graced with a birds-eye maple fireplace mantle and 100-year-old applique on French net curtains. The spacious master bathroom has a huge bathtub and a remarkable collection of antique combs and beaded purses.

Blue Room: Originally the Clark's family room on the second floor of the mansion, the room has been converted into a bedroom. This spacious room boasts a handpainted frescoed watercolor ceiling and its own half bath.

Rose Room: Originally one of the Clark children's bedrooms, this room has been elegantly decorated with an exquisite rose motif. Private sink in room.

Gold Room: Light and airy, this room features furnishings from the 1920s. In addition, the bed belonged to Club Foot George, a notorious outlaw in the early history of Montana. Private sink in room.

Butler's Bedroom: The butler had the privilege of being the only servant to live on the same floor as the Clark family. The room built for him is best described as "snug and cozy".

Enjoy fishing, skiing, hiking, wildlife viewing, hunting and photography.

Rates - $$ Map Location - SW

Raven Crest
844 W. Broadway Street
Butte, Montana 59701
(406) 782-1055

The Raven Crest, a three-story red brick Victorian, was built in 1891 by August Christian, chief engineer for the copper mine.

During the 1880s, Butte became the world's biggest copper producer. The mine still is in production today, and Butte now is known as the richest hill on Earth.

Full breakfast with special attention to dietary needs.

In Butte, you're within an hour of the finest fly-fishing in America. Or take a day trip to Glacier or Yellowstone national parks.

Rates - $$ Map Location - SW

CHOTEAU, MONTANA

Country Lane Bed & Breakfast
Route 2 Box 232
Choteau, Montana 59422
(406) 466-2816 or (505) 299-4468 - Winter

Country Lane is a modern bed & breakfast that reflects the peace, beauty and charm of Montana, while offering pure comfort and gracious hospitality.

A sign at the private lane directs guests to a contemporary split-level home of cedar and shake construction with vaulted ceilings and exposed beams. The cedar interior creates a cozy country feeling, and this spacious home has three fireplaces, an organ, and plenty of magazines for your enjoyment. Guests are welcome to swim in the indoor solar heated pool adjacent to the living room, or sit on the patio furniture outside and enjoy a barbecue.

As Country Lane is located on 58 wooded acres on the Spring Creek Game Preserve, it's common to see does and their fawns from your windows before breakfast or from the decks and patios at dusk. A gift shop features fine art and handmade clay sculptures, as well as jewelry and wearables. Shipping is available.

Five large guest rooms are available:. The Country Garden has a king-sized bed, TV, and a private deck; the Country Salsa has a king bed; the Country Plaid has queen and single beds; the Country Lace has a queen-sized bed; and the Country Tulips room has a single bed.

A full country breakfast—featuring fresh fruit, juice, coffee, tea, fresh baked breads, rolls, muffins and popovers— is served in the dining room. You'll also get a main dish, such as quiche, strata or homemade waffles with fruit and cream.

Enjoy wildlife viewing, photography, fishing, swimming, boating, waterskiing and picnicking.

Rates - $ to $$ Map Location - NW

COLUMBIA FALLS, MONTANA

Bad Rock Country Bed & Breakfast
480 Bad Rock Drive
Columbia Falls, Montana 59912
(406) 892-2829 or 1-800-422-3666

The Bad Rock Country Bed & Breakfast is an elegant country home on 30 acres, just 15 miles from the entrance to Glacier National Park. Look out on the majestic 7,200-foot-high Columbia Mountain two miles away and the majestic peaks of Glacier National Park. This beautiful valley is surrounded by open fields and groves of tall pine trees.

This inn is located near all of Flathead Valley's fabulous activities, including hiking, fishing, golfing, whitewater rafting, horseback riding, cross-country and downhill skiing and snowmobiling.

Three guest rooms have queen-sized beds, private baths, phones, living rooms, and Old West antiques, and hot-tub time is reserved exclusively for each guest.

Full hearty Montana style breakfast featuring fare such as Montana potato pie, huckleberry muffins and buffalo steaks.

Rates - $$ Map Location - NW

CONDON, MONTANA

33-Bar Ranch Bed & Breakfast
Hultman Road, P.O. Box 1068
Condon, Montana 59826
(406) 754-2820

The 33-Bar Ranch is located between the Bob Marshall and the Mission Mountain wilderness areas, giving access to 2.6 million acres of some of the world's most pristine wilderness. In the valley proper, less than 6 percent of the property is privately owned—U.S. Forest Service land adjoins the ranch on two sides, and you can ride on horseback from the ranch directly into "the Bob."

The 33-Bar's main lodge was built of logs in 1933 by skilled woodsmen. Each log is 45 feet long, has no splices, and is hand polished. The ranch offers modern conveniences in an old-fashioned setting. And if you like to relax with a good book, the library material dates back to the 1920s.

The 33-Bar has five guest rooms both, some with private baths and some with shared ones. Separate, full housekeeping, log guest chalet with breathtaking views of the Swan and Mission ranges also is available.

Sit around the kitchen table and watch the ranch-style breakfast being prepared on the Elmira wood cookstove.

Enjoy wildlife, hunting, fishing, horseback riding, hiking, mountain biking, pack trips and cross-country skiing.

Rates - $$ Map Location - NW

DeBORGIA, MONTANA

Hotel Albert Bed & Breakfast
P.O. Box 30018
DeBorgia, Montana 59830
(406) 678-4303

Built in 1911, the Hotel Albert is a fine example of frontier spirit and late Victorian decor. Located in the Bitteroot Mountains and the Lolo National Forest, you'll be near U.S. Forest Service trails for hiking and mountain biking.

A car tour will take you to the "World's famous $10,000 Bar," just 2 miles away, plus river rafting, canoeing and fishing on the Clark Fork River 14 miles to the east, or one of the best antique stores in Montana, in St. Regis.

The Hotel Albert Bed & Breakfast has four bedrooms and two baths.

Continental breakfast is served.

The area's activities include fishing, hunting, hiking, wildlife photography, cross-country and downhill skiing, to name just a few.

Rates - $ Map Location - SW

EMIGRANT, MONTANA

Paradise Gateway Bed & Breakfast
P.O. Box 84
Emigrant, Montana 59027
(406) 333-4063

Paradise Gateway Bed & Breakfast, nestled in the majestic Absaroka Mountains, is just minutes from Yellowstone National Park. The surrounding area boasts a milieu of activities, including hiking, horseback riding, fishing, rafting, windsurfing, sightseeing and much more. The inn is spacious and sits on the banks of the pristine Yellowstone River, a blue-ribbon trout stream.

Just down the road, you can enjoy fine dining or relax in the natural spas at Chico Hot Springs Resort. The Paradise Getaway is a great stopover if your journey takes you on to Bozeman, Big Sky, Flathead Lake or Glacier National Park. It offers two quiet, comfortable guest rooms, with a shared bath and relaxing parlor.

The Wildflower Room: A comfortable queen-sized antique bed greets you in this bright, cheery room. Complete with homemade quilts, antiques and river views.

The Blueberry Patch Room: Decorated in Country English with a queen-sized antique Rice bed. Snuggle under the quilts at night and open your eyes to Emigrant Peak in the morning.

Enjoy breakfast by the banks of the Yellowstone: Choose from a "Hearty Country" or a "Healthy & Light" menu. Fresh flowers adorn the dining table each morning.

Rates - $$ Map Location - SE

ENNIS, MONTANA

9T9 Ranch Bed & Breakfast
99 Gravelly Range Road
Ennis, Montana 58729
(406) 682-7659

High in the Northern Rockies of southwest Montana flows the famous Madison

River, rushing to the headwaters of the mighty Missouri. Midway along its run—in the valley near the old frontier town of Ennis—nestles the 9T9 Ranch. From the house deck overlooking the river's edge, experience a 50-mile view of the Madison Mountain Range, snowcapped most of the year. Enjoy the peaceful solitude of the meadows where the deer and antelope really do play. This is Big Sky Country at its finest.

The 9T9 Ranch provides spacious rooms furnished with family antiques and an eye toward rural comfort. The guest level of the house has its own living room, providing privacy and an atmosphere made for genuine rest and relaxation.

Rose Room: Double bed and shared bath. This lovely room is decorated with pink roses, lilacs and white eyelet lace. It is spacious, with an over-stuffed chair, and presents a view of the lawn and garden and the Gravelly Mountain Range.

Bunk House Room: Bunk beds and shared bath. This smaller room has a seashell decor and is perfect for children or fishermen. It features a rocking chair and lamp for comfy reading, plus a view of the lawn and garden.

River Room: Twin beds and private bath. This charming room has a wondrous view of the river and mountains and features a Western motif.

Breakfast is served at your convenience, and features fresh-baked pastries, granola and fruit bowl and sumptuous omelets with hash browns, or biscuits and gravy served with eggs, a Montana favorite.

The 9T9 Ranch offers a wide range of activities. A four-minute walk steers you to the river's premier rainbow- and brown-trout fishing. Your hosts have boats, rafts and other sportsmen's equipment and services for float trips.

Visit nearby Virginia and Nevada cities, sites of gold rush and vigilante fame. Play golf at Ennis; soak in Norris Hot Springs; and enjoy photography, hiking, mountain biking, or hunting in the Gravelly Range, where deer, elk, antelope, moose and grouse abound. Yellowstone is just 60 miles away.

Guests are invited to help gather eggs or harvest the vegetables at the 9T9 Ranch if they'd like.

Rates - $ to $$ Map Location - SW

EUREKA, MONTANA

Trail's End Bed & Breakfast
57 Trail's End Road
Eureka, Montana 59917
(406) 889-3486

Trail's End Bed & Breakfast is located six miles northwest of Eureka, the town known by some as the "Christmas Tree Capital of the World." Snuggled in the To-

The Whitney on Fifth Avenue, Kalispell, MT

bacco Valley, Eureka is 70 miles north of Kalispell and eight miles south of the Canadian border at Roosville. Sophie, Moran, Tetrault and Koocanusa are just a few of the nearby lakes, where trout, bass and salmon are in abundance. Ice fishing is popular in the winter.

Trail's End is just two miles from the Tobacco Plains boat ramp on Lake Koocanusa, and there's plenty of room to park your boat in the inn's yard during your stay. Part of the attraction to this area is the elk, deer and moose hunting. Just a few miles of driving puts you on public land or on private land, where you can hunt with permission.

This bed and breakfast is in a three-level Amish designed log home, with a wrap-around covered deck and a beautiful view of the Canadian Rockies. The loft has two bedrooms and a shared bath tucked under the eaves. The ground level features three bedrooms and a shared bath.

Cooking is ranch style, with specialty sourdough pancakes. Coffee is a special blend, fresh-ground in either regular or decaf.

Rates - $ to $$ Map Location - SE

GLENDIVE, MONTANA

The Hostetler House Bed & Breakfast
113 North Douglas Street
Glendive, Montana, 59330
(406) 365-4505

The Hostetler House is a charming 1912 historic home with two comfortable guest rooms, done in a casual country decor. Relax in the hot tub and gazebo, the sitting room full or books, the enclosed sun porch, or on the deck. Watch color cable TV or movies in the living room, or play board games at the dining-room table.

Wake up to the smell of fresh-ground gourmet coffee, tea and homemade breads and muffins.

The Hostetler House is located one block from rafting or floating on the Yellowstone River and two blocks from downtown shopping and restaurants. It also is close to parks, a swimming pool, tennis courts and churches.

Other possible activities and points of interest in Glendive include a golf course, antique shops, a water-slide park, Dawson Community College, a museum, fishing, hunting, cross-country skiing, hiking, or just enjoying the prehistoric landscape amid the fossils at Makoshika.

Rates - $ Map Location - SE

GOLD CREEK, MONTANA

L.H. Ranch Bed & Breakfast
471 Mullan Trail
Gold Creek, Montana 59733
(406) 288-3436

The L.H. Ranch Bed & Breakfast is in a log house, built in 1970 to replace the original 1850 house that burned down. This was one of the first bed & breakfast inns in Montana, and sits on the Mullan Trail.

It is located in historical surroundings, where gold first was discovered. It also is the location where east met west on the railroad, and where the last rail-road spike was driven. While you're here, visit ghost towns, national forests and the ranch museum.

Stay in one of two guest rooms, each of which has a double bed and semi-private bath.

Breakfast is organically grown.

Enjoy cross-country skiing, hiking, horseback riding, swimming, fishing, hunting, birdwatching, and photography.

Rates - $ to $$ Map Location - SW

GREAT FALLS, MONTANA

The Chalet Bed & Breakfast Inn
1204 Fourth Avenue North
Great Falls, Montana 59401
(406) 452-9001 or 1-800-786-9002

Reflecting Great Falls' historic past, this former governor's Victorian chalet is alive with the wealth of detail that was fashionable in the early 1900s. Beautifully preserved interior appointments include warm dark wood, high-beamed ceiling, French doors and leaded glass. New improvements retain old-world charm, while providing modern comforts.

Linger on the carriage entry Veranda, or rev up the barbecue by the miniature pond. Spring buds, autumn foliage or branches dressed in sparkling white finery create seasonal artistry.

Make yourself at home in one of six unique guest rooms, which vary from quaint and cozy to spacious and elegant. Help yourself to refreshments in the Butler's Pantry. Enjoy a delicious breakfast featuring local products. Curl up with a book next to a crackling fire, take part in a parlor game, watch a video, or visit and relax in the manner of a bygone era.

Across the street from The Chalet, enjoy the C.M. Russell Museum. Or take a car tour of Yellowstone and Glacier national parks. Other accessible outdoor activities include fishing, hunting, hiking, golf, tennis, skiing, and swimming.

Rates - $ to $$ Map Location - NW

The Sarah Bed & Breakfast Inn
626 Fourth Avenue
Great Falls, Montana 59401

As a guest of The Sarah, you will experience the simple elegance and quaint character of a grand Victorian mansion. The authentic historical residence, built in 1903 for Herman and Anne Afflebach, is endowed with warmth and character. Restored in 1989, this mansion features original maple hardwood floors, quarter-sawn oak woodwork, oak wainscoting, leaded-glass windows and decorative fireplaces.

Located on the original townsite of historical fourth Avenue North, The Sarah sits in the heart of Great Falls. Within walking distance is the famous C.M. Russell Museum, Gibson Park and the downtown area. You can also visit Yellowstone and Glacier national parks, and enjoy the area's fishing, hunting and rafting.

The Sarah includes six spacious guest rooms, each of which has a personality of its own.

Enjoy a full gourmet breakfast served in the wainscoted dining room, and linger over fresh-ground coffee while you read the morning paper.

Rates - $ to $$ Map Location - NW

Sovekammer Bed & Breakfast
1109 Third Avenue North
Great Falls, Montana 59401
(406) 453-6620

The Sovekammer, located in historical downtown Great Falls and built in the early 1900s, is furnished with antiques and collectibles.

Evergreen Room: With the look and feel of Christmas, this room features a queen bed, cable TV and private bath with tub/shower combination. Curl up on the plaid loveseat and soak in the warmth of red and green. The purple bathroom displays a matching purse and hat collection.

The Master Bedroom: This honeymooner's favorite will surprise and delight you, from the black floral wallpaper with accents of red and pink to the collection of hats and apparel from yesteryear. Includes queen bed, table for two, large closet and newly installed private bath with shower.

Guest Quarters: Springtime bright describes this room, with a full-sized bed and private bath—an old-fashioned tub sits right in your room. In cheery blue with splashes of flowers, this wallpaper will make you smile, and the coral carpet will welcome you. Treasures from the past are tastefully displayed throughout the room.

Brandee's Chamber: Wallpapered in burgundy and teal, this quaint room has one full-sized bed and one twin. The private bath in the hallway has the original claw-foot tub with added shower.

Full breakfast includes Danish family recipes.

Visit the C.M. Russell Museum, Giant Spring Park and the Great Falls at Ryan Dam, or enjoy fishing, hunting, photography, rafting and hiking.

Rates - $$ Map Location - NW

HAMILTON, MONTANA

Bavarian Farmhouse Bed & Breakfast
163 Bowman Road
Hamilton, Montana 59840
(406) 363-4063

This late-1800s traditional farmhouse has been remodeled so as to maintain its original country charm.

It has five bedrooms, each with a sink/vanity. Two rooms have queen beds and three have two doubles each. Four new baths.

Sit in the Bavarian dining room for a German farm breakfast of juice, cereals, boiled eggs, sliced cheeses, cold cuts, rolls, breads, jams, coffee and teas.

The Bavarian Farmhouse is encircled with big trees. The scenic Bitterroot Range of the Rockies Mountains is nearby, and the area affords plenty of space for hiking and biking, as well as national-forest access for fishing and big-game hunting. With advance notice, your hosts can arrange guided floats, fly-fishing trips, big-game hunts and pack trips on horseback.

Rates - $ Map Location - SW

HARDIN, MONTANA

Kendrick House Inn
206 N. Custer
Hardin, Montana 59034
(406) 665-3035

The Kendrick House Inn, built in 1914 by Elizabeth Kendrick, originally served as a boarding house. The Dec. 10, 1914 *Hardin Herald* of deemed it an "elegant new rooming house with hot and cold water in all the rooms." It was considered "strictly modern" for its time and locale.

In 1943, the Kendrick House was converted into Winn Hospital, which served the Hardin community until 1945.

It then was reverted to a room-and-board facility and, later, to private residences. The old rooming house stood empty and deteriorating from the 1970s until the current owners began restoring it in 1988. They filled it with period antiques and turn-of-the-century memorabilia to give it an authentic and romantic feel, and the Kendrick House now is listed on the National Register of Historic Buildings.

Guest areas include a library and TV room, an old porch swing on the first-floor veranda and a second-floor veranda. The comfortable living room lends itself to warm conversation with the host and other guests.

The Kendrick House Inn offers seven graciously decorated guest rooms that reflect turn-of-the-century living. Each room is furnished in a late Victorian style with comfy old-fashioned beds, antique dressers, period prints, framed lace, and memorabilia of yesteryear.

Two guest rooms on the main floor share a full old-fashioned bathroom with claw-foot bathtub, plus shower and pull-chain toilet. Five guest rooms on the second floor also share an old-fashioned bathroom with shower. Each room is equipped with a pedestal sink.

A hearty, homecooked Montana breakfast is served family-style in the formal dining room, with your choice of two settings. Coffee is always available.

The Kendrick House is uniquely situated in an area rich in Western history. Nearby are the Crow and Northern Cheyenne Indian Reservations, Fort Custer and Custer Battlefield, Bozeman Trail, Fort Phil Kearney and the abundant bird and wildlife watching opportunities for which Montana is famous. You'll also find blue-ribbon trout fishing and fabulous hunting opportunities, plus rafting, hiking, photography and mountain biking.

Rates - $ to $$ Map Location - SE

HELENA, MONTANA

The Barrister Bed & Breakfast
416 North Ewing
Helena, Montana 59601
(406) 443-7330

This 1874 Victorian mansion is centrally located in Montana's capital city. Enjoy more than 2,000 square feet of common area, featuring a parlor, formal dining room, den, TV room, library, office, air-conditioning and enclosed sun porch.

The original home of Herman Gans boasts six ornate fireplaces, original stained-glass windows, high ceilings and carved staircases. The magnificent St. Helena Cathedral is directly across the street, so don't forget your camera!

The five bedrooms are spacious and carefully decorated to provide an intimate atmosphere. All rooms have private baths, color TV and queen beds. The decor in each room varies from charmingly nostalgic to eloquent.

A full breakfast is served in the dining room or on the sun porch.

Take a car tour to Gates of the Mountains, Canyon Ferry Lake, Great Divide Ski

Area, Montana Historic Museum, State Capital, Old Govern's Mansion, ghost towns, and some of the greatest fishing and hunting Montana has to offer.

Rates - $$ Map Location - SW

KALISPELL, MONTANA

Blaine Creek Bed & Breakfast
727 Van Sant Road
Kalispell, Montana 59901
(406) 752-2519

Blaine Creek Bed & Breakfast is a Country Chalet with fireplaces, sauna, hot tub and beautiful mountain views.

It has three guest rooms—one with queen bed and private bath, one with double bed and shared bath, and one with twins beds and shared bath. Full breakfast included.

Blain Creek is just 20 minutes from West Glacier Park. Enjoy skiing, fishing, boating, hunting, swimming, rafting, hiking, biking and summer theater.

Rates - $ to $$ Map Location - NW

The Whitney On Fifth Avenue
538 Fifth Avenue East
Kalispell, Montana 59901
(406) 755-3456 or 1-800-426-3214

The Whitney will add the perfect touch of turn-of-the-century charm to your Montana visit. This stately red-brick mansion was built in 1910 and commands a corner of the finest street in town. It recalls bygone days of the young West, when a proud new city boasted private rail cars, remote buffalo herds, fancy balls and English pocket watches.

The inn reflects a rich past with a natural blend of Mission-Victorian, with Pennsylvania Dutch influences. Throughout the parlors are exquisite appointments of maple and oak. The two-story tower also features high bay windows, massive oak pocket doors, and a wrap-a-round porch with a classic view of green lawn and lush flower gardens, all framed by the wide Montana sky. The cozy library, the music room and the spacious living room are still scenes of friendly conversation.

This elegant 27-room mansion is filled with art and joy, and this is an area that emanates health, beauty and safety. The glorious snow-capped peaks of the Bob Marshall Wilderness can be glimpsed through the high-standing maples.

The staircase was crafted by a commissioned artisan from Chicago. Each bedroom is special, beginning with the master suite, with its own sitting parlor and distinctive jade-floored fireplace. Each room has a sense of privacy and the romance of soft evening air. The windows, original stained- or curved-glass, are complemented by unique furnishings.

At Whitney, you'll get an enchanting sense of another day, when time was counted in the slow ticking of the hallway clock and the measured hoof-beats of passing horses. Full sit-down breakfast with gourmet coffee, tea and fresh juice.

Enjoy rafting, horseback riding, hiking, fishing, hunting, boating, canoeing, Glacier National Park, antique stores, Flathead Lake, and the Bigfork Theater Playhouse.

Rates - **$$** to **$$$**   Map Location - NW

LAKESIDE, MONTANA

Deer Creek Inn
430 Deer Creek Road, P.O. Box 863
Lakeside, Montana 59922
(406) 857-2337

The Deer Creek Inn sits on 12 forested acres on the side of a mountain, with a fantastic view of Flathead Lake and the Mission Mountain Range. It is a large cedar home, with deer and horses feeding in the meadow, plus a firepit and large deck for your enjoyment.

The Inn has two guest rooms—one double and one single. Shared bath.

Breakfast includes homemade muffins, fresh fruit, pancakes, waffles, French toast, and assorted breakfast casseroles, all served with sausage or bacon.

Enjoy fishing, hunting, hiking, skiing, swimming, and Glacier National Park.

Rates - **$$**   Location - NW

LAUREL, MONTANA

Riverside Bed & Breakfast
2231 Thiel Road
Laurel, Montana 59044
(406) 628-7890 or 1-800-768-1580

The Riverside Bed & Breakfast is an old remodeled farmhouse. Just outside, you can fish on the Yellowstone River, linger with the llamas, or soak away your troubles in the screened-in hot tub. During breakfast, listen to the singing birds or the honking waterfowl. Play bocci or horseshoes in the back yard.

Garden Room: Large bedroom with queen bed. Bath with shower is across the hall.

Rose Room: Double bed with private bath.

Enjoy a delightful complimentary breakfast of juice, fruit, coffee or tea, and a main dish. Add eggs and toast, blue-ribbon "Healthy Homeground Homebaked Whole Wheat Honey" bread, egg quiche, sourdough pancakes, muffins, or tasty French toast.

Take a spin on the bicycle built for two, golf at the nearby 18-hole Laurel Golf Course or, in the winter, downhill or cross-country ski at nearby Red Lodge.

Rate - $ to $$ Map Location - SE

LEWISTOWN, MONTANA

Spring Creek Bed & Breakfast
HC 87 Box 5050, Heath Star Route
Lewistown, Montana 59457
(406) 538-9548

From the Spring Creek Bed & Breakfast, enjoy the scenic, quiet comfort over-looking beautiful Spring Creek. From the large deck, see beautiful hills and trees and watch the trout fishermen on the creek.

The deck is perfect for breakfast in warm weather, with birds, squirrels and rabbits surrounding you. Unique landscaping is surrounded by lush green hills for hiking. Or take a quiet walk along the creek.

The Spring Creek inn is near the Montana Fish Hatchery, a park-like area with picnic facilities and a pond of unusual fish to feed, and is a short drive from gold mines, the Belt Mountain camping areas, Crystal Lake, Camp Maiden, Maiden Canyon, and Warm Springs swimming and picnic area.

The Central Montana area is a hunters' and fishermen's paradise and a natural vacationland for the tourist and recreation enthusiast. Lewistown is in the center of the state, amid vast natural resources and beauty, plus business and industry. Lewistown exemplifies the hospitality and warmth that is so common to Montana.

The Spring Creek Bed & Breakfast offers two comfortable guest rooms, one with a double bed and one with twin beds. Shared bath. Downstairs is a family room with telephone and TV.

A full breakfast of juice, bacon, omelet, toast, homemade jams and coffee is served. Eat on the deck when weather permits.

Rates $ Map Location - NE

LIBBY, MONTANA

Kootenai Country Inn
264 Mack Road N. Hwy 37
Libby, Montana 59923
(406) 293-7878

The Kootenai is located in the country, on a 40-acre ponderosa forest but is just four miles from the Libby Shopping Center. The Kootenai River runs below the inn, and you can take trail walks or hike into the mountains from here.

One suite consists of a full kitchen and dining room area including a refrigerator and microwave, plus a large living room area with a large stone fireplace. The suite has a private entrance and views of the Cabinet Mountains through sliding-glass doors. Down the hall are three bedrooms, with private baths. Each has handmade quilts and antiques.

Wake up to a full ranch-style breakfast or Continental breakfast, your choice.

Your hosts also offer guided photography tours for a wilderness experience that likely will include deer, elk, moose, mountain lion, scenery, birds, waterfowl and a wealth of other small critters. Visit Libby Dam, Kootenai Falls, Cabinet Wilderness, Kootenai Springs Wildlife Museum and Heritage Museum.

Rates - $ to $$ Map Location - NW

LIVINGSTON, MONTANA

Greystone Inn Bed & Breakfast
122 South Yellowstone Street
Livingston, Montana 59047
(406) 222-8319 or (406) 222-8350

This turn-of-the-century inn was built of quarry sandstone and features hardwood floors, oak pillars, antiques, and leaded-glass windows. Whether your pleasure is to socialize, read, sightsee or just relax, Greystone offers a quiet, unhurried getaway.

Muriel's Room: Double bed and private bath, on the main floor.

Sunset Room: Double bed and shared bath, on the second floor.

Lockhart Room: Queen-sized bed and shared bath, on the second floor.

Sunrise Room: Queen-sized bed, daybed and shared bath, on the second floor.

A hearty country breakfast is served in the sunlit dining room.

Your hosts will be happy to help arrange guided fishing trips or a day's car tour of Yellowstone National Park. Try hiking, river rafting, hunting and mountain biking.

Rates - $ to $$ Map Location - SE

The Talcott House Bed & Breakfast
405 West Lewis
Livingston, Montana 59047
(406) 222-7699

The Talcott House is an elegant but unpretentious bed & breakfast, just three blocks from downtown Livingston, Montana. It was built in 1903 by the Talcott Family and now is on the National Historic Register. Tiffany lamps, wood parquet floors and chandeliers bring back the flavor of historic Livingston.

This inn includes five finely furnished bedrooms, one downstairs and four upstairs. Relax in the upstairs living room, or join others in front of a fire in the formal living room on the main floor. The Talcott House has a large yard and wide verandas for those who want to linger outdoors. Big screen cable TV, in-room phones and full exercise equipment are available, as well.

The Teal Room: Queen-sized bed and private bath, downstairs.

The Yellowstone Room: King-sized bed, shared bath and fireplace, upstairs.

The Lewis and Clark Room: Double bed, shared bath and fireplace, upstairs.

The Sleeping Giant: King-sized bed, private bath and superb view, upstairs.

The Suite: Queen-sized bed, double and single beds and private bath, upstairs.

A filling Montana breakfast is included.

Livingston is 50 miles north of Yellowstone National Park, has an upbeat Western atmosphere, plus great restaurants, galleries, shops and the fascinating Livingston Depot Museum. The Yellowstone River, Sacajawea Park, public golf course, tennis courts and swimming pool are within walking distance of the Talcott House.

Depending on the season, your hosts offer guided fishing on blue-ribbon trout streams. Or you may choose to try river rafting, mountain biking, cross-country or downhill skiing, or snowmobiling. Upland game bird and waterfowl hunts on private lands are offered through the inn's outfitting service.

Rates - $$ to $$$ Map Location - SE

MISSOULA, MONTANA

Goldsmith's Bed & Breakfast
809 E. Front Street
Missoula, Montana 59802
(406) 721-6732

Goldsmith's is a beautiful turn-of-the-century brick home on the banks of the Clark's Fork River. Next door is the inn's famous ice cream parlor and restaurant and four blocks away is downtown Missoula, with plenty of shops, good restaurants and friendly people. If you have business at the university, the nearby footbridge over the river provides a pleasant stroll to the campus.

Goldsmith's Bed & Breakfast formerly was the residence of Clyde Duniway, second president of the University of Montana. Your hosts have painstakingly restored this 1911 home to reflect its original splendor. Beautiful sleigh, pewter and porcelain, and wicker and Victorian beds are complemented by hardwood floors of maple and oak.

Available to all guests is the downstairs common room downstairs, with a big easy chair, fireplace and TV. Also, a small nook offers a library, refrigerator and microwave.

The inn's six bedrooms are accented by Oriental carpets and hand-tiled private bathrooms—and telephones, if you wish.

Parlor Room: Queen-sized bed with private bath down the hall and a bay window overlooking the Clark's Fork River.

Blue Room: Queen-sized bed and private bath.

Green River Room: Queen-sized bed and private bath. Overlooks Clark's Fork River.

Red River Room: Queen-sized bed and private bath. Also overlooks the river.

Fireplace Room: Has its own fireplace, plus queen-sized bed and private bath.

Twin Bed Room: Features wicker twin beds and private bath.

Whitewater Suite: Charming suite has a queen-sized bed, private bath and sitting room with TV.

Enjoy your breakfast and fresh-ground coffee while taking in an unparalleled view of the Sapphire and Bitterroot mountains and the sparkles of the Clark's Fork River in the morning sun. Breakfast is served in the dining room or on the outdoor deck.

Summer or winter, Goldsmith's is ideally located in the heart of the Rocky Mountains. Fishing just outside the inn's front door, or take a 20-minute twenty drive to either of two ski areas. Canoeing, cross-country skiing and pack trips are just some of the other recreational opportunities here. Of course, your hosts can put you in touch with guides and outfitters who will help you design your dream vacation.

Rates - $$ to $$$ Map Location - SW

Greenough Bed & Breakfast
631 Stephens Avenue
Missoula, Montana 59801
(406) 728-3626

The Greenough Bed & Breakfast is a spacious turn-of-the-century home, recently renovated to retain the charm and qualities of an earlier era. Beautiful antiques adorn the tastefully furnished rooms.

The Greenough is centrally located in Missoula, with easy access to local attractions and shopping. Missoula is in the hub of five valleys where the Bitterroot River, the Blackfoot River and Rattlesnake Creek converge with the Clark's Fork of the Columbia. The Missoula area is rich with history and has always been an important center of commerce in western Montana. The city also is home to the University of Montana.

Missoula offers pleasant shopping in a thriving downtown area—with a full-sized mall and several other shopping centers. The city has numerous parks and an extensive system of walking paths and nature trails as well. The Historical Museum at Fort Missoula, the Ninemile Remount Center and the Smokejumper Museum offer insights into local history. Culture is alive in this city and the university, where you'll find notable art museums and galleries. Choose from a vast selection of restaurants as well.

Surrounded by mountainous natural areas, Missoula is convenient to Glacier and Yellowstone national parks, the National Bison Range, the Flathead Indian Reservation, wilderness areas and national forests. The area offers excellent opportunities for hiking, fishing, photography, bird and wildlife watching.

Ol' Joe's Room: Features a double bed, summer balcony, and private bath with claw-foot tub and shower, downstairs.

Green Room: This room features a queen-sized bed and a private bath with shower. Prints by Monte Dolack, a noted Missoula artist, adorn the walls.

Master Bedroom: Features a charming Victorian queen-sized bed and a private bath with the original claw-foot tub, a pull-chain toilet and a separate tiled shower. This room is connected to the "Maid's Quarters."

Maid's Quarter's: Adjoined to and shares a bath with the Master Bedroom. Two beds are available.

Breakfast included.

Rates - $$ Map Location - SW

NOXON, MONTANA

Bighorn Lodge
710 Bull River Road
Noxon, Montana 59853
(406) 847-5597

Bighorn Lodge is a combination country Inn, hunting lodge and home accommodating eight to 10 guests in four large bedrooms with private baths. Designed for comfort and beauty, it is a unique blend of Southern plantation and Western contemporary architecture, tastefully decorated and landscaped. The food is exceptional.

The Bighorn is in the beautiful Bull River Valley of northwest Montana, between two wilderness mountain ranges. It is 1,500 feet off of Highway 56, a Montana scenic by-way. Most guests fly into the Spokane Washington Airport, two and a half hours away. Sandpoint and Coeur d'Alene, Idaho are one and two hours away, respectively. Both towns have small jet capabilities, and Sandpoint is served by Amtrak. The meadow river behind the lodge easily accommodates helicopters.

The Bighorn offers a great variety of recreational opportunities, including fishing, hunting, canoeing, hiking, wildlife viewing, photography, swimming, cross-country skiing and trail riding.

Rates - Vary with the type of vacation package; please call.   Map Location - NW

POLSON, MONTANA

Hawthorne House
304 Third Avenue East
Polson, Montana 59850-2345
(406) 883-2723

Hawthorne House is located in the small western Montana town of Polson, established in 1910, when the Flathead Indian Reservation was opened for a white settlement.

The house is a two-story English Tudor with seven gables. The quiet shady street is just a block from the shores of Flathead Lake. From here, you'll get a wonderful view of Flathead Lake and the beautiful mission Mountains. Inside, you'll find a piano and organ in the music room, a cozy living room with TV and VCR, and a lovely collection of antiques and plates.

The inn has six rooms with three shared baths. Your stay includes a full or Continental breakfast with fresh strawberries, raspberries and cherries, in season, plus homemade muffins and cinnamon rolls.

Visit the National Bison Range, Historical mission Church, and Glacier National Park. Or test your skill on the 18-hole golf five minutes away or on any of the six other golf courses within 60 miles. Enjoy the Port Polson Players, Bigfork Summer Playhouse, scenic boat rides, whitewater rafting, swimming and Montana's only winery.

Rates - $ Map Location - NW

Hidden Pines Bed & Breakfast
792 Lost Quartz Road
Polson, Montana 59860
(406) 849-5612

This well-crafted bed & breakfast is guarded by a stand of stately pines in front of its large circular driveway. A large porch announces the entrance to the home. Once inside, a lovely brick fireplace greets you.

Feel the stress and tension melt away in the quiet and peaceful surroundings of Hidden Pines Bed & Breakfast. Relax on the deck and watch the deer graze in the yard, and take your swimming suit for a romp in the water or hot tub. Your binoculars are a must for viewing Wild Horse Island. Try hiking in the summer and cross-country skiing in the winter.

Hidden Pines has three guest rooms—a double and queen with a shared bath, plus a queen with a private bath.

Choose from a full, delicious breakfast from your host's kitchen or Continental breakfast for the lighter appetite.

Boat-docking facilities and boat rentals are available nearby on Flathead Lake. Also enjoy the National Bison Range, Kerr Dam, Historical Mission Church, Glacier National Park, golfing, fishing, waterskiing, Big Mountain winter sports, Bigfork and Port Polson summer theaters, and plenty of good restaurants.

Rates - $ to $$ Map Location - NW

Ruth's Bed & Breakfast
802 Seventh Avenue West
Polson, Montana 59860
(406) 883-2460

At Ruth's Bed & Breakfast, you will enjoy the friendly, small-town atmosphere of Polson, the beautiful view of Flathead Lake and the majestic Mission Mountains.

The inn has two separate guest rooms with port-a-potties, and one room in the main house. One room in the cottage has a double bed and the other has a queen bed and daveno. They both have televisions and are heated. Clean towels are provided.

Choose from four breakfasts—A Continental breakfast of juice, fresh fruit, homemade cinnamon rolls, coffee, tea or milk; hotcakes served with maple syrup, bacon, eggs and beverage; bacon and eggs, hash brown potatoes, toast and beverage; or hot or cold cereal, toast and beverage.

Rates - $ Map Location - NW

Willows Inn, Red Lodge, MT

RED LODGE, MONTANA

Willows Inn
224 S. Platt Avenue, P.O. Box 886
Red Lodge, Montana 59068
(406) 446-3913

Nestled in a serene valley below the majestic Beartooth Range of the Rocky Mountains, the quaint village of Red Lodge will sweep you back to simpler times. Situated along the spectacular Beartooth Highway that Charles Kuralt described as "the most beautiful drive in America," Red Lodge offers fishing, hunting, hiking, skiing and just plain relaxing—all amid the scenic grandeur of Big Sky Country.

Complementing your stay in this magnificent retreat is the Willows Inn, a home away from home captured in turn-of-the-century Victorian splendor. Here, travelers are luxuriously accommodated in the five distinctively appointed guest rooms, each with its own bath and breathtaking view of the surrounding countryside. For social-izing, reading, or relaxation, the Willows Inn also features a cozy parlor and sunny patio. Awake in the morning to a scrumptious Continental breakfast served in the wicker-furnished dining room. Gather around an authentic wood-burning stove, savor de-lightful homemade pastries. In the afternoon, cool down with a frosty glass of lemonade or warm up with a cup of hot chocolate or mulled apple cider, as the season dictates.

A milieu of recreational pleasures await you during your stay at Willows Inn. Nature lovers will thrill to the abundance of wildlife and wildflowers teeming in the countryside. Picturesque Rock Creek, noted for its trout fishing, runs behind the inn. Also, try downhill or cross-country skiing, tour Yellowstone National Park, or enjoy the quaint shops and homey restaurants in the alpine setting of Red Lodge.

Rates - $ to $$ Map Location - SE

SEELEY LAKE, MONTANA

The Emily A. Bed & Breakfast
P.O. Box 350
Seeley Lake, Montana 59868
(406) 667-FISH or (206) 782-4929

The Emily A. commands a sunny valley tucked between ranges of the Rocky Mountains at the headwaters of the Columbia River. Wide porches and woodland paths offer the peace and vitality of the Montana wilderness, coupled with the gra-cious hospitality of the Old West.

The Emily A. is built in the center of the Circle Arrow Ranch. Its larch logs were harvested from nearby hills. Broad picture windows frame views of an eight-acre lake, wildflower meadows, the Clearwater River and the rugged mountains of the Mission and Swan ranges.

The lodge's interior spaces are generous and comfortable. Furnishings include a world-class collection of sports memorabilia and Western art.

Gett lost in a novel or snooze the afternoon away on the porches of the Emily A. Meet around the hearth on cool evenings—the stones of the two-story fireplace have their own stories to tell. Or head to the television room/library and adjoining atrium for more private getaways.

The Emily A. has five guest rooms, two with private baths, plus a two-bedroom family suite with kitchen facilities on the lower level. Rooms are complete with pe-riod furniture, feather duvets and fresh flowers.

Breakfast is served in the spacious, sunny dining area.

Day activities can include exploring 158 acres of hiking and cross-country trails, as well as boating, fishing, hunting and bird and wildlife watching. Osprey, eagles, loons, ducks, geese, deer and other wildlife frequent the area. Take your fishing pole, camera and binoculars!

Summer activities include theater at the Big Fork Summer Playhouse, plus rodeos, swimming, horseback riding and whitewater rafting. A championship golf course is 80 miles up the road and the Bob Marshall Wilderness Area is right across the way. Winter recreation here is becoming as popular as its summer fun!

Rates - $$ Map Location - NW

SOMERS, MONTANA

Osprey Inn
5557 Highway 93 South
Somers, Montana 59932
(406) 857-2042 or 1-800-258-2042

The Osprey Inn is located on the shore of Flathead Lake, at the center of Mother Nature's most spectacular outdoor playground. The three-story lakeside inn offers a panoramic view of northwest Montana's lake, islands and mountains.

The well-kept lawn extends to the shore of the lake, where you'll find a gentle, pebbled beach and boat dock. Relax on the deck and watch the morning sun play on the Mission Mountains or kick back in the hot tub after a day of touring.

Let your tension and stress melt away as you watch the osprey, geese, loons, grebes and other shore creatures that frequent the area. In the summer, feel free to take your own boat or canoe. And, in the winter, take your downhill or cross-country skis.

The Osprey is conveniently located at the hub of the Flathead Valley, eight miles south of Kalispell. Amtrak and major airline services are just 30 minutes away.

The inn has four guest rooms—two with a shared bath and two with private baths—plus a rustic, but new log cabin for two overlooking the lake.

Breakfast includes Western or Continental fare, including fresh strawberries, raspberries, or cherries in season. Muffins and cinnamon rolls are a house speciality, as is the homemade syrup on your pancakes.

Other amenities at the inn include a TV lounge, VCR, library, fireplace, player piano and cribbage board.

In the area, you'll enjoy Glacier National Park, seven golf courses within 60 miles of the inn, lakes and streams for boating, fishing, waterskiing, whitewater rafting and sailing, Big Mountain winter sports area 45 minutes north, and guided birdwatching tours and photography opportunities.

The city of Kalispell also offers great shopping, casinos, museums, antique shops and art galleries.

Rates - $$ Map Location - NW

SWAN LAKE, MONTANA

Stoney Creek Ranch
P.O. Box 133
Swan Lake, Montana 59911
(406) 886-2002 or 1-800-538-4804

Stoney Creek Ranch is located in northwest Montana's community of Swan Lake, which is surrounded by national forest, in the heart of one of the most spectacular areas Mother Nature has to offer.

Relax on the deck of the rustic but modern three-story ranch house built in 1990. Watch the deer graze in the fields of one of Swan Lake's original homesteads, hike to one of the three alpine lakes five to seven miles from the ranch, try your hand at fishing or just kick back in the hot tub after a day of sightseeing.

Amenities at Stoney Creek include a sunroom with hot tub, TV lounge, VCR, library, fire ring, volleyball, horseshoes and gopher hole golf.

Feel free to take your own boat, canoe, and water skis and enjoy the breathtaking Swan Lake Recreation area. A boat ramp and picnic area are just one half mile from the ranch.

Master Suite: Brass king-sized bed, jet tub, shower, sitting area, TV and VCR.

One Guest Room: Large bedroom with a queen bed and private bath, tub and shower.

Two Guest Rooms: Two large bedrooms with queen-sized beds and a shared bath.

Enjoy a Continental or full Western Breakfast. Huckleberry muffins and pancakes are a house specialty.

Rates - $$ Map Location - NW

THREE FORKS, MONTANA

Sacajawea Inn
5 North Main Street, P.O. Box 648
Three Forks, Montana 59752
(406) 285-6515 or 1-800-821-7326

This was named after Sacajawea, who guided the expeditions of Lewis and Clark in the Three Forks area. Designed by architect John Willson, the hotel was founded in 1910 by John Quincy Adams to serve the travelers of the Milwaukie Railroad and Three Forks residents. Adams purchased the Madison House, built in 1882, and moved it from old Three Forks on log rollers. Today, that encompasses the kitchen, dining room and other rooms of the Sacajawea. The 1910 construction houses the main lobby, with its lofty wood beams and polished hardwood floors.

Savor the casual elegance of this newly renovated landmark, which is listed on the National Register of Historic Places. A large veranda with rocking chair welcomes you to the spacious lobby, fine dining, and 33 nostalgic guest rooms, all with private baths.

Breakfast includes homemade pastries and seasonal fruits.

Sacajawea is a perfect base from which to explore the historic and beautiful Gallatin Valley, including the Lewis and Clark Caverns, Madison Buffalo Jump State Monument, Three Forks Museum and the Museum of the Rockies. Blue-ribbon trout fishing on the Jefferson, Madison and Gallatin Rivers, the area also offers excellent deer, elk, goose, duck and pheasant hunting. The public golf course is within walking distance of the inn, and biking and hiking trails abound. Skiing, horseback riding, Yellowstone National Park, Virginia City, Nevada City and Frontier Town all are accessible.

Rates - $ to $$ Map Location - SW

TOWNSEND, MONTANA

The Bedford Inn
7408 Highway 287, P.O. Box 772
Townsend, Montana 59644
(406) 266-3629

The beautiful Bedford Inn, built in the earl 1900s, once was the house at the historic Cook Ranch in the Canton Valley. With construction of the Canyon Ferry Dam in the early 1950s, the valley flooded, forcing the home's removal. It then was sectioned, moved to its present site and reconstructed, so as to preserve some of the area's history.

Relax with the homestyle hospitality while enjoying the panoramic view this Colonial inn has to offer. Take a stroll to the warm springs that run through the tree-studded grounds.

The Bedford Inn has five guest rooms—one with private bath and sun porch and four with shared bath.

Wake up to the aroma of fresh-brewed coffee and a full country-style breakfast Close by is Canyon Ferry Lake and the Missouri River. Enjoy fishing, hunting, hiking, canoeing, and waterskiing.

Rates - $ to $$ Map Location - SW

TURAH (Missoula), MONTANA

Colonial House Bed & Breakfast
13655 Turah Road
Turah (Missoula), Montana 59825
(406) 258-6787

Colonial House Bed & Breakfast is located in western Montana, on 25 acres of forest and meadows, just minutes from Missoula and midway between Glacier and Yellowstone national parks.

The inn is furnished with family heirlooms and period pieces that depict the Colonial era. The library with fireplace and TV is a welcome place to enjoy afternoon refreshments and relax.

Colonial House has three guest rooms, which all share a bath. Fresh flowers and luxurious feather duvets await you in your room.

Full breakfast and snacks.

Close to the Colonial House are ski areas, golf courses, fishing, rafting, swimming, hiking, picnicking, cross-country skiing, theater, museums, art galleries and shopping.

Rates - $$ Map Location - SW

VALIER, MONTANA

Pine Terrace Country Bed & Breakfast
Route 3, Box 909
Valier, Montana 59486
(406) 279-3401 or 1-800-446-6924

Pine Terrace Country Bed & Breakfast sits on 160 acres, about a hour and a half from Canada, Glacier National Park and Great Falls. The inn is decorated with antiques, including old clothes that date back to the 1800s. Wander around the yard and help yourself to fresh fruit and vegetables, in season. Or enjoy the flowers from the deck.

You may be wakened by the guineas, turkeys, peacocks, pheasants or bantam chickens that live in the park-like setting of Pine Terrace.

The bed & breakfast has two guest rooms—one done in antique Victorian decor with a double bed and the other done in country antique decor with two single beds. Shared bath.

Lake Francis, five miles from the inn, offers boating, camping, canoeing and fishing.

Rates - $ Map Location - NW

VANDALIA, MONTANA

Double J Bed & Breakfast
P.O. Box 75
Vandalia, Montana 59273
(406) 367-5353 or (406) 259-7993

The Double J is a new cedar home with vaulted ceiling. It sits on a hill overlooking the Milk River, one and a half miles of which is owned by your hosts. On the main floor, you'll have a magnificent 360-degree view, wildlife included. Enjoy the 52-inch TV, plus swimming pool and hot tub.

Vandalia has been around since the late 1800s. Ranchers traveled for days to sell their grain at the towns grain elevator. And though the town now is gone, the original school still stands, and now is used as a post office and pottery art store.

The Double J has four guest rooms: Two share a bath in the inn and two share a bath in the trailer.

Breakfast features homemade jams and bread.

Area attractions include Country School Antiques and Pottery, Pioneer Museum, Fort Peck Summer Theatre, Fort Peck Museum, and Fort Peck Dam and Lake.

Rates - $ Map Location - NE

WEST GLACIER, MONTANA

Mountain Timbers Lodge
P.O. Box 94
West Glacier, Montana 59936
(406) 387-5830 or 1-800-841-3835

Mountain Timbers is a small intimate lodge, built with 450-year-old logs and situated just one mile outside Glacier National Park. It sits on 250 acres and is surrounded by national forest.

The lodge has seven guest rooms, four with private bath and three with shared bath. Full breakfast.

Hike in Glacier National Park, or go swimming, cross-country skiing, mountain biking, horseback riding or golfing.

Rates - $$ to $$$ Map Location - NW

WEST YELLOWSTONE, MONTANA

Rainbow Point Inn
P.O. Box 977, Rainbow Point Road #6954
West Yellowstone, Montana 59758
(406) 646-7848

The Rainbow Point Inn is located on the shore of beautiful Hebgen Lake, near the west entrance of Yellowstone National Park.

Evenings begin in the Great Room, with delicious hors d'oeurves served before a roaring fire, and a magnificent view of the lake, where mallard ducks swim in and out of the cattails.

Yellowstone Room: This 800-square-foot room features cathedral ceiling, fireplace, dual king bed, extra large shower, private deck overlooking Hebgen Lake, study, sofa, telephones and TV.

Madison Room: Has a queen-sized canopy bed and large bathroom. Shares a deck with the Gallatin Room.

Gallatin Room: Features a double bed and large bathroom. Shares a deck with the Madison Room.

Guest Cabin: Two bedrooms, one double bed and two bunk beds, plus shower, fully equipped kitchen, small sitting/dining area and TV.

Enjoy a delicious breakfast in the dining room, with a view of Hebgen Lake and Hebgen Mountain. Watch osprey, Canadian geese, bald eagles, swans, cranes and white pelicans fly by as you eat.

Come prepared to fish, hunt, snowmobile, cross-country ski, and sightsee. Hebgen Lake is rated the best wild-trout reservoir in the state, and the Yellowstone area is the snowmobile capital of the world and the fly-fishing headquarters for the United States.

Rates - $$ to $$$ Map Location - SE

WHITEFISH, MONTANA

The Castle Bed & Breakfast
900 S. Baker
Whitefish, Montana 59937
(406) 862-1257

Enjoy the ambiance of one of Whitefish, Montana's most unique homes at the Castle Bed & Breakfast. Built in 1931 on one and a half acres, it provides panoramic views of the nearby Rocky Mountains, and features the unusual architecture and charm that have earned it a place on the National Register of Historic Places. Relax by the fire in the living room, enjoy the sauna by the family room, or stroll the grounds and make yourself at home in the quiet elegance of the past.

The Castle has three guest rooms—one with a private bath and two with shared.

Breakfasts are hearty and tempting, Montana style, and include homemade breads and fresh fruits to compliment the menu feature of the day.

Beautifully located in the foothills of the northwestern Rocky Mountains, Whitefish offers four seasons of diversified recreational attractions, selective dining and lively night life. Local festivals, such as the Winter Carnival and the Summer Games, add color and interest. Winter or summer, Montana has it all—Big mountain Ski Resort, Glacier National Park, golf, canoeing, rafting, hunting and fishing.

Rates - $$ Map Location - NW

Eagle's Roost
400 Wisconsin Avenue
P.O. Box 518
Whitefish, Montana 59937
(406) 862-5198

Eagle's Roost was established in 1992 and has three guest rooms—one with a private bath and two with a shared one.

Breakfast is Continental.

Enjoy Glacier National Park and Big Mountain Ski Resort.

Rates - $ to $$ Map Location - NW

The Edgewood Bed & Breakfast
12 Dakota Avenue
Whitefish, Montana 59937
(406) 862-WOOD (9663)

Built in about 1914, The Edgewood is one of the oldest homes in Whitefish. The two-story farmhouse was remodeled by your hosts, and is decorated with family antiques throughout. It also provides a showcase for an extensive collection of dolls, which are changed frequently, according to the season.

A nice lawn provides summer guests an opportunity to play croquet or have a picnic under the large old apple tree.

The Edgewood offers a warm, friendly atmosphere at any time of the year. Each of the three bedrooms is decorated differently, yet all provide a feeling of comfort. Single and double beds are available, all with shared bath. A full breakfast is served from 7:30-9:30 am. Hot coffee is always available. The full-breakfast menu may include sourdough waffles made from an original Yukon starter or baked goods served with jams and jellies made from the fruit grown on the property. A Continental breakfast is provided for those who wish to eat before 7:30 a.m. or after 9:30 a.m.

During your stay at The Edgewood, try fishing Whitefish Lake or elsewhere in Flathead Valley, dog sledding, ice skating, downhill and cross-country skiing, hiking, golfing, rafting and Western wagon rides. Visits museums, concerts, theatre, shops, restaurants, Big Mountain Ski Resort and Glacier National Park.

Rate - $ to $$ Map Location - NW

The Garden Wall Inn
504 Spokane Avenue
Whitefish, Montana 59937
(406) 862-3440

The Garden Wall Inn was built in 1923 by a railroad engineer, and the farmhouse detailing and gambrel-style roof have been redone to the style for that period—including Persian rugs, tiled bathroom, specialty linens and antiques.

The Inn has three guest rooms with private baths, and one two-bedroom suite, also with a private bath.

Enjoy downhill and cross-country skiing, ice fishing, ice skating, snowmobiling, fishing, hunting, hiking and golfing.

Rates - $$ to $$$ Map Location - NW

WHITE SULPHUR SPRINGS, MONTANA

Foxwood Inn
P.O. Box 451
White Sulphur Springs, Montana 59645
(406) 547-2224

The Foxwood Inn was built in 1890 as a county poor farm, and later served as a rest home until 1975. It has since been remodeled as a bed & breakfast that retains the old-country charm and comfort.

The Foxwood has 15 guest rooms—six with two beds and nine with one bed. The guest rooms are nicely decorated. All shared baths.

Full breakfast at a minimal charge.

Enjoy downhill and cross-country skiing, fishing and hunting. Visit Yellowstone and Glacier national parks.

Rates - $ Map Location - SE

WIBAUX, MONTANA

Nunberg's Ranch
HC 71 Box 7315
Wibaux, Montana 59353
(406) 795-2345

The Nunberg Ranch house, built in 1913, is a two-story home furnished with antiques and collectibles. It is located on Highway 7, just seven miles from Interstate 94 and the historic town of Wibaux, where President Theodore Roosevelt often visited and which an area cowboy nicknamed "Old Four Eyes." A quiet den is set aside for reading, writing or just relaxing, and TV is available with the family in the spacious living room.

A large gambel-roof barn is still home to farm livestock. This is one of the few large barns left in the area, its rafters still ringing from the early day barn dances.

Nunberg's Ranch includes three bedrooms—one with a queen-sized waterbed, one with two double beds, and one with two single beds. All have a shared bath and are complete with handmade comforters, hand-painted pictures and crocheted afghans.

A full Montana country-style breakfast is served.

Join in the excitement of farm/ranch operation by planting crops and calving in the spring, haying in the summer, and with harvest and roundups in the fall. Or help care for the animals anytime of the year.

The area's wildlife is abundant. Deer and antelope roam the hills, and beaver are at home in nearby creeks. Birds of all kinds flock to the area as well.

Nunberg's Ranch is just an hour's drive from Medicine Rock State Park, with its spectacular sandstone formations. A half-hour drive on I-94 takes you to Makoshika State Park, with badland buttes, gullies, hills, rocks and fossil hunts.

The highway leads to the Battle of the Little Big Horn or to the Black Hills and gambling in South Dakota. The Inn is less than an hour from the Theodore Roosevelt National Park at Medora, North Dakota. Skiing on Montana's western mountain slopes at Red Lodge and Bozeman is only a six-hour drive. Don't forget your camera!

Rates - $ Map Location - SE

BETTER
Bed &
Breakfast
Inns

WYOMING

• Buffalo

New Castle •

• Kaycee

• • Jackson Hole   • Dubois
Wilson

• Afton   • Pinedale

• Rawlins

• Rock Springs   Saratoga •   Laramie
                              •   Cheyenne
                    Centennial   •

AFTON, WYOMING

Star Valley Bed & Breakfast
308 Jefferson
Afton, Wyoming 83110
(307) 886-9480

Star Valley Bed & Breakfast is 90 miles west of Jackson Hole and 120 miles from the west entrance of Yellowstone National Park. It features two rooms with three double beds an a snack room. There's also a large dormitory with two double beds, a refrigerator, microwave and coffeemaker. And there's one small bedroom, with double bed, shared bath, and color TV.

Afton has a small-town atmosphere, with plenty of fishing, hunting and scenery. Full country breakfast includes fresh cinnamon rolls and fresh-brewed coffee.

Rate - $ Map Location - SW

ALTA, WYOMING

High Country Comforts
Alta North Road
Route 1, Box 3720
Alta, Wyoming 83422
(307) 353-8560

This 18-year-old custom hand-hewn log lodge is situated on a small farm on the east slope of the majestic Teton Valley. The interior has been completely renovated over the last several years, with emphasis on total comfort. The ground floor features a massive lava-rock fireplace, surrounded by the game loft, pool table, bar and the T.V., stereo and reading area. The upstairs is supported by highly polished burlwood throughout the dining and living areas. Each of the four guest bedrooms is tastefully decorated with down comforters, flannel sheets, handmade quilts, and antique or rich pine furnishings.

The Inn also features one of the finest local art collections in the Teton area. The second floor deck overlooks the Valley and the Bighole Mountains to the west and north, as well as Grand Targhee Ski & Summer Resort, the Jedediah Smith Wilderness, the Targhee National Forest, and the top of the Grand Teton to the east. The inn is surrounded by wide, open spaces, mountain vistas and lush ranchland.

In the summer, get a magnificent view of the mountains from the inn's hot tub, and enjoy the patio with a barbecue and picnic tables, volleyball, horseshoes and a firepit. The area also offers golf, tennis, fishing, hiking, mountain biking, shopping in Jackson Hole, chair-lift rides to the top of Grand Targhee, fine dining and dancing, and either whitewater rafting down the Snake River or gentle river floating on the Teton River.

In the winter, the Grand Targhee Resort draws skiers from around the world to experience its bottomless champagne powder, short lift lines, snowcat and backcountry skiing, fine dining and dancing. If snowmobiling appeals to you, Teton Valley offers some 250 miles of groomed trails to suit your fancy. Guided day-trips through Yellowstone National Park's magnificent winter scenery (with door to door service) are available as well.

At High Country Comforts, you can start your day out with a hot cup of coffee by a cozy fire, or on the porch as the sun rises over the mountains. Breakfasts here are hearty, with an emphasis on traditional country cooking.

Rates - $$ Map Location - NW

BUFFALO, WYOMING

This Olde House Bed & Breakfast
365 North Main
Buffalo, Wyoming 82834
(307) 684-5930

This Olde House, built in 1893, originally served as a hospital, then a boarding house, before becoming a bed and breakfast in the 1940s.

The house has four bedrooms, two baths, a living room, dining room, large kitchen and a big front porch. It is located in walking distance of Buffalo's historic downtown area, the fascinating Jim Gatchell Memorial Museum, Wyoming's largest outdoor swimming pool, golf and Buffalo's scenic nature trail/bike path.

Take your time and enjoy a community that will make you feel welcome. Your stay with This Olde House will include evening snacks and a big country breakfast. Something is always cooking in the kitchen.

Rates - $ Map Location - NE

CENTENNIAL, WYOMING

Brooklyn Lodge
P.O. Box 292
Centennial, Wyoming 82055
(307) 742-6916

Brooklyn Lodge, offering a special bed and breakfast experience, is nestled in a tall pine and spruce forest between two babbling trout streams. Come and sit on the porch or the corral fence and overlook breathtaking flowered mountain meadow.

The warmth of this historic lodge is found in the native hand-hewn logs and the two huge stone fireplaces. Here, you'll be part of the same clear, pristine setting that lured Buffalo Bill Cody's sidekicks, Hoot and Hattie Jones, to build on this spectacular site, high atop the Snowy Range Mountains at the 10,000 feet elevation.

Brooklyn Lodge is located 700 feet off the snowy Range Highway 130, thus affording easy access. The Lodge is in the middle of Medicine Bow National Forest, and gives you spectacular views.

You'll wake to fresh-brewed coffee and a family-style breakfast. Then you can take a quiet walk through wildflowers or sit on the porch swing and take it all in. In the quiet of the evening, prop up your feet and relax around the campfire or read a good book.

Now Lilly: A romantic, warm room, which includes a sitting area, north facing window, king-sized bed, large pine closet, glass-top wagon wheel table and Western prints.

Indian Paintbrush: A cozy, intimate room, with a sitting area, east-facing windows, king-sized bed, large closet, glass-top wagon wheel table and Western prints.

Guests share a modern bath with tub and shower. It has a large mirror plus heat and cosmetic lights to make it warm and comfortable. You'll also be pampered with plush towels, cozy bathrobes, a crackling fire and chocolates at bedtime.

Breakfast may start early with coffee in the country kitchen or on the porch swing facing a spectacular sunrise. Or you may decide to sleep in and enjoy a delicious family-style breakfast a bit later.

Things to do: Fishing, hunting, hiking, backpacking, horseback riding, biking, birdwatching, river floating, photography, four wheeling, horseshoe pitching, picnicking, swimming, plus a variety of winter recreational activities.

Rates - $$ Map Location - SE

Twin Trees Bed & Breakfast, Jackson, WY

CHEYENNE, WYOMING

A. Drummond Ranch Bed & Breakfast
399 Happy Jack Road
Cheyenne, Wyoming 82007
(307) 634-6042

This is a quiet retreat on 110 acres at 7,500 feet, near Curt Gowdy State Park and Medicine Bow National Forest—with a view of the Rocky Mountains.

In nearby Cheyenne, visit the State Museum, Historic Governor's Mansion, Old West Museum, Terry Bison Ranch, F.E. Warren Air Force Base, the Mountain Music Festival in June, or the Sierra Trading Post Outlet Store, or ride the historic trolley. In Laramie, see the Fine Art Center, Geological Museum, Children's Museum and Nature Center, Ivinson Mansion, Territorial Park and Dinner Theater, UW Planetarium, or take the one-day Wyoming/Colorado Scenic Railroad excursion.

Go for a short walk or take a lunch on an all-day hike in the state park or national forest. You'll find old gold and copper mines, birds, wildlife, and plenty of peace and quiet. Granite Reservoir and surrounding streams offer promising rainbow, brown, brook and cutthroat trout fishing. Try mountain biking, horseback riding, rock climbing or skiing. Or hunt for antelope, deer, or elk nearby.

One room at Drummond Ranch has a queen bed and private bath; one has a double bed and shared bath; another has a double and single bed and shared bath. Roll-away bed or a futon also is available. Outdoor hot tub for guests year-round.

Family-style breakfast provided as early as you wish, featuring sourdough waffles and homemade breads. Lunch and dinner available with advance notice. Some dietary restrictions accommodated according to advance requests..

Rates - **$$$$**   Map Location - SE

Adventurers' Country Bed & Breakfast
3803 I-80 S. Service Road
Cheyenne, Wyoming 82009
(307) 632-4087

Adventurers' Country Bed & Breakfast is situated on a knoll above I-80 and is surrounded by 102 acres of the prairies and green pastures of Raven Cry Ranch.

The expansive front lawn, tree-lined adobe courtyard with flower gardens and the comfortable front porch welcome you to this Southwestern style ranch home. Each of the four large guest rooms includes a private bath. A comfortable sitting room with a cozy fireplace, library, videos and games is available for your enjoyment and relaxation.

The Paint Brush Room: An elegant room with a queen-sized bed, warm colors and coordinated bedding that enhance the Southwestern decor. Powder room, walk-in closet and private bath included.

The Wild Rose Room: Comfortable, cozy room with a queen-sized bed, sitting area, private bath. The decor is done in warm pinks and plums, with coordinated bedding.

The Cottonwood Room: A beautiful room with a queen-sized bed, sitting area, private bath, and large windows with a view of the rambling porch and the courtyard. Decorated with a Southwestern flair.

Sunset Room: Luxurious room with a queen-sized bed, sitting area, large private bath, and three large windows with a great view across the Wyoming prairie.

The Bison Room: Adjoining the Sunset Room, this is available as a suite or for additional guests.

Package deals available throughout the year, plus mystery game weekends, historical adventures, train buff tours and horseback riding instructions, barbecues and bon-fires.

Rates include a hearty homemade breakfast, fresh fruit, snacks and beverages.

Rates - **$** to **$$**   Map Location - SE

Howdy Pardner Bed & Breakfast
1920 Tranquility Road
Cheyenne, Wyoming 82009
(307) 634-6493

A big Wyoming welcome awaits you in this relaxed Western setting. The secluded Howdy Pardner ranch home is perched high on a hill, with spectacular views all around, yet it's just 10 minutes from Frontier Park, downtown Cheyenne, the airport, and interstates 25 and 80.

The Howdy Pardner is on the way to elk, deer, antelope and goose hunting, as well as great stream and lake fishing. Take a drive to old Fort Laramie and watch a typical 1800s day unfold, as costumed inhabitants go about their chores. Be sure to stop and see the wagon ruts on the Oregon Trail and Register Cliff, where pioneers carved their names. Take the round-trip train from Laramie to Fox Park on a one-day Wyoming-Colorado Scenic Railroad Excursion through the Snowy Range. And walk back in time during a visit to the Wyoming Territorial Prison Park.

The Doll Buggy: Queen-sized bed with private bath.

The Flour Grinder: Queen-sized bed with shared bath.

The Grand Teton: Twin bed with shared bath.

Rates - $ to $$　　　　　　　　　　　　　　Map Location - SE

DUBOIS, WYOMING

Badlands Bed & Breakfast
RR 31, Box 807
Dubois, Wyoming 82513
(307) 455-2161

The Badlands Bed & Breakfast is a solar log home nestled in the cottonwoods along the Wind River. The upper Wind River Valley is famous for its scenic beauty, wildlife, wilderness areas, Native American history and blue-ribbon fishing. It's also amid the greater Yellowstone ecosystem, so you can also enjoy access to some of the most spectacular wilderness in the world.

Enjoy backpacking, horsepacking, fishing, hunting, photography, boating and rocking hunting.

One room with two double beds and shared bath.

Menu includes homegrown garden vegetables and fresh trout and meats, by reservation.

Rates - $　　　　　　　　　　　　　　　Map Location - NW

GUERNSEY, WYOMING

Annette's White House
239 South Dakota
Guernsey, Wyoming 82214

Annette's is just 13 miles from Old Fort Laramie, and features two bedrooms with shared bath.

Continental breakfast served daily.

Enjoy touring the city, swimming, boating at Guernsey Lake, or golfing.

Rates - $ Map Location - SE

JACKSON HOLE, WYOMING

H.C. Richards Bed & Breakfast
P.O. Box 2606
160 West Deloney Street
Jackson Hole, Wyoming 83301
(307) 733-6704

Your host's grandfather homesteaded in the Jackson Hole valley in the early 1920s, and the current home was built for their 50th wedding anniversary.

This bed and breakfast has three rooms, all with private baths, One room has a queen-sized bed; two others have two double beds. All rooms have cable TV and telephone.

Full homemade breakfast and afternoon tea is included.

Things to do: Fishing, hunting, boating, camping, rock climbing, live theater, hiking, snow skiing, ice climbing, museums, art galleries and plenty of gift shopping.

Rates - $$ Map Location - NW

Moose Meadows Bed & Breakfast
P.O. Box 3647
1225 Green Lane, Wilson
Jackson Hole, Wyoming 83001
(307) 733-9510

Moose Meadows sits on three acres near the foot of Teton Pass, with wonderful views of the Jackson Hole Ski Area and the Teton Range. It's mid-way between the town of Jackson and Teton Village, where the ski resort is located. In the winter, relax in the breakfast room and watch the sun settle on the slopes. Then ski the longest vertical drop of any U.S. ski resort—with plenty of runs for beginner, intermediate and advanced skiers. You'll also find great cross-country skiing in the area, as well as snowmobiling, ice-fishing, sleigh rides, snow-cats into Yellowstone and even dogsled trips. Your host will point you in the right direction.

Numerous summer activities are on tap in Jackson Hole as well—including camping, Western horse pack trips, trout fishing, and whitewater rafting. All of these adventures will be on your doorstep at Moose Meadows, with Yellowstone National Park and all its natural wonders just 50 miles north. In the fall, the colors change again, and the hunting season begins.

Moose Meadows Bed & Breakfast offers a pleasant mix of family antiques, wild animal mounts and paintings by local artists. The four guest rooms have great views, plus cozy flannel sheets and warm duvets on the beds. You're very much a part of the family here. Enjoy a large lounge with a woodstove and TV, and make yourself at home. Don't be surprised if a couple of real cowboys stop by. Your host spent 10 years as a working cowboy, then as the cook for her son's camp.

In the winter, homemade snacks and tea, coffee or hot chocolate are available when you return from skiing. For dinner, try one of the numerous excellent restaurants in Jackson Hole or Teton Village.

Grand Teton Room: One queen bed plus two single beds. Private bath. Large window looks out at the Teton Range. Sleeps four or more.

Meadows Family Room: One queen bed plus an adjoining room with two bunk beds. A view across the meadows to Teton Pass. Shared bath. Sleeps up to four.

Teton Pass Room: Mountain views toward Wilson and the pass over to Idaho. Brass bed and shared bath. Sleeps two.

Southern Comfort Room: A cozy room with grandma's antique bed. Private bath. Sleeps two.

Full breakfast included with all rooms.

Rates - $$ to $$$ Map Location - NW

Nowlin Creek Inn
660 East Broadway
P.O. Box 2766
Jackson Hole, Wyoming 83001
(307) 733-0882 or 1-800-54BB

Nowlin Creek Inn sits in a quiet section of Jackson Hole, bordering the National Elk Refuge. Jackson Hole has become one of the world's most celebrated communities. With Yellowstone and Grand Teton national parks nearby, it offers a taste of civilization and a taste of wilderness—of tomorrow and of yesterday. Towering lodgepole pines rise above the grounds at Nowlin Creek. Off the living and dining room sun deck, a cozy outdoor hot tub invites you to kick back and relax. With its woodsy setting, custom-designed interiors and hand-crafted furnishings, Nowlin Creek Inn reflects a romantic Western appeal.

Enjoy morning coffee and breathe crisp mountain air on the rustic deck. Fresh, hot coffee and gourmet teas, homebaked breads and muffins, and fresh fruits, as well as traditional breakfast entrees, are served in the dining area.

No matter what the season, Nowlin Creek Inn offers a central location for your daily activities—be it skiing, hiking, music, shopping, rafting, tennis, golf or business. Your hosts are happy to help you make arrangements.

After a day of sightseeing in Yellowstone and Grand Teton national parks, return to the quiet privacy of Nowlin Creek Inn and relax in the comfort of the living room, with overstuffed couches and chairs and the Nowlin family's collection of original artwork and historical prints. Or enjoy the intimate second-floor library, complete with regional literature. Views of the Elk Refuge and Teton mountains are breathtaking. Take a moonlight stroll on the refuge, or head downtown to shop, attend wild west shows, browse museums and art galleries, or dine in one of the many top-notch restaurants.

Light, airy and spacious, the bedrooms extend a warm welcome with fresh, polo linens, comfy chairs, Victorian antiques and Western furnishings. All guest rooms have private baths with pedestal sinks and tubs/showers.

Jenny: Overlooking the Elk Refuge, with queen-sized bed and private bath.

Emma Matilda: Overlooking the Elk Refuge, with queen bed and private bath.

Two Ocean: Overlooking Snow King Mountain, with twin beds and private bath.

Goodwin: Overlooks Snow King Mountain, with queen-sized bed and private bath.

Solitude: Overlooking Snow King Mountain, the Elk Refuge and the Grand Teton, with king-sized bed and private bath.

Amenities include a country breakfast, use of the hot tub, and an evening beverage.

Rates - $$$ Map Location - NW

The Painted Porch Bed & Breakfast
3755 N. Moose-Wilson Road
P.O. Box 3965
Jackson Hole, Wyoming 83001
(307) 733-1981

Country elegance is apparent at this beautifully restored turn-of-the-century farmhouse nestled in three acres of aspen and pines trees. The Painted Porch is located just off the Teton Village Road, eight miles from the town of Jackson, four miles from the Jackson Hole Ski Area, six miles from Grand Teton National Park, and 60 miles from

Yellowstone. It is within minutes of skiing, golf, tennis, horseback riding, biking, hiking, fishing, a health club, shopping and dining. Moose and deer share this setting.

The living room has a warm and inviting ambiance with it's cozy fireplace, lovely antiques, hardwood floors and view of the Tetons.

Two Rooms are available,.each with a private bath, Japanese soaking tub, TV, porch, separate outdoor entrance.

The Cowboy: This room depicts a 1950s Western. Cow Camp mixes with traditional Western decor to create a wonderful flavor. Two extra-long twin beds can be transformed into a king-sized bed upon request.

The Garden Cottage: Country romance is apparent in every detail of this suite. Florals mixed with chambray, chintz, ticking and plaids make this suite a garden in itself. The bedroom has a queen-sized bed, and the adjoining sitting room has a double-sized sleeper sofa.

Breakfast is served in the cheery dining room, on the porches, or in your room.

Rates - **$$$**   Map Location - NW

The Sassy Moose Inn
HC 362
Jackson Hole, Wyoming 83001
(307) 733-1277

The Sassy Moose is a new large log home established in 1992. It has five guest rooms, all with a view of the Tetons. Each has a private bath, and two of the five have fireplaces.

Jackson Hole, last of the Old Wild West, is home to two ski areas and the Snake River, where you'll find some of the finest fly fishing in the world. Visit Yellowstone and Grand Teton national parks.

Gourmet breakfast included.

Rates - **$$** to **$$$**   Map Location - NW

Twin Trees Bed & Breakfast
575 S. Willow
P.O. Box 7533
Jackson Hole, Wyoming 83001
(307) 739-9737

Twin Trees Bed & Breakfast is a lovely country-style home located at the base of Snow King, Jackson's own ski mountain. Three rooms, each with its own personality,

The Painted Porch, Jackson, WY

benefit from sunshine and close-up mountain views. They are outfitted with luxury appointments—including spa, down comforters, plush linens and bathrobes for your use.

Twin Trees is located less than 30 minutes from Grand Teton National Park and the Jackson Hole Airport, and is just an hour's drive from Yellowstone National Park's southern entrance.

At Twin Trees, you are within easy walking distance of the Snow King Ski Area, with transportation readily available to other nearby ski areas. You're also just up the street from Jackson Hole's Town Square, where you'll find plenty of shopping and restaurants. Enjoy the many recreational opportunities the area has to offer, including skiing, snowmobiling, hiking, whitewater rafting, fishing, hunting, canoeing, horseback riding, swimming, golf, biking, photography or wildlife viewing.

A full breakfast, prepared and served by your hostess, is offered in a sunny dining room or, weather permitting, on the deck. Your innkeeper is responsive to special dietary requirements.

Rates - $$ Map Location - NW

The Wildflower Inn
Teton Village Road
P.O. Box 3724
Jackson Hole, Wyoming 83001
(307) 733-4710

The Wildflower Inn is situated on three beautiful acres covered with aspens, cottonwoods, and wildflowers.

It has five sunny guest rooms and is located one-eighth of a mile from the Jackson Hole Racquet Club and Teton Pines Golf Course, and four miles from the Jackson Hole Ski Area at Teton Village. While visiting the Wildflower, you will enjoy the added convenience of nearby skiing, tennis, golf, fishing, climbing, hiking, rafting, fine dining and shopping.

The guest rooms are a pleasurable experience, from nestling under down comforters to viewing the aspens and nearby mountains out your window. Each room has a private bath, and four of the five rooms have a private deck.

Your hosts will serve you a delicious mountain breakfast in the dining room or, weather permitting, on the deck overlooking the pond and Teton Range. Make yourself at home in the rest of the house, especially in the solarium with hot tub—a great way to relax at the end of your day, or before exploring the rest of Jackson Hole.

Rates - **$$$**   Map Location - NW

KAYCEE, WYOMING

Graves Bed & Breakfast
1729 Barnum Road
Kaycee, Wyoming 82639
(307) 738-2319

Graves Bed & Breakfast is a fourth-generation ranch, in the heart of the famous Hole In The Wall. The accommodations include a rustic log cabin and a small house. Bath available within walking distance.

Things to do: Fishing, photography, swimming, hunting, touring the Hole In The Wall and Dull Knife Battlefield.

Rates - **$**   Map Location - NE

LaGRANGE, WYOMING

Bear Mountain Back Trails
P.O. Box 37
LaGrange, Wyoming 82221
(307) 834-2281

Experience Western hospitality at its best on this working cattle ranch, homesteaded in the late 1800s and located just 50 minutes from Cheyenne, Wyoming. Private bedroom and dormitory-style room in the main house with shared bath, plus a separate guest house with two bedrooms.

Enjoy the many outdoor activities in clean, fresh air under sunny blue skies. Hike, climb or fossil hunt on 3,000 acres. Fish for trout, bass and pike at a nearby lake. Take a nature walk and enjoy the beauty of the open prairies and rugged sandstone formation.

Abundant wildlife is readily viewed, especially during the summer. Observe or hunt deer, antelope, ducks, and pheasants. Or try your skill at horseback riding, boating and waterskiing. Visit Fort Laramie National Historical Site and Scottsbluff National Monument.

Full breakfast included. Additional meals available for an extra charge.

Rates - $ Map Location - SE

LARAMIE, WYOMING

Annie Moore's Guest House
819 University
Laramie, Wyoming 82070
(307) 721-4177

After receiving the land from the U.S. government in 1864, the Union Pacific Railroad Company transferred certain plots of land in Laramie to public use in 1879. The railroad held this land until 1910, when Sayer and Mary Hansen bought it for $1,500. Available documentation suggests that Sayer Hansen, an early Laramie rancher and laborer, built the original structure, a Post Victorian Princess Anne style home.

The University of Wyoming Delta Phi Sigma sorority occupied the home from 1928-29. In the mid-1930s, Annie Moore moved into the house and, by 1937, was advertising it as a boarding house. The UW Phi Kappa Catholic fraternity leased the property for the 1950-51 academic year, while it was still part of the Moore estate. In 1952, the Wyoming Farmhouse Association bought the property for its fraternity, and used it until 1971.

The property then was called the Chaparral Boarding House, and was owned and operated under various names until 1977, when it again was sold and rented for semi-private lodging until 1981. That year, the property was purchased for use as a bed & breakfast by a group of friends who found the home in a serious state of disrepair. Due to negligence by previous tenants, a three-month fix-up plan turned into an 18-month major renovation.

The Yellow Room: Very bright and roomy, with queen bed, personal sink area, and lots of drawer and closet space. Overlooks the University of Wyoming campus.

The Blue Room: Quaint and cozy with antique white iron double bed, and pedestal sink. Opens out onto the sundeck.

The Purple Room: Large, romantic room with king-sized bed and antique furnishings, personal sink, and southeast-facing bay window. Overlooks the UW campus.

The Sunrise Room: On the southeast corner, this room boasts lots of wood and windows, and has a double bed.

The Green Room: Large, bright and comfortable with deck and queen and twin beds.

Annie's Room: Annie Moore lived in this cozy room, with double bed, personal sink and old-fashioned decor.

All rooms have shared bath.

Continental-plus breakfast includes fresh muffins or rolls, juices, yogurts, cereals, homemade maple nut granola, imported coffee, teas, and fresh fruits in season.

Things to Do: Fishing, hiking, biking, hunting, visiting museums and riding the Wyoming-Colorado Excursion Railroad.

Rates - $ to $$ Map Location - SE

NEWCASTLE, WYOMING

Flying "V" Cambria Inn
23726 Hwy 85
Newcastle, Wyoming 82701
(307) 746-2096

The Flying "V" was built by the Cambria Fuel Company in 1928, in a European Castle Fashion. It's located in the Black Hills, home of the "friendliest residents found anywhere." Within 50 miles of the inn is Mount Rushmore, Devils Tower, Crazy Horse, Jewel Cave and many other attractions.

The Flying "V" includes three single and four double bedrooms.

Breakfast is typical American. The inn also serves dinner, with a seafood and Italian cuisine.

Rates - $$ Map Location - NE

PINEDALE, WYOMING

Window On The Winds
10151 Highway 191
P.O. Box 135
Pinedale, Wyoming 82941
(307) 367-2600

The Green River Basin originally was inhabited some 10,000 years ago, and those that followed left their legacy. Later, the pioneers passed through "The Winds on the Lander Cutoff" of the Oregon Trail.

Pinedale was the location for the Green River Rendezvous. In the early 1800s, trappers, traders, Indians and other folks would get together to trade their goods. Now, every year, the mountain men and Indians of Pinedale re-enact the Rendezvous. At the base of The Winds, Pinedale is a trailhead for the Bridger Wilderness and the Bridger Teton National Forest. Many consider The Winds to be the premier hiking and camping mountains in the United States.

The Window on the Winds is a large rustic log home offering a spectacular view of the Wind River Mountains. The entire second floor is for special guests. Four rooms share two full baths. Each room has a queen-sized lodgepole pine bed. One room has an additional single bed, and another has bunk beds. A corral and pasture space for boarding horses are on site.

A grand room with a breathtaking view of the Wind River Mountains offers warmth and comfort as you relax by the hearth. Or take the time to relax in the hot tub.

Year-round recreational opportunities area abundant—stream and lake fishing, whitewater rafting, horseback riding, wildlife viewing, photography, cross-country skiing, hunting, mountain biking, hiking, birdwatching and snowmobiling.

A delicious breakfast is served in the main-floor dining room. Special dietary needs are considered. Coffee, tea, and cold beverage are always available.

Rates - $$ Map Location - SW

RAWLINS, WYOMING

Ferris Mansion Bed & Breakfast
607 West Maple
Rawlins, Wyoming 82301
(307) 324-3961

The Ferris Mansion is a classic Queen Anne style Victorian home. The three-story brick home was designed by Barber and Klutz of Knoxville, Tennessee. It was placed on the National Register of Historic Places in 1982.

Julia Ferris built the mansion in 1903, after the death of her husband George. He was killed in 1901 by a runaway team of horses as he returned from his copper mine in the Sierra Madre Mountains, southwest of Rawlins. Julia lived in the mansion she died in 1931 at the age of 76.

In the 1940s, the mansion was converted into apartments. Restoration to its original grandeur then began in 1979. The bed & breakfast was started in 1986, then including just one guest room, where today there are four.

Ascend the grand oak stairway to your second-floor room. Rooms are spacious and quiet with authentic Victorian decor. Some have a fireplace. All have private baths and TV. Telephones are available. The downstairs parlours and reception room with grand piano are open to guests as well. Enjoy the evening swinging on the porch.

The Maids Room is available for a single traveler or for a third person traveling with a couple. The bathroom then is shared.

Breakfast is served buffet-style. Choices include homemade granola, muffins, breads croissants, or cooked cereal on request, plus coffee, tea, juices and fresh fruit.

Rates - $ to $$ Map Location - SE

ROCK SPRINGS, WYOMING

Sha Hol Dee Bed & Breakfast
1116 Pilot Butte Avenue
Rock Springs, Wyoming 82901
(307) 362-7131

The Sha Hol Dee originally was a 1901 miner's shack, before being remodeled and turned into a warm, simple home.

It includes one large guest room with private bath and two rooms with shared bath. You'll also enjoy the large gathering room with a TV, reading material and tables, where you'll be served a full homecooked breakfast as early as you like.

People in Rock Springs are friendly and ready to share their town with you. Visit the museum, the beautiful 18-hole golf course, shopping malls and recreation centers—two of which offer swimming, racquetball, weights and all the latest in exercise equipment.

Within walking distance, you'll find the downtown area, including some unique gift and craft shops

Rock Springs is the perfect stopover between Denver, Cheyenne and Salt Lake City. It is located 160 miles from Jackson Hole and the beautiful Teton Mountains. It's a one-day drive to Yellowstone National Park, or 60 miles to Flaming Gorge Dam, where you'll find excellent fishing and camping.

A full breakfast and a bedtime snack are served. Dinner available by reservation.

Rates - $ Map Location - SW

SARATOGA, WYOMING

Hood House Bed & Breakfast Inn
214 Third Avenue
P.O. Box 429
Saratoga, Wyoming 82331
(307) 326-8901 or (307) 326-8772 or (307) 326-5624

This Victorian inn was built in 1892, restored and furnished in period pieces, antique china, Laura Ashley wallpaper and bed linens. Hood House is situated three blocks from downtown Saratoga, on a quiet residential street.

Saratoga was settled around a natural mineral hot springs and named after Saratoga, New York. The area consists mainly of ranching, agriculture and tourists.

Three queen-sized rooms and one with two single beds, plus two full baths upstairs.

Things to do: Hiking, fishing, hunting, floating or whitewater rafting, fish hatchery, historic tours and museums.

Full breakfast includes homemade granola and muffins.

Rates - $ to $$ Map Location - SE

WILSON, WYOMING

Teton Tree House
P.O. Box 550
Wilson, Wyoming 83014
(307) 733-3233

The Teton Tree House is a secluded mountain lodge that combines rustic charm and elegance. The inn is post-and-beam construction, with four stories, each with a ground-level entrance. It offers remote feel, though you are just a mile from Wilson.

The Tree House borders Grand Teton National Park and is 60 miles from the south gate of Yellowstone National Park. Jackson Hole boasts a world renowned ski area.

The great room has a fireplace, piano and walls of books.

The inn has six guest rooms, all with private baths, and most with decks and wonderful views of the mountains or forest.

Full, low-cholesterol breakfasts featuring coffee cakes, muffins, yeast bread, homemade granola, hot cereal, fresh fruit and huckleberry pancakes.

Enjoy fishing, hunting, whitewater rafting, hiking, golfing, photography, art galleries, history tours, canoeing, rodeo and skiing.

Rates - $$ to $$$ Map Location - NW

Teton View Bed & Breakfast
2136 Coyote Loop, P.O. Box 652
Wilson, Wyoming 83014
(307) 733-7954

The Teton View features one room with private bath and two rooms with shared baths.

Only 57 miles to Yellowstone National Park and 11 miles to Grand Teton National Park.

Full breakfast included.

Rates - $$ Map Location - NW

INDEX